Asian Perspectives in Counselling and Psychotherapy

In the last few decades we have entered a new area of multiculturalism, which has created a demand for indigenous therapies. Deep-rooted cultural issues must be considered, alongside issues of racism and political correctness.

Asian Perspectives in Counselling and Psychotherapy considers what exactly cross-cultural counselling and psychotherapy mean. Topics covered include:

- A detailed analysis of the concept of culture, which is examined from subjective, anthropological, sociological, psychological and post-modernist perspectives.
- The relationship between culture and therapy.
- A comparative study of western cultures and eastern cultures.
- The historical development of counselling and psychotherapy in western countries.
- The controversies related to the problem of 'matching' clients with therapists.

Illustrated by stimulating case studies, the theoretical knowledge and practical advice presented in *Asian Perspectives in Counselling and Psychotherapy* will be invaluable reading to all practising and training counsellors and psychotherapists.

Pittu Laungani is a Senior Research Fellow at Manchester University. He has published works in the areas of counselling and psychotherapy, death and bereavement, stress, mental illness, child abuse, and health and illness.

Pittu Laungani is co-editor of the following books:

Death and Bereavement Across Cultures, 1999, Routledge.

Stress and Emotion: Anxiety, Anger and Curiosity, Vol. 15, 1995, Taylor & Francis.

Stress and Emotion: Anxiety, Anger, and Curiosity, Vol. 16, 1996, Taylor & Francis.

Asian Perspectives in Counselling and Psychotherapy

Pittu Laungani

HOVE AND NEW YORK

First published 2004 by Brunner-Routledge
27 Church Road, Hove, East Sussex, BN3 2FA

Simultaneously published in the USA and Canada
by Brunner-Routledge
29 West 35th Street, New York, NY 10001

Brunner-Routledge is an imprint of the Taylor & Francis Group

Copyright © 2004 Pittu Laungani

Typeset in Times by RefineCatch Limited, Bungay, Suffolk
Printed and bound in Great Britain by
TJ International Ltd, Padstow, Cornwall
Cover design by Hybert Design

All rights reserved. No part of this book may be reprinted or reproduced or utilized in any form or by any electronic, mechanical, or other means, now known or hereafter invented, including photocopying and recording, or in any information storage or retrieval system, without permission in writing from the publishers.

This publication has been produced with paper manufactured to strict environmental standards and with pulp derived from sustainable forests.

British Library Cataloguing in Publication Data
A catalogue record for this book is available from the British Library

Library of Congress Cataloging in Publication Data
Laungani, Pittu.
Asian perspectives in counselling and psychotherapy / by Pittu Laungani.
p. cm.
Includes bibliographical references and index.
ISBN 0-415-23300-3 (hardback : alk. paper) – ISBN 0-415-23301-1 (pbk. : alk. paper)
1. Asians–Mental health. 2. Psychotherapy–Cross-cultural studies. 3. Psychiatry, Transcultural–Case studies. 4. Cross-cultural counseling. 5. Asians–Counseling of. I. Title

RC451.5.A75L386 2004
616.89'14'08995–dc22

2004000669

ISBN 0-415-23300-3 (hardback)
ISBN 0-415-23301-1 (paperback)

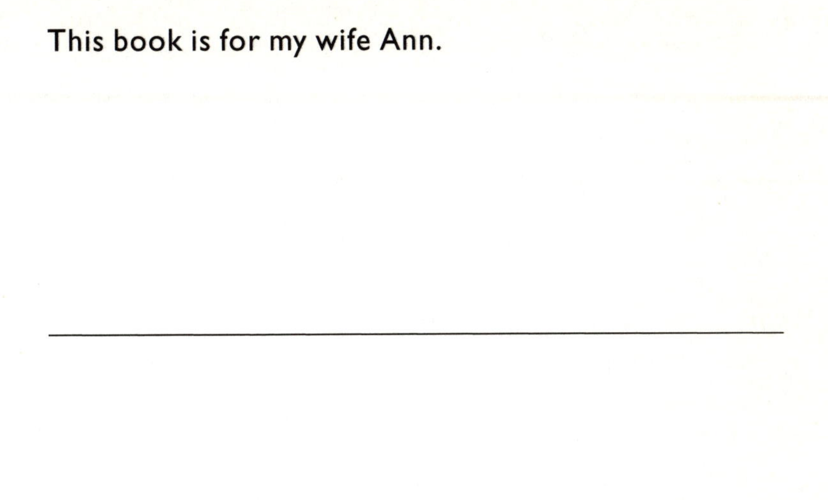

This book is for my wife Ann.

Contents

Acknowledgements

Acts of selfless kindness are impossible to redeem.

Firstly, I would like to mention the constant medical help and attention given to me by Dr Derek Coffman, Dr Adrian Richardson and Dr Lucy Abrahams, all part of The Law Medical Group Practice. Without the beady eye with which they monitored my health, I might not have been able to complete the book. Although at times, I was more than a damned nuisance, they chose to see it differently. Tests, examinations, referrals, admissions, home visits, all part of the service – provided with a smile. To the three doctors I shall remain permanently indebted.

Waseem Alladin, and Professor Stephen Palmer, and Dr William West helped me to clarify many of my own ideas related to counselling and psychotherapy within cross-cultural settings. Waseem, as Chief Editor of the *Counselling Psychology Quarterly*, provided me with the marvellous opportunity of writing a regular article in his esteemed journal – an offer, which I was not always able to fulfil with the regularity he expected. Stephen Palmer and I have worked together on several occasions and despite his own hectic schedule of work, he was always able to find the time to go through the material I sent him, offering me valuable advice along the way. William West has always been a source of great comfort. Many of his suggestions helped me to rethink and rewrite several chunks in a couple of chapters.

In America and Canada, my friends and associates Professor Charles Spielberger, Dr Ann O'Roark, Professor Uwe Gielen, Dr Greesh Sharma, Professor Victor Sanua, and Professor John D. Morgan, all went through many of the chapters when the book was in the making and offered suggestions, many of which I have been able to incorporate in the book. Needless to say all the mistakes in the book are mine.

My special thanks go to Nadine Malcolm and Yaffa Sassoon, who have helped me with the additions and the corrections that were required for the book.

I cannot end this without thanking the staff at Routledge – Joanne Forshaw and Helen Pritt in particular – for the patience and the forbearance they showed while the book was being written.

Introduction

Asian perspectives in cross-cultural counselling and psychotherapy

The reader is entitled to ask: why publish a book on Asian perspectives in counselling and psychotherapy? Isn't there a surfeit of books on counselling and psychotherapy already? Isn't the clinical, academic and popular journalistic 'market' on books of this nature flooded, or even over-flooded? Why add yet another book? These are fair and legitimate questions.

The need to write such a book would not arise if counselling and psychotherapy were like the natural sciences, such as physics, where one does not need multiple theories to understand and explain the nature of gravitation, the planetary movements and other such natural phenomena. Newton's theory alone clearly demonstrates how the planets circle (or move elliptically) round the sun with inexorable regularity. No such consistency and regularity can be attributed to human beings, other than the fact that all human beings are born as tiny little infants, who grow, develop and, passing through various stages of life, eventually die. But between the two stages of birth and death (or from one nothingness to another nothingness, as Ernest Hemingway so eloquently put it) they all lead their own varied individual lives, which are subject to a variety of influences, including those of their family, their friends, the society in which they live and the culture into which they are born.

It would be impossible to find in any one individual the consistency and the regularity of planetary movements. Even identical twins vary. In keeping with the sentiments expressed by Heraclitus, the pre-Socratic philosopher, who remarked that 'the only thing permanent in the Universe is change', one might extend the same remark to humanity: 'the only thing permanent about human beings is change!' Given that variation and change in humanity is the norm, it stands to reason that one finds differences both within and between individuals and groups and of course within and between cultures. The term 'variation' must not be equated with randomness; human behaviour, to a large extent, is motivated, goal-directed and purposive. This allows us to understand, explain, and even predict not only our own behaviours but those of others as well. The extent to which we succeed is related to our depth of knowledge and the understanding that we bring to bear on our encounters with others, and the knowledge and understanding that we acquire or possess *of* others. Encounters become more meaningful and successful when the two parties involved share a set of common assumptions, which may be linguistic, metaphorical, religious, culture-specific etc. This, as we know, is also the case in counselling and therapy.

A therapeutic encounter, where the therapist and the client are of the same culture, speak the same language, share the same assumptions and values and understand the same metaphors (it is often forgotten by therapists the important role played by metaphor in our day-to-day encounters) is likely to proceed more smoothly. But even in such situations misunderstandings can easily occur, thus upsetting the smooth flow of the therapeutic process.

Clients and therapists who come from different cultures do not always share mutual assumptions, and therefore may have difficulty in understanding one another. In a broader sense, they may find it difficult to get a deep and penetrating insight into the worldview of the other.

Until recently, therapists of all persuasions were not unduly disturbed by these cultural problems. Counselling and psychotherapy were seen as western enterprises. And given the belief of many therapists that their own models had universal applicability, few serious attempts were made to examine the role of any cultural factors in their therapeutic practices. Over the years the western models of therapy acquired 'world supremacy' and were used in virtually all parts of the world. To a large extent they still are. Their hegemony, which until recently has remained unchallenged, has now come to be questioned. There is a felt need to consider non-western perspectives, which as we shall see are in many ways different from western models.

How has such a situation come about?

The world, to use the well-worn cliché, has turned into a global village. Travel has become inexpensive and easy – so much so that many people live in one country and commute to work in another country every day, thus adding a completely new dimension to the concept of work and travel. At the other end of the scale, an increasing number of people in the West work from home, but they have little reason to feel deprived of the experiences enjoyed by those who travel. Multiple satellite transmissions make it possible for people to 'invite' the outside world into their homes. Moreover, by clicking their 'mouse' they are able to explore and surf through cyberspace and enjoy the exhilaration of virtual reality. It is clear that the outside world is catching up with the world inside our homes and heads.

In the last few decades, people from different countries have come to Britain. There has been a steady flow of people from the European Union (EU) countries, including a significant number from eastern Europe, Africa, Asia, Pakistan, Afghanistan, Hong Kong and from countries in South-East Asia. Those coming to Britain have included a vast assortment of political refugees, asylum seekers, tourists and other types of 'settlers'. In addition to the newcomers, Britain, as a result of its past historical associations, has been the beneficiary of several groups of Asians (from India, Pakistan, Bangladesh, Sri Lanka, East Africa, South Africa and the West Indies), most of whom emigrated to Britain and set up homes in what was referred to as their 'mother country'.

We have entered the new world of multiculturalism, political correctness and racism. All these three factors, directly or indirectly, have created a demand for indigenous therapies.

Some politicians in Britain have expressed concern over what they see as an influx of outsiders wishing to settle. There is a belief, shared by many others in this country, that when migrating to Britain people ought to jettison their cultural baggage. It is believed that such a course of action will assist greatly in the rapid process of assimilation to the norms of the host country. Such a belief is naïve, false, and potentially dangerous. It is naïve because it is unworkable. It is potentially dangerous because it is in direct infringement of fundamental human-rights. Such a belief also rests on the false assumption that the norms of the host country are the only ones that matter: regardless of the norms and values the outsiders might have imbibed in their own cultures, it is incumbent upon them to acquire the dominant norms of the host culture. However, no country or culture can claim to set up a 'gold standard' of norms and values, which the rest of the world is expected to follow.

What the politicians advocating the policy of assimilation have failed to realize is that people do not jettison their cultural baggage when migrating to another country. All of us are firmly rooted in our own culture. These roots run deep. They extend over several centuries. One can no more sever one's attachments to a culture than a tortoise can its shell. Thus, when people migrate they bring with them not just their unique skills, qualifications and experiences: they bring their hopes, their aspirations, their ambitions and of course their fears (known and unknown), and their uncertainties. Their own cultural beliefs and values, their traditions, their religious practices, their customs, their rites, rituals and ceremonies, their dietary practices, their family structures and (equally importantly) their own language(s) are an integral part of their upbringing. No immigrant in that sense ever travels light. No immigrant ever sheds his or her cultural legacies and acquisitions easily. One is, in that sense, handcuffed to one's culture by past history.

From a social psychological point of view, the mixture of cultures within the mainstream of British society provides exciting opportunities to academics, scholars, artists, poets, writers, clinicians, doctors, health professionals and a host of other interested care providers for learning and acquiring insights into a variety of cross-cultural issues. For instance, several fundamental questions can be raised. How do people from different cultures bring up their children? What constitutes child abuse in their culture? What are the parameters which they consider important in the socialization process? What are their attitudes and values towards women, towards the sick, the infirm and the elderly? What rules govern their family structures and kinship patterns? How do they grieve and mourn for their dead? What constitutes a mental and/or a psychiatric disorder? How is it dealt with? What roles do rituals, religion and worship play in daily life? How do they perceive members of the host culture and vice versa? How do they attempt to relate to one another? To what extent do they succeed or fail to succeed in forming meaningful relationships with members of the host culture? What are the factors which lead to failures and successes? What effect do the dominant values of the host culture have on their own system of values? How far do their own values impinge upon the values of the host culture?

In addition to clear psychological insights it also becomes possible to tease out the social, economic and political consequences which are likely to occur when people of different cultures, speaking different languages, imbibing different moral values, share and/or compete for available resources related to occupations, housing, medical care and so on. What are the short-term and long-term consequences that are likely to occur in such a culturally diverse society?

Although the need for alternative indigenous therapies has been expressed with great fervour, its implementation raises a variety of problems. Despite the few inroads that have been made in that direction, the situation as far as cross-cultural therapy is concerned is far from clear. What does cross-cultural or indigenous therapy and psychotherapy mean? How is cross-cultural therapy different from 'trans-cultural' therapy? How do the two in turn differ from or how are they similar to culture-centred therapy, cultural therapy etc? How do all these indigenous approaches differ from the current western models of therapy? Who can be called a cross-cultural therapist? Who is best qualified to be a cross-cultural therapist? What are the attributes a cross-cultural therapist possesses or ought to possess? What are the training requirements for those wishing to become cross-cultural therapists? Are cross-cultural therapists in any way different from 'mono-cultural' therapists? Do the therapists who claim to be experts in cross-cultural or indigenous therapies have the necessary expertise to justify such claims? How has such expertise been defined and acquired?

Many conscientious counsellors and therapists also undergo training courses in multiculturalism, cultural diversity and other related issues. But (based on my own observations) a large number of such training courses tend to veer more towards a dissemination of issues related to racism and political correctness than deep-rooted cultural issues. As a result, ideas of culture, what constitutes a culture, and the subtle manner in which it impinges upon one's life tend to become conflated with political, ideological and racial issues.

For trainers in multiculturalism to discuss culture largely in terms of political, ideological and racial perspectives is unwise and potentially dangerous. Firstly, it may allow the trainer to promote his or her own private agendas under the guise of 'multiculturalism'. Secondly, it does not provide a systematic, objective and rational understanding of culture. This is not to deny that political, ideological and racial issues do not enter into an understanding of culture. They do. But to focus on them to the exclusion of all the other factors which go to make up our understanding of a culture is unlikely to be of great value in counselling and psychotherapeutic encounters.

In this context, there is another related problem which needs to be aired. There is an assumption among many white health professionals, including counsellors, psychotherapists and clinical psychologists, that an Asian health professional, by and large, is more knowledgeable about his or her own culture than a white Caucasian. At first sight this seems a reasonable assumption. The possession of a brown or a black skin is occasionally seen as the required 'certificate' that guarantees 'expertise' in the Asian health professional. The Asian health professional, 'elevated' to the position of an expert, may often be more than willing to play the role of the expert. Yet a moment's reflection should make it clear that the possession of a given skin colour and the fact that one comes from a particular cultural background does not *ipso facto* transform that individual into an expert in his or her own culture. Not all Italians living in Florence are experts in Renaissance art! To claim expertise by virtue of possessing a brown or black skin is akin to claiming racial superiority by virtue of possessing a white skin. Both claims are false. As Abraham Lincoln was reputed to have said, one can fool some of the people all the time, most of the people some of the time, but not all of the people all of the time. If life were only that simple! And deceptions that easy!

Even within an 'ideal' mono-cultural setting (what constitutes 'ideal' remains an open question) the field of counselling and therapy is beset with known and unknown difficulties. For instance, one is not always clear whether one is actually helping one's clients to determine their own life goals, or whether one's involvement as a therapist has had any positive effects upon the psyche and the eventual behaviour of the client. Sometimes it becomes inordinately difficult to define what one means by a 'positive outcome'. One may find that one's definition is at total variance with those of other therapists. Although one may formulate a set of interesting hypotheses, one may not be clear as to what it is about the counselling process that leads to a positive (or negative) outcome. One feels handicapped by one's inability to objectively test these hypotheses. What complicates the problem further is the fact that there isn't any one guiding theory of counselling to which all counsellors subscribe. There are several competing and complementary theories of counselling, each with its own traceable origins, its own sets of assumptions, its own formulations and approaches, its own methods and its own expected outcomes. Followers of a given theoretical approach often tend to ignore if not deride other theoretical approaches. This of course makes the task of evaluating the efficacy of theories an exciting but extremely difficult proposition.

When it comes to counselling people from different ethnic and cultural backgrounds, the above problems get compounded. Cross-cultural counselling is like venturing into uncharted psychic territories. One might find oneself moving into areas about which very little is known. For instance, one may be unfamiliar with the language of the client, one may have little knowledge of the cultural background of the client, one may find that the client's worldview is different from the therapist's, and so on. Moreover, what may be known may not, upon reflection, turn out to be of any significance. There are several such issues, including the cultural and racial settings within which counselling occurs, to which competent and informed counsellors would need to be sensitized.

Let us take a few trivial examples to illustrate the influence of culture on people's beliefs and behaviours. Most Hindus do not eat beef, but Muslims do. Muslims do not eat pork, but some Hindus do. Divorce is anathema among Hindus; among Muslims, under certain conditions, marriage is seen as a social contract, which can be revoked by mutual consent. Muslims believe in the *yaum-al-qiyamah*, the final resurrection, or The Day of Judgement. Hindus subscribe to the idea of an unending cycle of birth and rebirth, encapsulated in the 'law of karma'. These are seemingly ordinary, day-to-day examples which most health professionals are familiar with and even encounter in the course of their professional work with some of their multicultural clients. However, it should be pointed out that the above examples are disparate items of information and do not necessarily constitute 'knowledge'. These items of information acquire deeper meaning only when one understands them from within the broader context of knowledge related to the religious practices, rites, rituals and notions of pollution and purification (*haraam* and *halal*) of Hindus and Muslims. Without such in-depth knowledge, one merely succeeds in peddling stereotypes, which are devoid of their contextual origin and meaning.

As T. S. Eliot (1969) expresses with great beauty and simplicity in his poem, *Choruses From 'The Rock'*: 'Where is the wisdom we have lost in knowledge? Where is the knowledge we have lost in information?' It is clear, therefore, that one needs to distinguish between information and knowledge and not confuse one with the other. Information can be gleaned from encyclopaedias, libraries and other electronic sources. But the way to knowledge – objective, scientific knowledge – alas is not that simple.

Interestingly enough, until the 1950s, even such culturally differentiated items of information were relatively unheard of and therefore unknown to most western psychologists. The narrow and rigid framework from which they chose to see the world was a form of 'cultural myopia', which remained uncorrected. But in recent years noticeable shifts have begun to appear in the thinking of western therapists. They are beginning to take into account the important role of cultural factors in therapy. One hopes that in the years to come both western and non-western therapists will be able to work together, each lending a hand in the creation of a genuine multicultural society.

Just a few more words need to be said, concerning the arrangement of the chapters in this book. The book starts with a detailed analysis of the concept of culture, which by all accounts is open to diverse interpretations and misinterpretations. A historical approach has been adopted, which allows us to see the different meanings and interpretations which the term has gone through over the years, moving from stereotypes and subjective interpretations to psychological and postmodernist interpretations of the term. Chapter 1 then examines the relationship between culture and therapy and ends with a hypothetical case study.

Chapter 2 follows the migratory patterns of Asians into Britain soon after Indian independence, and their subsequent attempts to settle down in the country. It then moves on to discuss the lifestyle of the second and third generation Asians living in Britain and their attempts to find their identity in an alien country. The chapter ends with a case study.

Chapter 3, which is the longest in the book, is a comparative study of western cultures (in particular, England) and eastern cultures (in particular, India). A model of cultural differences is presented in depth and the salient behaviours emerging therefrom are discussed in depth. The chapter discusses the powerful impact of one's cultural upbringing on one's beliefs, attitudes, values and behaviours. Given the comparative and analytical approach, the chapter allows us to describe and also understand the 'whys' of behaviours, not only of Asians, but also of the English. The importance of this chapter in understanding culturally related behaviours in eastern and western cultures cannot be overstated.

In Chapter 4 I have traced the historical development of counselling and psychotherapy in western countries, starting with the period when counselling was not called counselling and mental disorder was not called mental disorder. Instead it was interpreted as a visitation from malevolent gods or demons, and mental patients were not 'treated' in the modern sense of the word but were incarcerated in dreadful institutions. The chapter goes on to discuss the humane methods of treatment which later came into being, and with them the rise of the major theoretical models of therapy, including Freudian, behavioural and humanistic, which to a large degree form the basis of therapeutic work in western countries today.

How clients get to meet therapists in India and in England forms the substance of Chapter 5. What transpires when they get to meet? What kind of mutual assumptions are shared, if any, at such a meeting? What kind of therapeutic strategies are advocated or suggested by therapists, both in England and in India? Does the therapeutic strategy change in any way when white therapists meet Asian clients and vice versa?

Chapter 6 offers a systematic account of the indigenous therapeutic strategies that are available to Indians in India and also in England. Unlike western therapies, which have a viable theoretical, empirical and secular basis, most Asian therapies are hallowed by ancient tradition, with deep-rooted religious and ritualistic underpinnings.

Chapter 7 considers the controversies related to the problem of 'matching' clients with therapists (whites with whites and Asians with Asians). Factors such as racism, political correctness, ethics, cultural relativism etc. all have a strong bearing on the problem of matching and are critically examined.

The penultimate chapter consists of case studies, with which I was involved during the course of my work. To create the necessary impact and 'mood' on the mind of the reader, the case studies have been written in a personalized, literary style and, where necessary, dialogue has been introduced.

The final chapter sums up the discussions throughout the book and formulates a set of rules which might be of help to therapists.

Chapter 1

Understanding culture: its influence on counselling and therapy

Introduction

In 1932, Mahatma Gandhi came to England to attend the Second Round Table Conference in London. The purpose of the visit was to discuss with the British government the issue of Indian independence. His presence, partly because of the simple clothes he wore, partly because of his seeming frailty, and partly because of the 'halo' of saintliness which the Indians had imbued him with, aroused a great deal of interest and curiosity. Several journalists accosted him, each jostling for an exclusive interview. One of the journalists asked him what seemed an interesting question.

'Mr Gandhi,' asked the journalist, 'what do you think of British culture?'

With a twinkle in his eye, an impish smile lighting up his face, Gandhi answered: 'I think it is a wonderful idea!'

It is possible that Mr Gandhi's reply is apocryphal. But it has entered the legends of Indo-British history. Gandhi's answer, uttered no doubt in a mood of levity, was cryptic, sardonic, moralistic and even judgemental.

There are several important points that can be raised from this brief encounter. What did the journalist mean by the word 'culture'? What did Gandhi understand by the word culture? Were the meanings of the term mutually shared? In describing British culture as a wonderful idea, was Gandhi merely teasing the journalist? Or was he actually adopting a superior moral stance, which carries the implication that what the British might refer to as culture is not what Indians would call culture? Did Gandhi's reference to British culture as an abstraction (translatable into reality) carry within it the unvoiced judgement that conquerors, whoever they might be, whatever period of history they may emerge from, by their very actions cannot be said to be a cultured group of people?

Can one speculate on the motives of the journalist who asked the question? Was he seeking approbation? Or was he attempting to extol in a subtle (and yet not-so-subtle) way what might have seemed to him the self-evident virtue of British culture? Alas, we shall never know.

Since further speculation may lead to some elucidation, allow me to ask you the same question. What does the term 'culture' mean to you? How would you define culture? Would you try and define it with reference to yourself, the kind of person you are, your family background, the country in which you were born, and so on? Or would you try and define it in abstract terms? Or both?

A few years ago I put similar questions to my undergraduate students at the university. They had elected to do a course in cross-cultural psychology and seemed the most appropriate group to which I could put such questions. Their answers surprised me. Most of them answered with reference to themselves: they said they were white and British. Most of the non-white students were second-generation, and a few even third, and they described themselves as being black British, or Asian. Only a few chose to describe themselves in terms of their ancestral origins. They defined culture as *being with people of their own kind*. They spoke of people who shared their interests and values, their preferences in food, music, books and sports, who spoke their own language, who were of the same religion as they; people who understood them, accepted them for what they were and in whose company they felt comfortable, safe, wanted, loved and could 'let their guards down'. Hardly any of them chose to explain the concept of culture in abstract terms.

Subsequently, I extended my enquiries to other groups of students; their answers were very similar to the ones given by the first group. There were hardly any differences in their responses. Even from this cursory 'survey' it became clear that the term 'culture' holds a variety of meanings for people: nationality, skin colour, country of birth, religion, a shared language, patterns of relationships, acceptance, warmth etc. A few were critical of what they saw as the dominant values of British society, which they felt unable to identify with and wanted changed. There was among them a small group of feminists who were critical of the patriarchal values of western society as a whole and felt that subscribing to such values undermined their own identity.

Last year, I was able to extend this form of enquiry to a few groups of students in Bombay, where I had been invited to give a set of lectures. I was surprised by their answers. The students in London saw themselves initially in terms of their inherited or acquired nationalities – black British, white British, Irish etc. and from there they moved on to other specifics, such as religion, country of ancestral origin, region, language etc. But the students in Bombay operated on an inverse set of parameters. They defined themselves largely in terms of their religious and caste-related denominations, (e.g. 'I am a Saraswat Brahmin', 'I am a Sunni Muslim', 'I am a Gujarati *bania* [of the Vaishya caste – see Chapter 3]', 'I am a Marwari Jain'). And then in a descending order, they identified themselves in terms of their sub-caste, their family, their region, and finally their nationality. Thus, while the students in London moved from the general to the particular, the students in India moved from the particular to the general. It was obvious that they were more concerned about emphasizing their caste and hierarchical *differences* than talking about their national *similarities*. Although one would be loath to call this form of enquiry a robust empirical study, similar findings have been corroborated by several sociologists, including Bougle (1992) and Gupta (1992, 2000).

Popular conceptions of culture

Many people construe the word 'culture' from their own, subjective, idiosyncratic, individual perspectives. Sometimes, the generic term 'culture' is confused with the idea of a *cultured person*. Persons subscribing to an 'elitist' view of culture may talk about a cultured person and may come to define culture in terms of desirable qualities possessed by an individual. They would see a cultured person as being well behaved, considerate, sensitive, sophisticated, tactful, perhaps even a classicist, with impeccable manners. An uncultured person, on the other hand, would be seen as being uncouth, ill mannered, coarse, ignorant, bigoted and uneducated. If the desirable qualities are possessed by a large group of people, they are then said to be a cultured people, and the society in which they live is said to be a cultured society. Thus, education, manners, learning and one's bearing come to be equated with the term 'culture'. Then there are those who refer to culture as highbrow and lowbrow, superior and inferior, advanced and developing, scientific and superstitious. But such definitions, because of the implicit value judgements contained in them, may become unprofitable digressions.

The word 'culture' becomes even more difficult to grasp when it is prefixed by other words, such as *agri*culture, *bio*culture, *horti*culture, or when a microbiologist studies and examines *cultures*. Although in this instance the word 'culture' carries a specific occupation-centred or profession-centred meaning, its usefulness as far as our own interests are concerned is limited.

At a common-sense level, culture may also be seen in historical terms, as a historically created system of beliefs, attitudes, values and behaviours of people enjoined by a common language and religion, and occupying a given geographical territory or region. These factors allow individuals living in that society to structure their lives in accordance with the sets of established norms of that society. They also allow them to regulate their individual and collective lives.

The term 'culture', like many such global terms (e.g. intelligence, personality, consciousness, creativity etc.), is best understood as an umbrella term, which covers a variety of meanings and perspectives. Little purpose will be served in attempting to examine all the different nuances, meanings and perspectives attached to the term. Let us therefore restrict ourselves to understanding culture from the following three perspectives:

- subjective;
- academic;
- postmodern.

A brief discussion of the above perspectives will hopefully help us to understand, analyse and sift through the difficulties involved in coming to terms with the nebulous concept of culture. Let us turn to the first one.

Subjective perspectives

In our own, private, personal, subjective way, we all know what we mean by culture. We are each born into a particular family, which has a history of its own. Through the process of socialization we learn (hopefully) to imbibe and internalize the language, the rites and rituals, religion and religious practices, rules, habits and customs, beliefs, attitudes and values, and patterns of appropriate conduct which our family members (and other members of the community) endeavour to inculcate in us. The lessons we learn are generally in accordance with the norms prevalent in our wider society and the extent to which parents express a willingness (and are able) to influence them. We learn to tell the difference between right and wrong, good and bad, beautiful and ugly, appropriate and inappropriate, acceptable and unacceptable, secular and sacred etc.

A family is a microcosm of a wider section of our community, which in turn is a microcosm of the society in which we live and grow up. Society provides us with a structure which regulates our lives, our beliefs and practices, and we are able to make sense of ourselves, of our own lives, of others, and of the world around us. We tend to see society in tangible terms because it consists of groups of people who also occupy a given territory and live together. We also notice, even within our own society, variations in people: skin colour, language, dietary practices, patterns of worship, social interactions and relationships, and even climatic and other ecological variations. As we learn to make sense of our society we notice that the differences also extend into political, social, economic, physical and other environmental domains. Despite this, we tend to experience a sense of belongingness, a feeling of 'oneness' among the diverse groups around us. This occurs when we come to understand that all the diverse groups in our society are united by a set of core values – religious, aesthetic, political, legal, nationalistic, social – which form an integral part of our culture.

If perchance we move away from our own culture into another culture (e.g. through migration, education, political asylum etc.), what comes as a huge shock (culture shock) to us are the vast differences which separate us from the people of that culture. Everything seems different, strange and alien: the people, their mode of dress, their mannerisms, their accents, their colloquialisms, their buildings, their food, their climate, their rules, their norms etc. The entire pattern of life appears bewildering, even quite intimidating. We lose our bearings; the familiar reference points, which we took for granted in our own culture, lose their meaning. We feel intimidated at the idea of having to start all over again, to learn afresh the new patterns of life which would allow us to make sense of the new culture, eventually becoming part of it. We become aware – sometimes quite painfully – of the powerful impact which culture exercises in shaping our personality and our view of the world. We are as though chained to our culture. Our condition is like those of the chained prisoners described by Plato in the *Republic* (Book VII). All that the prisoners could see were blurs and shadows, all they could hear were echoes, mistaking appearance for reality. We too, when we migrate to another culture, tend often to feel that way. And so long as we remain chained to our own culture and immobile, we are unlikely to acquire any deep understanding of the adopted culture. Any knowledge that we gain *en passant* is likely to be superficial, stereotypic and irrelevant.

Does one ever succeed in breaking out of the chains of one's own culture? Whether we succeed in achieving an understanding of the adopted culture and accepting (or rejecting) its dominant values is related to a variety of factors. They include the age at which one migrated to another culture, one's level of education, one's occupation, one's area of residence and the kinds of experiences one has in the course of living in the adopted culture. We also come to feel that in the process of trying to make sense of the new culture, we may not be able reconcile the conflicting cultural values which impinge upon us, and might lose sight of and even abandon the values of our own culture.

Academic perspectives

Here we shall confine our discussion to three major perspectives, which are: anthropological; sociological; and psychological.

Anthropological perspectives

The study of cultures has been of interest to anthropologists (Kroeber and Kluckhohn 1952; Leach 1964; Murdock 1964; Tyler 1969; Geertz 1973) to sociologists (Shweder and Sullivan 1993) and more recently to cross-cultural psychologists (White 1947; Whiting 1964; Triandis 1972, 1994; Kakar [1979] 1992; Brislin 1983, 1990; Barnlund and Araki 1985; Roland 1988; Berry *et al.* 1992; Smith and Bond 1993; Laungani 1996, 2000c, 2001d; Segall *et al.* 1999). Anthropologists were the early pioneers in their studies of cultures. Their early writings were speculative, naïve and even quite absurd (Harris 1968). Early anthropology, as Bock (1980), Harris (1968) and several others have pointed out, was also blatantly racist in its formulations (see Rivers 1901; Woodworth 1910; Bartlett 1923, 1937). Differences between Negroes (as they were referred to then) and Europeans were often explained in terms of naïve and ill-founded theories. Non-European and non-white societies were judged as being backward, primitive and inferior. White, western societies were seen as being enlightened and superior.

It was not until the early twentieth century that anthropology began to acquire academic respectability. Following the lead of Franz Boaz (1911), anthropologists started to undertake ethnographic field studies. Starting with the pioneering investigations of Malinowski among the Trobriand Islanders in the South Pacific (1927), other field studies were also undertaken. To the anthropologists, culture includes the 'total attainments and activities of any specific period and group of humans' (Triandis 1980: 1). Culture therefore is best seen as an abstract concept, an overarching symbolic configuration, created by the people in society. It incorporates within it all the distinctive human forms of adaptation and the distinctive ways in which different human populations arrange and organize their lives on earth (Levine 1973). It regulates and lends legitimacy to the relationships and the practices of members of society. All cultures are symbiotically related to their societies. Although the two are not identical, one cannot conceive of a society without culture, nor culture without some society (Carrithers 1992; Parekh 2000). Cultures evolve, grow, change, and in some cases wane, and may even die and become extinct (e.g. the ancient Hellenic culture).

Thus each culture is seen as having a structure and a pattern. And each part of the pattern includes beliefs, attitudes, values, rules, laws, symbols, rites, rituals, taboos, patterns and networks of communication, etc. The study of whole societies has been the main concern of anthropologists. In their concern to describe a system, they often chose to adopt a *relativistic* position. Conceptually and methodologically their discipline is more allied to psychiatry and psychoanalysis than to psychology (Klineberg 1980; Jahoda and Krewer 1997). But with increasing collaboration the dividing lines separating disciplines have blurred and in recent years new specialist areas such as psychological anthropology, cognitive anthropology, cultural psychology and so on have emerged (Munroe and Munroe 1980).

Sociological perspectives

To sociologists, culture is best seen as 'that complex whole, which includes knowledge, beliefs, art, law, customs and other capabilities and habits acquired by man as a member of society' (Taylor 1989).

The attributes of culture are that it is shared by all, learned and transmitted, not inherited, constantly being created and recreated, undergoing change and providing knowledge and techniques of survival. Culture also enables human beings to stand on the shoulders of their ancestors and bring forth a heritage of wisdom from one society to another.

In recent years diverse uses of the word 'culture' have proliferated within sociology and cultural studies. Diverse inputs, instead of making the meaning any clearer, have tended to cloud the concept even further. For instance, the term 'culture' has been divided and subdivided into other diverse terms. Sociologists have written about popular culture, media culture, mass culture, minority culture, ethnic culture, aborigine culture, black culture, white culture, feminist culture, gay culture, lesbian culture, drug culture, colonial culture, modernist and postmodernist culture, Marxist and post-Marxist culture, highbrow, middlebrow and lowbrow culture, techno culture, organizational culture, managerial and executive culture, culture of complaint, culture of violence, culture of the classes, culture of the underclasses – the list is virtually endless. Some writers, for reasons which are not easy to understand, have felt it necessary to add further divisions into each of these concepts by adding the prefix 'sub' to the word culture. So now we have a subculture of violence, a subculture of drugs etc. If one were being pedantic one could subdivide a subculture into a sub-subculture, creating a meaningless fragmentation of the concept.

Psychological perspectives

Within psychology too, there is lack of agreement as to how culture should be defined and conceptualized. Triandis (1980) points out that societies vary with respect to their ecology, their subsistence system, their sociocultural system, their individual systems and their inter-individual systems. Others (e.g. Murdock and Provost 1973) have proposed different classification systems.

Regardless of the lack of consensus on the number and type of parameters which would best define a culture, the necessity of a classification system cannot be denied. It allows us to understand the nature of variation in different societies and in so doing permits us to go beyond a descriptive classificatory system and pose fundamental theoretical questions concerning the nature and the causes of such variations. Let us sample a few definitions of culture.

Barnlund and Araki (1985) tend to construe culture from a *behaviouristic perspective.* To them, cultures 'have no existence except as they are manifest in the behaviour of people who constitute them. A culture is only an abstraction based on common [characteristics] . . . displayed in the behaviour of a given community of people' (p. 9). Clearly there is a problem with this definition. How would the authors promoting such a view of culture explain the deviant, bizarre, uncommon, anomalous and even one-off behaviours exhibited by some of the people of such a society? Valsiner (1989) on the other hand sees culture in terms of *organized psychological functions*, which may be intrapersonal and also interpersonal. Geertz (1973) identified culture as a 'historically transmitted pattern of meanings embodied in symbols' (p. 89). Many psychologists have emphasized several factors which constitute a culture: ecology, physical geography, climate, common language, dietary practices and so on (e.g. Leach 1964; Murdock 1964; Whiting 1964). Some on the other hand have focused on value systems and networks of communication as being the essential ingredients comprising a culture. A few have argued that a proper definition of culture would need to include the geographical territory occupied by the people one referred to as belonging to a culture. Most of the definitions and interpretations appear to be 'discipline driven' and reflect in one form or other the theoretical orientations and the differing research methodologies of the contributors. There is however a shared belief among academics that there are differences and similarities among all cultures all over the world. In other words, all human beings share several common universal attitudinal, behavioural and emotional characteristics. At the same time, each culture or each society has its own unique features which vary along several important dimensions, such as ecology, climate, levels of education, technological development, politics, social, economic and environmental conditions, beliefs, attitudes and value systems. Value systems have a significant bearing on a variety of factors, including, childrearing techniques, patterns of socialization, development of identities, kinship networks, work habits, social and familial arrangements, and the religious beliefs and practices of people in that society (Kakar [1979] 1992; Roland 1988; Laungani 2001d).

Given the cultural specificity of certain values, it follows that many of our beliefs, attitudes and behaviours, both private and public, are also likely to be culture-specific. Thus one would expect to find, both within and between cultures, *similarities* and *differences* in the manner in which a variety of problems such as health, illness, mental illness, grief, bereavement, patterns of infant rearing and socialization, acquisition of identity, attitudes to work, relationships etc. are defined, conceptualized and acted upon by peoples of those cultures.

Let us now turn to the third view concerning culture.

Postmodern perspectives

Postmodernism, despite its increasing popularity, defies an acceptable definition. Before we turn to the term 'postmodernism', let us briefly look at the term 'modern'. 'Modern' derives from a Latin adverb meaning *just now*. In English it is used in its *current* sense, meaning 'now'. Following this line of argument, the modern period – just now – has given way to a postmodern period, meaning that we have just gone past *just now*! It is clear that the term postmodern is not to be taken literally – since it is impossible to live beyond just now. To arrive at some understanding of the term we need to disentangle modern from postmodern. This, of course, raises intriguing questions.

Has the modern stopped and the postmodern begun? Did the modern begin at any one point in space-time? Who signalled its birth? How was it signalled? Or has postmodernism 'grown out' of the modern? Is postmodernism a sunrise which has permanently eclipsed the modern? Or is postmodernism the child of the modern, grown to manhood? Is postmodernism a 'universal era'? Are there reliable sets of criteria, or markers, by which we could specify a) the commencement of postmodernism and b) its main features?

There is, it would seem, an unvoiced sentiment shared by many postmodernists that the postmodern is a western 'phenomenon', or 'age' or 'period' – a 'way of thinking', 'a way of life' an 'advancement'. One gets the impression too that the promoters of postmodernism, among other things, seem eager to implant the rapidly changing value systems (including commercial, economic and technological) in western societies into non-western societies. Let us transport a few intrepid postmodernist scholars into a few small, time-frozen villages in Orissa, Bihar and Mahya Pradesh in India, and a few into small towns such as Thato, Mirpurkhas, Kotri, Larkana in Pakistan. The day-to-day lives of the people living in such places has moved hardly beyond the medieval period. What would the postmodernists see? How would they reconcile or explain away the glaring contradictions confronting them? No clear answers, other than a refuge into rhetoric, can be offered.

Even today, there are serious disputes among professional historians concerning the distinction between medieval and modern. The criteria by which the medieval can be distinguished from the modern keep changing. The medieval period has been 'pushed back' from the fifteenth and sixteenth century to the twelfth century (Brinton 1962). It is virtually impossible to answer all the above questions, leaving us no choice other than to accept postmodernism on 'faith' or reject it altogether. One might be inclined to take it on trust, if one was given a clear idea about what it means, what it symbolizes, what it stands for, what its major assumptions are, what its historical pedigree is and why it has become part of the modern intellectual folklore. One would need to be an extraordinarily brave person to offer a clear precise and objective definition of the term postmodernism.

All we can do is to try to understand the problem by highlighting the conflicting, contradictory and confusing ways in which the term has been explained. Several exponents of postmodernism (Habermas 1981; Huyssen 1984; Featherstone 1988; Boyne and Rattansi 1990; Giddens 1991; Bauman 1992; Gellner 1992) have pointed out that it means different things to different people. The following are some of the meanings and labels ascribed to postmodernism:

- Licence to do whatever one may fancy, without taking anything seriously; a life without truths, without standards, without ideals.
- Emergence of a new historical condition, a contemporary, social, cultural, political condition, with an acceptance of cultural diversity and plurality; its resultant coexistence and the flattening of all forms of hierarchies and any form of ordering.
- Subjective standards of ethical judgements and the consequent refuge into ethical relativism.
- Abandonment of any yardsticks by which any meaningful comparisons of any kind can be made; lack of commensurability; the impossibility of making any final judgement; in other words, 'anything goes'.
- The end or the dissipation of objectivity, and the end of positivism.

- Epistemological anarchy.
- The triumph of a liberal, democratic way of life over other social and political systems.

When one sifts through the massive literature on postmodernism, one gets the impression that the concept appears to lack a core. It seems to be covered by unending layers upon layers of metaphorical, and sociological aphorisms. One peels off layer after layer in the hope that one will, after painstaking effort, eventually arrive at some definite understanding of the central ideas underlying postmodernism – the 'core' – which will reveal its true essence. What one is left with are the vague vestiges of a vaporizing, vanishing dream.

I would like the reader to appreciate that the above is not meant to be a critical commentary on postmodernism; it merely expresses the difficulty which one is likely to encounter in attempting to understand and reconcile some of the contradictory ideas underlying postmodernism. But since, despite its crudity, the term has come to stay and we shall stay with it. In contemporary postmodern western society, the term 'culture' is seen as *passé*; it appears to have given way to the concept of multiculturalism. The trend toward multiculturalism has gathered considerable momentum in recent years. Cultures coexist alongside each other. Such coexistence inhibits any form of ordering of cultures into hierarchies. The cultural 'windows' have already begun to open, at least as far as Britain is concerned. Britain is no longer seen as a mono-cultural society, but as a multicultural society. It has been argued that with the exception of very few cultures dotted around the world, virtually all cultures are influenced by, and in turn influence, other cultures (Parekh 2000).

The mix of cultures within the mainstream of British society is seen as an invaluable asset and not a crippling liability. It provides exciting opportunities to academics, scholars, clinicians, doctors, health professionals and a host of interested organizations for learning and acquiring insights into a variety of cross-cultural issues. Many people believe that the visible cultural diversity (or multiculturalism) in Britain has made it easier for people of different cultures to understand and relate to one another in meaningful ways. However, the critics of postmodernism have argued that postmodern culture remains fragmented, disorderly, pluralistic and devoid of any direction. It is no doubt true that people of all cultures frequent the same department stores and supermarkets, visit the same types of restaurant, avail themselves of the same health services, watch similar television programmes, go to the same cinemas, and are often the hapless victims of the mass media etc. But one must not be misled into believing that this has made it any the easier for people of different cultures to understand and relate to one another.

The cultural mix seen from the outside conveys the impression of assimilation, even integration. But behind closed doors, when each individual enters his or her own home, the apparent similarity ends and life takes on a specific culture-centred dimension.

We have travelled a long way. Of the various approaches and perspectives we have examined thus far, the postmodernistic one has perhaps been the least useful in our attempts to understand culture. To use a popular postmodernistic phrase, 'doubts remain'. But let us distil the main points from the foregoing to encapsulate the concept with some rigour, after which we can examine the influence of culture on counselling and psychotherapy.

Final comments on culture

What constitutes a culture? All cultures possess a set of core (primary) features and a set of peripheral (secondary) features. The core features constitute the essential requirements of any culture. The peripheral features, although important, may vary from culture to culture.

Core features

- A past history (recorded or oral).
- Regulated political, legal and social systems, and communication networks.
- A dominant, organized religion within which the salient beliefs and activities (rites, rituals, taboos and ceremonies) can be given meaning and legitimacy.
- A set of core values and traditions, including regulatory norms of personal, familial and social conduct to which the people of that society subscribe and attempt to perpetuate.
- Artefacts unique to that society, such as literature, works of art, paintings, music, dance, drama, religious texts, philosophical texts etc.

Secondary features

- Freedom from religious, political and social persecution.
- Shared common language(s).

- Internationally recognized common physical and geographical boundaries within which people of that particular society live.
- Housing and other living arrangements.
- Socially accepted dietary, health and medical practices.

We have discussed the concept of culture at some length. We have also accepted the view that cultures vary with respect to their value systems, which in turn influence the private and social behaviours of people in those cultures. It is obvious therefore that one would expect to observe differences (and similarities) in values and behaviours between, say, the indigenous (native-born white) English and Indians in India, and persons originating from the Indian sub-continent living in Britain.

Objective knowledge of such similarities and differences, and *how and why they arise* would be of immense value to teachers, educators, doctors, health workers, psychotherapists *and* counsellors – to name but a few. The differences between eastern cultures and western (largely English) cultures are discussed in Chapter 3.

Having examined the issues of culture (without having 'settled' them) it is now time to examine the impact (if any) culture has on counselling and therapy. The term 'therapy', in this instance, should include the physical presence of the therapist as well, because it is difficult to visualize therapy without a therapist. Even this caveat is not strictly true, for it is possible in the postmodern era to obtain some form of therapy over the internet. This possibility eliminates the need for the physical presence of the therapist. In the not too distant future it should become possible to link up sound and audio-visual contact between the client and the therapist, regardless of the thousands of miles which may separate them. I shall, however, err on the side of caution, if not conservatism, and examine the problem from a situation which presupposes a face-to-face encounter between the client and the therapist.

The influence of culture on counselling and psychotherapy

From the foregoing it is obvious that the influence of culture on counselling and psychotherapy cannot be underestimated. Whether you happen to be sitting behind a therapist's desk or facing the therapist, cultural differences come into play right at the outset. One would need to be extremely naïve not to notice differences (and similarities) in one's encounter with the client. How can one fail to notice the client's skin colour, gender, age, accent, class, mode of dress, language, and all the other differential details which may surface upon one's first meeting with the client? Yet there are several therapists who take pride in asserting that in the course of their work (and even in their private life) they operate as though they were 'culture blind'. What in fact they are saying is that they choose to ignore the cultural differences which separate them from their clients, or that they do not consider cultural differences as of significant importance in therapy. To ignore such salient variables which might determine not only the process of therapy but also the outcome, seems strange to say the least. This is an intensely debatable issue to which we shall return later.

What further adds to the complication is the fact that the field of counselling (psychotherapy, psychoanalysis, behaviour therapy, transactional analysis, Gestalt therapy, person-centred therapy – to name but a few) is itself a disparate, non-unified discipline. It is not 'united' by a single, all-embracing theoretical framework, or paradigm, in the Kuhnian (Kuhn 1967) sense of the word. There are several hundred diverse models of therapies (see Chapter 4), each of which is founded on different assumptions, requires different skills, calls for different training programmes, accepts different forms of accreditation (or not, as the case may be), uses different techniques and predicts different outcomes.

Such is not the case in the natural sciences. Here, the theoretical and the applied scientists tend to work within an accepted paradigm, which Kuhn refers to as 'normal science'. Failure to predict outcomes, failure to validate the theoretical models, failure to digest or explain away anomalies, leads to a crisis of confidence in the paradigm, which in turn leads to a scientific revolution. Scientists turn away from the model and the model is abandoned. Subsequently it is replaced by another paradigm, leading once again, to a state of 'normal science'.

To ignore the problem of a lack of a single theoretical framework for counselling in relation to culture (as has largely been the case so far) or to deny its salience is dangerous. To continue to operate with 'free for all' therapeutic strategies may eventually tarnish the image of this noble profession, and lead to a state of epistemological anarchy.

It is important that therapists of all persuasions and theoretical orientations from all over the world meet, put their heads together and discover acceptable ways of dealing with the complex issues related to culture and psychotherapy, and find rigorous ways of testing their diverse approaches and strategies before it is too late. These are complex issues. In the following chapters they will be discussed at length. To give the reader a 'flavour' of the complexities involved in cross-cultural therapy, I have sketched below a short summary of three hypothetical, cross-cultural case studies. The reader is invited to examine each study carefully and work out the best way in which he or she might tackle the problem.

Given the wide-ranging sets of variables that come into play right at the outset, the question that arises is this. On what sort of basis is the therapy likely to proceed? What are the mutual assumptions (both of the client and the therapist) that will guide the process of therapy? How will each make sense of the 'other's world'? How would you as an experienced therapist deal with the case studies described below? Given the above caveat that therapists do not subscribe to a unified paradigm, your approach in dealing with a specific problem is likely to be quite different from that of another therapist whose theoretical model differs from yours. For instance, the assumptions made by a psychoanalyst will be significantly different from those of a person-centred therapist, which in turn will differ from those of a cognitive behaviour therapist, and so on. How is one to determine which of the diverse approaches is the most effective one to use, and how is one to make such an assessment? This leads us straight into the problems of commensurability (Laungani 1999c) or, in other words, how does one compare one therapeutic approach with another? Failure to find ways of testing and comparing one approach with another can lead to a state of 'anarchy' within the entire field of counselling and psychotherapy. We shall return to this vital issue later.

Although the case studies selected are all hypothetical in nature, they are not entirely dissimilar from some of the cases that some of my friends and associates in England and in India have encountered. Thus, although they are not 'real life' cases, they are close to real life.

Hypothetical case studies

Case study 1

The case concerns a second-generation Hindu Indian female born and brought up in England. Her parents are caring, loving, traditional and quite orthodox. They plan and discuss her arranged marriage to an engineer living in India. The girl refuses the proposal. Unbeknown to her parents she is in love with a young English guitarist, who is desperately trying to get into a 'big time' pop group. She has no desire whatever to go and live in India.

Imagine the usual predictable scenario.

Parents find out and threaten to send her to India to 'cool her heels'. With the help of one of her English friends, the girl leaves home and stays with her friend. Not a glimmer of reconciliation on the horizon. Parents distraught, the girl torn by guilt, anger and conflict. Loves her parents dearly but will not accept an arranged marriage, and will not go and live in India.

It is the *parents* who seek you out and come to you for help.

Case study 2

A Muslim family originally from Pakistan: father, mother, a daughter and two sons, all in their teens, all born in England. Father works as a weaver in a carpet factory in Bradford. Has lived in England for over 20 years. Has no formal education. Can speak a bit of conversational English, enough to get by.

Mr Rahman is eager to get his teenaged daughter married in Pakistan. The daughter has no strong opinions one way or the other. Has been to Pakistan on several occasions, has stayed with her relatives and loves it there. On one of her trips to Pakistan, she met the prospective husband and is quite fond of him. He runs a wholesale dry-fruits business in Lahore. Mr Rahman's wife, however, is very concerned and deeply unhappy about the proposal, not because of the proposal but because her husband is anxious to marry his prospective son-in-law's older sister, who is a widow. She does not wish her husband to have another wife and has no desire to be relegated to an inferior position were he to acquire one. Mrs Rahman feels isolated and alienated from the family.

This of course leads to unrest and violent quarrels at home. Arguments occasionally end in fisticuffs. The daughter sides with the father and dislikes the mother for standing in her way. She is keen to get married and despite being born and brought up in England, is happy at the idea of living in Pakistan. In desperation Mrs Rahman turns to the social services for help. The case is then referred to you.

Case study 3

This concerns an affluent Indian businessman, Mr Sharma, and his wife Shakuntala. They live in Taipei, in Taiwan. The husband has testicular cancer, and he and his wife have come to London for his treatment. They have a daughter who is doing a masters degree at Princeton University in New Jersey. The husband and wife lead relatively independent lives: he is totally absorbed with his business, and she, over the last ten years, has 'taken to' religion in a big way, to the neglect of all else. Much to her husband's unvoiced annoyance she has built a small temple in their large flat in Taipei, to which she invites all her Indian friends. Prayer meetings are held every day, devotional songs are sung, and visiting spiritual gurus are fêted and feasted with unfailing regularity. She has acquired the reputation of being a holy person.

During her husband's postoperative convalescence in London, she visits all the temples, meets a variety of gurus and eventually forms a strong attachment to a religious group, 'The Brahmakumaris' in London. An alarming change has come over her. Sex, meat, alcohol and television have become taboo subjects; she has taken to wearing plain white cotton saris; she spends most of the day either with the Brahmakumaris or at home, absorbed in prayers for her husband's recovery.

Mr Sharma, anxious about his own health, his business interests that he has left behind, and about his wife's 'sanity', contacts his daughter in New Jersey, asking her to come to London. In less than two days, the daughter gets in touch with you for help.

Conclusion

I need to emphasize once again that all the above case studies are fictitious; they bear no resemblance to any person or persons, living or dead. Please feel free to deal with each problem situation in your own way and in accordance with your own theoretical and intuitive orientations. Should you care to put your ideas and approaches on paper, nothing would give me greater pleasure than to receive them from you. It would be a singular honour.

Chapter 2

Asians in Britain: historical and intergenerational perspectives

Introduction

To understand the present it often becomes necessary to understand the past. To ignore the past and merely concentrate on the present often leads to a distorted and even a simplistic understanding of the present. There is another danger too, which was pointed out many years ago by the Spanish philosopher, George Santayana. He believed that in turning one's back on history, one was likely to repeat the very mistakes which one had made in the past. Learning the lessons from history may teach us how to avoid the mistakes of the past.

Let us therefore turn the clock back and examine the nature of migratory patterns of people from different parts of the world, in particular from the Indian sub-continent to Britain.

Migratory patterns of Asians into Britain

India, as Winston Churchill never tired of claiming, was Britain's 'jewel in the crown'. This sentiment was also accompanied by a firm belief that so long as Britain continued to rule over India, the sun would never set on British soil, which included all her colonies, spread around the world. The loss of India, it was felt, would result in the loss of the British Empire. Little did Churchill realize that his utterances would turn out to be so prophetic!

Britain did lose India, and soon afterwards most of its Empire. India gained her independence on 15 August 1947. Upon independence, India was split into two countries: India and Pakistan. Pakistan was created or carved out of India and was itself divided into West Pakistan and East Pakistan, each part separated from the other by over a thousand miles of Indian territory. This was because the division of India was made largely on religious grounds. India had a high proportion of Hindus, and Pakistan (both West and East) a high proportion of Muslims. India was sandwiched between West Pakistan and East Pakistan. East Pakistan was controlled and governed by West Pakistan, but relations between West and East were far from friendly, to say the least. They worsened over the years. A civil war broke out between East and West Pakistan; a long, hard and bloody insurrection took place in which about 3 million Bengali Muslims were systematically and brutally butchered by West Pakistani forces. Kith had killed its kin. The horrors of the savage butchery remain unknown to people in the West. Eventually, East Pakistan broke away from West Pakistan and in 1971 declared its independence. And thus was Bangladesh born.

The splitting of India taught the displaced persons their first bitter lessons in migration. The Hindus, who had lived in what came to be called Pakistan, fled to India, and similarly the Muslims fled from India to Pakistan. This cross-migration led to unimaginable horrors. Ugly, unparalleled violence, brutality and savagery brought about the loss of over half a million innocent lives on both sides of the religious divide – a fact which remains unvoiced and even unknown in the West (Das 2000). It should be made clear that less than 2 per cent of Hindus decided to stay behind in the newly created state of Pakistan, and about 11 per cent of Muslims decided to remain in India. Whereas the Muslim population in India has now increased to a little over 14 per cent (Manorama 2002), the Hindu population in Pakistan has remained relatively static, at just under 2 per cent.

The entire course of savagery repeated itself when Bangladesh came into being. The lessons from history had not been taken to heart. The Hindus who had lived in East Pakistan fled to Bengal, and the Bengali Muslims who until then had lived in Bengal fled to Bangladesh. The cross-migration once again led to violence, butchery and senseless savagery. It also created a generation of more than half a million refugees both in Bangladesh and in India.

Britain – the mother country of its colonies

Since Britain was seen as the 'mother' country of all its colonies, there were many persons in India and Pakistan (and of course in other colonies) who decided to migrate there. During the 1950s there were no difficulties and hardly any obstacles (other than the usual bureaucratic and health-related ones) to prevent any of the 'subjects' of the colonies from coming into Britain. This facility was also extended to the ex-colonies, such as India and Pakistan. Due to an acute shortage of labour following the post-war period in the early 1950s, Enoch Powell undertook a much-publicized trip to the West Indies in the hope of wooing the West Indians to migrate to England, where they would be made welcome and secure, and well-paid jobs would be made available. Several thousand people from the colonies, which included India, Pakistan, South Africa, East Africa and the West Indies, took advantage of the 'open door' policy and migrated to Britain. Most of them came to make a 'new life' for themselves, in social, economic, and cultural terms. They saw themselves as an integral part of Britain. Many of their forefathers had fought on the side of Britain during the two World Wars, and Britain was truly regarded as their mother country.

But by 1963, for a variety of reasons, Britain decided to close its immigration doors to members of their colonies and ex-colonies, excluding Australia and New Zealand. There were fears expressed among the influential members of the public and in Parliament that a continued open door policy would soon 'swamp' the country, which could ill-afford to accommodate the uncontrolled influx of immigrants from the Third World countries. (Even the phrase 'Third World' was maliciously referred to as 'turd world' by those who were opposed to any form of migration into Britain.) Shutters were lowered and migration into Britain, regardless of an ex-colony's past historical association, became increasingly difficult. Visas, employment vouchers, permits and other forms of documentation were required of persons wishing to come and settle in Britain. The mother country had decided to disown her 'children'.

During the late 1960s and early 1970s Britain's immigration policies were put to a severe test when Asians of Indian origin were compelled to leave Uganda where they and their forefathers had lived for over a century under British rule and British protection. The Africanization policies of the newly independent country made it impossible for the Asians to live there. And given that they were British 'subjects' and held British passports, they saw it fit to come to Britain, which after all was their mother country. Given their commercial and mercantile acumen, many Asians were able to transfer their assets to economically and politically stable countries such as Britain, Canada, Sweden and the USA. Their affluence meant that they had little difficulty migrating to countries of their choice, including Britain.

Some, however, were less prepared or lacked the shrewdness of many of their compatriots, and were taken by surprise by the sudden and dramatic changes that took place before their disbelieving eyes. They soon became poor and homeless. Like bits of flotsam, these homeless refugees were pushed around from country to country in search of a permanent home. Eventually they were offered succour by several countries, including Sweden, the Netherlands, Denmark, Germany, Canada, India and a few others. After a long and bitter period of political wrangling, Britain relented, and allowed the East African Asians to enter Britain.

First-generation migrants

Those who had entered Britain prior to the new immigration laws being enforced might be regarded as the first-generation immigrants. There are some who may disagree with this formulation. They might argue (and they would be right in so doing) that the post-war Indians who migrated to Britain were by no means the first to set foot on British soil. Given the historical association with Britain there were thousands of Indians from all walks of life, ranging from students to politicians, from retired military personnel to sailors who jumped ship, from doctors and engineers and entrepreneurs, to those with family connections, who had been living in Britain from well before the large-scale immigration started. In fact, many of the Indian princes and maharajahs had built their own manor houses in England, and lived a life of exclusive luxury. In addition to these, there were numerous highly educated entrepreneurs, politicians, lawyers and journalists who came to Britain in the nineteenth century. Several of them, including Dadabhai Naoroji, Mancherjee Bhownaggree and Shapurjee Dorabjee Saklarvala became Indian members of the British Parliament. Dadabhai Naoroji, a sharp and astute politician, returned to India where he founded the First Indian National Congress. Although many of these people returned to India to fight for Indian independence, they were the first generation immigrants to Britain (Luhrmann 1996).

However, those immigrants who arrived during the major influx of the 1950s and 1960s were, in the main, from uneducated working-class backgrounds. A few of them were skilled workers, but most were unskilled. They had little knowledge of the language and hardly any understanding of the social customs, religion, family life and dietary practices of the British. Initially it was the male working population that came to Britain. They came with the hope that as soon as they became 'settled' they would arrange for their families to join them. They came with no material assets to boast of, other than the social, religious and familial values which they had imbibed in their own ancient cultures.

Despite the sense of security which their own ancient cultural values offered them, the culture shock experienced by the immigrants must have been immense. Not being able to speak English with any degree of fluency (or hardly at all), not being familiar with western ways, not being able to obtain 'ethnic' food (Indian restaurants were virtually unheard of during this period), not being able to bask in the warm sunshine, not having the know-how to protect themselves from the piercing winters, life to them must have appeared bewildering, to say the least. I can testify to these feelings from my own experiences when I first came to England in the late 1960s. As I have stated elsewhere:

> England, to me, came as a shock! There were as many accents there as there are dialects in India – or almost. Each of them as though spoke in a different tongue, and a few, even in forked tongues! It was difficult to distinguish between levity and seriousness, between jest and truth, between praise and censure, between affection and affectation, between acceptance and rejection. I found it exasperating not being able to read correctly their feelings and emotions on the rare occasions they chose to express them. In India I had been born into a particular caste and had learnt through childhood what was expected of me in a variety of social situations, which involved a mingling of castes. But with the English it was difficult to place them in their appropriate class categories; the class divisions, it seemed to me were blurred and not as clearly defined as the castes were (and to large extent, still are) in India. I could not always work out what was expected of me in different situations and of different people. What distressed me even further was that hardly any of the English friends I made (or thought I had made), showed any curiosity concerning my own cultural origins and upbringing. They avoided personal exchanges as assiduously as an orthodox Brahmin might avoid contact with an untouchable. Either they were too reticent to ask and find out, or they were totally

> disinterested. In my own statc of paranoia, I chose to believe the latter. How, in the name of heaven, I kept asking myself in my increasing state of despair, will I ever begin to understand them and hopefully befriend a few of them?
>
> Living in a foreign country, I soon realized was like fighting a lone battle on several fronts: the weather, the climate, the preserved and processed food, the strange customs and conventions, the patterns of day to day life, and of course the people.
>
> I committed unforgivable social blunders; I was guilty of all sorts of *faux pas*; I annoyed and exasperated people without meaning to. I asked questions, which the English considered private, personal, and sacrosanct. I volunteered information, which they found difficult to handle. By the same token, there were people who annoyed and even tormented me to such an extent that in my in state of anguish, I drove metaphorical stakes through their hearts! Although we spoke the same language, although we had past historical associations, although I had read the books, which I had assumed they would have also read, and although I dressed the way they did, I could tell that a vast ocean of differences separated me from them. I felt alienated. I felt like Moses, standing at the edge of the Red Sea. While the sea parted for Moses and his followers and they were able to cross over to the land of safety, I drowned and died a hundred deaths in the first waves of misunderstandings which engulfed me. Despite our historical associations, I found that we were divided more by our differences than united by our similarities. Although Rudyard Kipling's observation that 'The East is East and the West is West – and never the twain shall meet' was made almost a century ago, who would have imagined that his words were as appropriate then as they are today!
>
> (Laungani, 2002a: 387–8)

Although these are my personal sentiments, it would not come as a surprise that my own feelings and experiences pale into insignificance when compared with what many of the first-generation immigrants may have gone through in the course of 'settling down' to a new, unfamiliar and hostile way of life in a foreign country. Being closeted in an academic environment one is, to a large measure, protected (even pampered) from the harsh and hurtful 'realities' which could otherwise poison one's existence in the outside world.

It was hardly surprising that the first-generation immigrants chose to live close to their own compatriots from India, Pakistan, Africa and elsewhere. Regardless of where they lived – in Birmingham or Bradford, London or Leicester, Glasgow or Gravesend – they lived in close proximity to one another, thus acquiring the negative stereotype of creating ghettos. However, doing so enabled them to share the language, the food, the music, the clothes and the social and familial patterns of life, and acquire a sense of security and belongingness. It also allowed them to preserve their own cultural identity, which was all they had come with. In that sense, therefore, their behaviour was not significantly different from that of the British who set up their 'clubs' in India during the period of the British Raj. Among other things, the clubs engendered a sense of belonging and a sense of national identity – despite the fact that the British were the rulers who wielded awesome power over the people of India.

It has never been satisfactorily explained why most of the Indians who migrated to Britain came mainly from Gujarat, Punjab and the Sylhet district in East Bengal, which subsequently became part of Bangladesh. Gujarati Hindus and Gujarati Muslims, Hindu Punjabis and Muslim Punjabis, the Sikhs and the Bengali Muslims were the four predominant groups of people who migrated from India. This is not to suggest that Indians from other parts of the country did not venture abroad. They did. But their numbers were never as large as those of the above four groups. One might venture the explanation that these four groups have had a long history of being venturesome, opportunistic and adventurous. They have never been shy of taking risks involved with settling down in other countries. Many of them already had their relatives living in Britain, prior to their coming. The same four groups of people also migrated in the nineteenth century to South Africa and East Africa (which were then British colonies), to the Fiji Islands, to Mauritius and to other parts of the world, including the West Indies. While the migrant Gujaratis came from all over Gujarat, the Punjabis and Sikhs who migrated from India came largely from Jullunder and Hoshiarpur in the Punjab. The Bengalis came largely from different parts of West Bengal and from the district of Sylhet. The majority of Muslims came from the district of Mirpur, in Pakistan.

Being commercially orientated, it was not long before many immigrants to Britain began to acquire shops, businesses and other forms of commercial outlet including jewellery stores, grocery shops, newsagents, garages and Indian restaurants. As a result, they managed to change within a decade or so the 'landscape' of those parts of the country in which they lived. Gradually, as the years went by, the first-generation Asians began to acquire their own properties and arranged for their family members to join them. Since religion plays an extremely important role in the preservation and the perpetuation of the cultural identities of Hindus, Muslims and Sikhs, it was not long before one began to see Hindu temples, mosques, and Sikh *gurudwaras* (temples) in the areas in which they lived. Who would have believed that one day one would see magnificent mosques with their shiny, gilded domes in Kensington and Regent's Park!

As is only to be expected, the first-generation Asians to a very considerable extent remained ensconced within their own culture. English or British 'culture' to them was seen as being 'foreign', (*ferengi*) – a word which aroused in their minds all sorts of negative connotations. Coming as they did from collectivist and hierarchically structured societies, they found it difficult and in some instances alarming to make the required adjustments to live in a society which was individualistic in its orientation and structurally horizontal. To make the required adjustments would have involved a serious, if not irreconcilable, clash of values. Of course they all made the superficial cosmetic adjustments which allowed them to relate to the people of the host culture at a day-to-day, functional level. But as far as their own 'inherited' core values were concerned, they clung to them with even greater tenacity than they might have in their own country of origin.

Second- and third-generation Asians

There are several questions that are of great concern to us here. What kind of adults do the second- and third-generation children grow up to become? How does exposure to two cultural value systems, which in many significant ways are non-complementary, if not incompatible, influence them in becoming the kind of adults they do? How do they, initially as children and then as adolescents, learn to handle, juggle, accept, reject, revise, change and modify their linguistic expressions at home and outside? What kinds of relationship do they form with their own indigenous groups of people and with others? And above all, how do they learn to cope with the conflicting sets of values to which they are continuously exposed?

How do they learn to live amid different worlds, each with its own sets of unique expectations, attitudes, values and traditions? How do they attempt to create for themselves a socially constructed identity, firmly rooted in psychological and social reality?

To use an overworked cliché, do they grow up to see themselves as being 'black British', or as Asians, as Indians, or as Pakistanis, or whatever? Do they conceive of their personal identity in nationalistic terms, in cultural terms, in terms of the amount of melanin in their bloodstream or in cosmopolitan terms – the ancient Greek ideal of 'citizen of the world'? Or do they see themselves in terms of 'I' and 'me'? William James (1918), one of the greatest American psychologists, distinguished between the 'I', and the 'me'. According to James, the 'I' refers to the subjective self and the 'me', to the objective self.

Family life in western cultures

In the not too distant past – less than half a century ago – a family unit consisted of the father, the mother, their two or three children, and even the grandparents. The father was seen as the patriarch and the proverbial 'bread-winner'. He had no role to play in the day-to-day bringing up of children, which was left largely in the hands of the women at home. Day-to-day life revolved around the family. But in the last three to four decades the situation has changed, so much so that the concept of what constitutes a family has become difficult to define with any degree of accuracy (Levin 1990; Trost 1990). This is due to several factors. Formalized marriage has lost its status in western society (Dumon 1992). Cohabitation without marriage has increased. The rate of divorce has been rising in most European countries, including Britain. It is estimated that at least a third of all families are single-parent, headed by a female. Over 25 per cent of the English population lives alone. Other extraneous factors such as changes in demographic trends, economic recessions, wars, famines, migrations, technological innovation, urbanization and widening opportunities for women also account for the changes that have taken place.

The changes in the size and the structure of families, combined with high levels of social and occupational mobility, may have 'destabilized' society, creating a sense of loss of community life, particularly in the urban metropolitan cities (United Nations 1996). From a psychological point of view, major changes have occurred in collective values, particularly those that support individualism, where the needs of an individual take priority over the needs of the family and the group. Although the family is recognized as the basic unit – the microcosm of society – the changes in society have altered the roles and functions of both men and women in families. It is clear that the 'traditional' role of the family as a self-sustaining, self-contained, unified unit has changed almost beyond recognition. What impact a nuclear or a one-parent family (or a family of 'changing' parents due to living with different partners or remarriage), combined with increasing occupational, physical and social mobility has on the future growth and development of the child is an open question. In the absence of any clear, longitudinal evidence, it would be pointless to express a firm opinion on this issue. However, it needs to be said that in such a changing family situation the child is more than likely to be denied a sense of continuity and familiarity, not just in terms of being brought up by the same parents, but also in terms of friends and acquaintances.

It has been argued that families in western countries, particularly in the USA, have been unable to develop positive ways of adjusting to these rapid changes, and it is possible that the rapid speed of change may in itself be a major factor of stress in families.

Family life in eastern cultures

In sharp contrast to western society, Indian society, not unlike other eastern societies, is family-based and community-centred (Zaehner 1966a; Mandelbaum 1972; Lannoy 1975; Kakar 1981; Koller 1982; Lipner 1994; Flood 1996; Laungani 1997c, 1999d, 2001a; Klostermaier 1998; Sharma 2000).

In non-western cultures, particularly in India, Pakistan, Bangladesh and several other countries in South-East Asia, including Malaysia, Thailand, Indonesia and China, the size of the average family tends to be much larger. Non-western cultures even today follow an extended family network, which often includes the child's parents, grandparents, uncles, aunts, sisters-in-law, nieces, nephews and other siblings in the household. In many affluent Indian homes, there would also be a retinue of faithful and long-serving servants (or 'faithful retainers', to use a Victorian phrase) involved in the care and upbringing of the children (United Nations 1996; Laungani 2001a). Thus a child learns from an early age to be tended to by a variety of persons of different ages in the household.

The child also learns the nature of his or her individualized relationship with different members in the family. One of the obvious consequences of such a cultural arrangement is a sense of continuity and permanence which is created in the mind of the growing child.

Given the large number of members in the family, children of course become the beneficiaries of multiple caregivers. The child in an Indian home is likely to be subjected to a variety of influences (both contradictory and complementary) in the process of socialization. In other words, a growing child is likely to acquire a variety of role models.

The extended family needs to be understood in its psychological and functional terms. For a start, the patterns of relationships tend largely to be intrafamilial. Family life is organized along age- and gender-related hierarchical lines, with male elders being accorded a privileged and powerful position. Each member – right from childhood – learns to understand and accept his or her own position within the family hierarchy. Who can take 'liberties' with whom, who can shout at whom, who will defer to whom, who will seek comfort and solace from whom, who can confide in whom, are subtle emotional patterns of expression, which one learns in an extended family network.

Gender differences in socialization

It should also be recognized that there are significant differences in socialization processes between boys and girls in eastern cultures. Male children enjoy a more privileged position than their female siblings. The elders in the family allow a male child to 'get away' with behaviours which they would find hard to condone in a female child (Kakar 1981). This privilege also extends to food, clothing, toys and play. In an impoverished home or a home of less than adequate means, a larger share of food is given to the male children; they may also be fed first by the family members. The part played by the mother in the bringing up of children is of paramount importance, particularly her relationship with her son; a special relationship develops between the two. Whether this relationship can be construed in Oedipal terms is arguable, although several writers, including Kakar, Lannoy and Roland, and others operating from within a Freudian framework, have asserted that this is often the case. The male child is indulged, pampered, protected and as far as possible denied very little. While the mother may attempt to strike a balance between the male and female child's demands, it often transpires that the male child's impulsive wishes, wants and desires take precedence over the needs of the female child. The father, on the other hand, remains detached from the day-to-day cares related to the upbringing of the children, male or female. His role, at least during the first few years, tends to be minimal.

The needs of the female child seldom or hardly ever take precedence. In accordance with ancient Hindu scriptures, the birth of a male child in a family is considered to be a blessing, for a variety of reasons (Laungani 2002a). First, it ensures the perpetuation of the family name. Second, the son is seen as an economic asset and upon marriage will bring in a handsome dowry. Third, he is also expected to support and look after his parents when they become old and frail. Fourth, it is the son who, on the death of his parents, is expected to perform all the funeral rites and also light the funeral pyre, to ensure the safe passage and eventual repose of their souls.

The birth of a daughter on the other hand is treated with mixed feelings and even with some misgivings. As Kakar (1981) points out, the daughter in a Hindu family hardly ever develops an identity of her own. She is expected to remain chaste and pure and upon reaching marriageable age she may be seen as an economic liability because of the dowry she is expected to take with her to her husband's home. On entering her married home, her status changes. She is seen as a wife, as a daughter-in-law, as a sister-in-law in the new home, and then as a mother, a grandmother, and, should her husband predecease her, as a widow. Like a snake casting off its skin the daughter upon marriage is shorn of her own name. She acquires a new persona and is given a new name by which she is addressed in future. While the snake's discarding of its old skin and acquiring a new skin is a natural event, which has certain biological and evolutionary gains, the Hindu bride, upon entering her new home (her own feelings notwithstanding) is expected to bury her past, which includes her identity, and start her life with a new identity, which is *ascribed to her* by her husband and her in-laws. Such a staggering metamorphosis serves no biological or evolutionary advantage. On the contrary, it reinforces the defenceless if not 'subjugated' role which a woman is expected to play after marriage. Thus, her maiden name 'Geeta' may be changed to 'Seeta', and 'Mohini' to 'Rohini', and so on. She appears to have no individual identity other than the changing identities she acquires through reflected role relationships. Her private persona remains submerged within these changing and conflicting identities. From birth to death she does not possess an identity of her own. However, it is important to stress that several enlightened parents look upon the birth of a girl as 'a gift of the gods' and see it as their sacred duty, which is part of Hindu *dharma*, to have their daughter(s) handsomely and 'happily' married.

Despite the seemingly pitiful nature of the daughter-in-law's position in her husband's family home, there are compensatory psychological and power-related dramas that are played out in Indian families. Imagine a scenario: three brothers with their respective wives living in an extended and joint family network. The oldest daughter-in-law (the *jethani*), by virtue of being married to the oldest son is often in an extremely dominant position, delegating cooking, cleaning, washing and other household tasks to the two younger sisters-in-law (the *derani*). Even the care of her own children may be relegated to her younger sisters-in-law. The power exercised can in certain instances be extremely tyrannical. The second sister-in-law can exercise a certain amount of power over the youngest sister-in-law, and so on, moving down along age-related hierarchical lines. However, the power structure can change dramatically in a variety of subtle ways, which often remain unnoticed to an outsider. For instance, the eldest sister-in-law may be childless, or may not have produced a male child; the younger sisters-in-law may have produced sons; they may also have come from affluent homes, and may also be highly educated, or their respective husbands may have a far superior earning capacity to their oldest brother, etc., etc. The balance of power is by no means fixed; it is flexible and subtle, and changes from time to time. However, all the three sisters-in-law are expected to defer to the unquestionable power of their mother-in-law, who often 'rules' the house.

Upon the death of the mother-in-law, the balance of power shifts quite dramatically. Covert (and sometimes not so covert) battles may be fought by the three daughters-in-law, with each jockeying for a position at the top. At times, the husbands too may be brought into the fray, leading to severe turmoil within the family, until the dust settles and the situation reaches a new equilibrium.

One wonders the extent to which western counsellors and therapists have an incisive understanding of these subtle family dynamics in Indian families.

Development of identity in western cultures

One of the features (and there are several) which distinguishes Indian families from western families is the manner in which children develop their identities. In the West, the development of individual identity is generally seen in socio-psycho-sexual-cognitive terms.

Erik Erikson (1963) proposed an eight-stage theory of psycho-social (instead of psychosexual) identity development. Erikson was trained by Freud's daughter Anna to become a psychoanalyst. But he disagreed with Freud's portrayal of the ego as being involved in perpetual conflict with the irrational id on the one hand and the controlling superego on the other.

The process of identity formation starts in infancy and according to Erikson passes through several *critical stages*, from childhood, to adolescence, and into adulthood (Erikson 1963). To acquire an appropriate identity which asserts one's strengths, which is located in reality, which separates the individual from others and is thereby kept distinct from those of others, which reflects one's true inner being and which leads to the fulfilment or the realization of one's potential is by no means easy. It often results in conflict, which if unresolved, leads to severe stress, and in extreme cases to an identity crisis (Erikson 1963; Maslow 1970, 1971; Camilleri 1989). In other words, the individual concerned has to 'work' towards achieving an appropriate identity.

Erikson's theory has enjoyed great popularity, but it has not gone unchallenged, both within western cultures and across cultures. While there is significant support for his fundamental formulations concerning the concept of identity, some doubts have been expressed concerning the theory's empirical validity (Waterman 1981). There is, however, some support for Erikson's theory within the Indian context (Kakar and Chowdhry 1970; Kakar [1979] 1992, 1981).

Erikson's theory has distinct parallels in Piaget's theory of cognitive development (1970). Following seemingly uncomplicated 'experiments' carried out on his children, Piaget came to the conclusion that all human beings engage in cognitive attempts to construct a meaningful social world which is rooted in reality. In that sense therefore the attempts of an 'ordinary' person to find meaning and explanation are in no way different from those of scientists, other than in levels of thinking that may be involved.

In contradistinction to Erikson's theory was the one proposed by Freud. Freud argues for a four-stage (if one includes the genital stage) psychosexual model of the development of the ego. Each stage operates at an unconscious level and is beset with its own potential tensions, traumas and conflicts. If the traumas remain unresolved they may manifest themselves in neurotic patterns of behaviour in one's adult life. Freud ([1953] 1976) believed in the *universality* of his proposed model. In other words, all children all over the world would be expected to pass through these unconscious stages in the process of developing their identities. Massive amounts of research evidence gathered over the years do *not* bear out Freud's universalistic claims. Malinowski, for example, in his studies of the Trobriand Islanders in the South Pacific, pointed out in 1927 the importance of cultural factors on the development of identity.

All the above theories, it needs to be emphasized, are European constructions and reflect, to a large extent, European values. The theories offer reasonable explanations of ego, identity, personality and cognitive development. It is not certain, however, that they are able to predict with any accuracy how a particular child brought up in a *dual culture* is likely to develop, and what kind of a person the child is likely to become. The explanations offered by such theories often tend to be given after the event. Given the complex nature of these theories, such a strategy is understandable. But I should also like to alert the reader to the fact that from a strict scientific point of view the value of a post hoc analysis tends to be questionable.

The number of factors associated with the growth and development of identity – identity itself is an elusive construct – are so vast and varied that it is virtually impossible to give unconditional, unequivocal answers to all the questions concerning it. Causal explanations are impossible to establish with certainty. It seems foolhardy to even try. Yet, this has not prevented several western psychologists from hinting at (if not actually offering) causal explanations concerning the development of identity.

In this connection, one ought never to forget the writings of David Hume, the eighteenth-century Scottish philosopher, on the subject of causality. He argued that it is virtually impossible to establish cause and effect even in the most carefully controlled experiments. According to Hume, all methods – from the most stringent and objective to the very loose and subjective – are doomed when it comes to establishing cause and effect. For Hume, post hoc studies would have seemed to be almost entirely without meaning. Although his criticisms have not gone unchallenged, no one so far has been able to find satisfactory answers to overturn them (Popper 1963, 1972; Lavine 1984). David Hume teaches us a valuable lesson. In simple terms he is suggesting that little or no purpose will be served in jumping to hasty conclusions as a result of such methods of investigation.

Development of identity in eastern cultures

The development of identity within an eastern cultural setting constitutes a complex problem. To understand the development of identity, it would become necessary to understand the workings of the Indian caste system, which has a very strong bearing on the development of identity and its influence on behaviour in all areas of life – attitudes and values, patterns of relationships, choice of friends, marital partners, occupations, worship etc.

Also, the problem of identity would become more meaningful when placed within the framework of a theoretical model, and this has been developed and elaborated in the following chapter.

Let us end this chapter with a vignette. The purpose is to try and capture the essence of what we have been discussing so far. Since a vignette or a case study has the ingredients of a drama, it also makes interesting reading. A case study may allow us to tease out some consistent features within a particular case. This would then permit us to deduce a few testable hypotheses. And despite the fact that each case has its own unique features, its own history and its own sets of circumstances, we may find parallels between one case study and another, between one family and another, between groups of people, and also between cultural groups.

Case study

Since the reader will come across two detailed case studies concerning Asian families in England (see Chapter 8), I shall resist the temptation of offering a case study related to an Asian family living in England. Instead, I would like you to imagine an English family living in India. The following account is based on my brief but fascinating and illuminating encounter with an English family in 1973–4. A few days later, I made copious notes of the encounter, and what follows is an abbreviated and amended version of those notes. (Needless to say, serious attempts have been made to safeguard the anonymity of the persons mentioned.)

It was at the New Year's Eve Ball in Khandala, at the Naval Academy, that I first met this English family. Khandala is a hill station about 100 miles to the south of Bombay, or Mumbai, as it is now known. A friend of mine, a high-ranking officer in the Indian Navy had invited me to the Ball.

It was a chilly night, even quite cold. We circulated among the crowds of people – the men in their smart woollen suits and DJs, the officers in their immaculate uniforms and the women in their shimmering silk saris and western dresses. Presently, I was introduced to a Mr Robinson, and his two daughters, Carolyn and Mildred. They appeared to be on their own, isolated from the rest of the revellers. My friend had decided to introduce me to them on the assumption that because I lived in England, we would have a lot in common with one another.

I was surprised by Mr Robinson's appearance. He was in his late fifties; he was lean, even quite frail. He was wearing a frayed woollen herringbone overcoat, which had seen better years. What struck me was the 'dog-collar', which went round his neck – a man of the cloth. His two daughters were in smartly-tailored but old-fashioned dresses, and had cardigans wrapped around their shoulders. They had striking features and flaming red hair. They appeared to be in their late teens or early twenties.

Reverend Robinson appeared quite pleased to meet me. As I gleaned the story of his life, I learnt that soon after his confirmation he had decided to go and work in India. After being moved around from one vicarage to another, he had finally settled down in a small town, halfway between Bombay and Khandala. In the 30-odd years that he had lived in India, he had never once been back to England. In India, he had married an Anglo-Indian lady, whom he had met in Calcutta (now known as Kolkata). Sadly, she had died less than ten years after their marriage, and he had courageously brought up the two girls on his own.

He plied me with lots of questions, which were concerned almost entirely with life in London, which is where he said he had been born. Initially, the two daughters were rather shy when I tried to engage them in conversation, but gradually they too started to ply me with questions related to 'life in England'. Both of them spoke English with an Indian accent. It surprised me to learn that neither of the two sisters spoke any of the Indian languages. In India, one assumes that a child 'picks up' the local languages almost without trying; they form an integral part of the cultural atmosphere. Both girls could speak a few disconnected phrases in Hindi, which they spoke in an exaggerated anglicized accent.

To recount the entire conversation I had with Rev. Robinson and his two daughters would fill up more pages than are necessary; besides, a detailed account would not serve a significant purpose. It is best therefore to summarize the conversation based on the notes that I made.

Reverend Robinson

- Most of his questions were about life in London.
- They were all related to the past – 30 years back in time.
- He wanted to know if cafés such as J. Lyons and the ABC were still around, and whether one could still get tea at The Ritz for less than a pound.
- He referred to Asians as 'coloured' people and to the blacks as negroes.
- He asked questions about the cinemas, music halls, the London Palladium, and about film stars and other entertainers of yesteryear, most of who were unknown to me.
- He showed little awareness of the current social, economic and political situation in Britain, and the major role which Britain was playing in international affairs.
- Being a clergyman, he also asked several questions about Christianity, patterns of worship, the number of worshippers and other such matters.
- He knew very little about the mosques and temples that had appeared in Britain in the last 30 years.
- He was extremely concerned to find out the cost of living in England, and when I gave him what seemed to me a conservative estimate, his face fell – disappointment writ large on his troubled visage.

In short, his questions centred round the period during which he had lived in England and the pattern of life that prevailed during that period. One could see that he was trying to preserve the past, keep it intact, which perhaps gave him the feeling of 'permanence' which allowed him to identify and 'relate' to the country which he had left 30 years before. The present was alien, if not frightening to him (so I chose to believe) and he had elected to ignore it, or blot it out of his psyche. Whether such a rigid adherence to the past was an attempt to cope with a sense of alienation and desolation which he might otherwise have experienced, one cannot say. To me, he seemed to have chained himself to the past and had become a prisoner of his own making. I felt that his 'defences', although constricting, were by no means unique. Several psychoanalysts, poets and writers, including George Orwell, in his novel *Coming Up for Air*, have explored this theme in poignant detail.

Carolyn and Mildred – the two sisters

- As has already been mentioned, neither of them spoke any of the Indian languages with any degree of fluency. They showed not the slightest interest in learning any Indian language.
- Although they had both been born and brought up in India, and had not been to England, they looked upon England as 'home'. They were convinced that they would one day go back and live with their aunt in Kingston, Surrey.
- They had made no Indian friends, knew very little about Indian customs and traditions, or about the rites, rituals and religious festivals of the Hindus, the Muslims and the variety of other religious groups living in India. Nor had they expressed any desire to understand the people and the country.
- Although they came from an Anglican background, they had been educated in a convent school in Calcutta, and had acquired a few of the dominant values of convent schooling.

The two sisters were second-generation English who had been born, brought up, and educated in India. After talking to them, I brooded for a long period of time. It seemed to me that India was a country they lived in; but their hearts and souls lay in England, a country which they spoke about constantly (even dreamed about, I suspect). Whether they had been brought up to think along those lines by their father, one cannot say. At some stage during their growth, they must have acquired the idea that England was home, and that they were merely biding their time before they returned to live with their aunt and people of their own kind.

They had isolated themselves from the Indians living in their area. Again, whether this had been done by choice or by a set of circumstances, one could not say. As a clergyman, one might have expected their father to meet and befriend the few English people living in the area. But the area where he lived and worked had hardly any English people in it. The majority of his congregation consisted of Hindus from Goa whose forefathers had converted to Christianity.

The one obvious question which none of them had asked (perhaps not even dared to ask) was this: how would they raise the necessary funds to travel to England? As a clergyman, he earned a pittance; he was as poor as the proverbial church mouse. Yet the two girls firmly believed that some day they would go home. I did not dare ask what 'home' meant to them both.

Were they living a lie? If so, who had nurtured and implanted this lie into their psyches? How had it taken root? Did the pursuit of this terrifying illusion allow them to cope with their alienation in India? Was England the talisman which they clung to with schizoid tenacity?

Although I paid them a visit once or twice after our first meeting, I felt helpless, inept, even estranged from Reverend Robinson's private torments, which he had also inflicted upon his two daughters. There was little I could do about the Robinson family. After a while, despite their invitations, I stopped seeing them. At any rate, I had to return to England: my own sabbatical at the university was coming to an end.

A quarter century has gone by since my meeting Reverend Robinson and his two daughters. What has become of them, I do not know. Whether they finally realized their ambitions and came to England and are living here, or whether like the three sisters in Chekhov's famous play, *Three Sisters*, who constantly dream of going to Moscow they too still continue to cherish the illusion of going back home, I do not know. But I cannot help feeling desperately sorry for them.

Conclusion

We have examined, albeit briefly, the 'fate' of the Robinson family, living in India. Whatever further knowledge and detailed information that we might gather concerning their lives in India, it would still not allow us to pinpoint accurately which were the salient variables or factors that led to their leading the kind of life they live (or lived). In other words, it is difficult to drawn any causal connections based on a detailed case study. However, one may be able to tease out parallels between the lives the Robinson family lived in India and the lives which many Asian families live in England. Like the Robinson family, which to me appeared to be fairly close-knit, there are a large number of Asian families (Hindu, Muslim, Sikh, Parsee and others) who also live as close-knit family units in Britain. Because the second-generation children are exposed to two cultural value systems (like the two English sisters were in India) they acquire a mixture of values, through school, television, the media and a variety of other sources. How the two value systems (in some ways confusing and contradictory, and in other ways clear and complementary) are balanced into the minds of the growing children is hard to conceptualize. It would of course be easy to make glib and grandiose statements about the kinds of identities which the second- and the third-generation Asian children develop; but such pronouncements and pontifications are best left to politicians and self-acclaimed pundits – of whom, sadly, there is an ever-increasing multitude. What such people do is to mistake information for knowledge. Genuine scholars on the other hand are guided by a sense of detached, dispassionate and insatiable curiosity combined with a sense of Socratic humility. By temperament too, they tend to be cautious, conservative and sceptical in their approach to any problem that they pursue professionally. The idea that they could be wrong and mistaken becomes an integral part of their training and thinking.

It is now time to add the finishing touches to the theme of second- and third-generation Asians living in Britain. A few points need to be made here.

First, the socialization processes of children in terms of their day-to-day behaviours, familial and social relationships, linguistic development, religious and moral values are often culture-specific. However, even within a single, tightly knit culture, the patterns and processes may vary from family to family, leading to differences. In broad terms, however, there may be striking similarities between groups of people within a single culture. Second, the range of experiences which a growing child has outside the protective 'womb' of the family are also likely to have their own influences upon the growth and development of the child. Third, the child's own cognitive and emotional development, the manner in which he or she learns to construe the world in which she or he soon learns to see him- or herself as a member of a minority group also has its own range of influence on the child's development of identity. These factors, to a large extent, determine what a child grows up to *become*.

Let us turn to an interesting model which was proposed by Bochner (1982). I have modified the model slightly to bring home the points more succinctly. Bochner points out that persons living in another culture may choose one of four strategies in dealing with their host culture:

- They may hastily reject the values of the adopted culture (e.g. Asian adolescents or black Afro-Caribbeans turning away from English culture). They may reject the host culture on intuitive, experiential and even irrational grounds. The hiatus created by rejecting the dominant values of the host culture is filled by extolling the virtues of their own culture (e.g. the 'black is beautiful' symbol, which became the defiant, assertive and aggressive slogan of the blacks in America, Great Britain and many other European countries). Such an approach is likely to lead to attitudes of chauvinism, racism and nationalism. This form of posturing is potentially dangerous, for it can lead to fractures and divisions within the different cultural groups in Britain.
- They may choose to denigrate and reject their *own* culture. In so doing, they may turn away from their own parents and despise their ancestral country of origin, looking upon it and its people as being non-progressive, backward, superstitious, repressive and even primitive. Once again, the psychological vacuum (and the existential alienation) created by this rejection may be filled by a blind, 'swing' to the adopted culture. This may manifest itself in a variety of ways. They may attempt to 'pass off' as whites, and try to 'assimilate' into the mainstream of western society. They may engage in actions ranging from harmless acts of bravado (e.g. rejecting vegetarian food in a strictly vegetarian home) to those which may lead to psychological disruptions and fractures, affecting both the individual concerned and the family.
- The third type of response is to vacillate between two cultural norms, unable to work out the means by which the norms and values of the two cultures may be reconciled. Painfully aware that they belong neither to the host cultural group, nor to their own cultural group such people may feel marginalized. This is likely to result in their being in a state of perpetual conflict, and in a state of uncertainty concerning their own ethnic identities. In terms of Erikson's theory, this group, more than the other two, is likely to experience 'identity confusion', leading to an 'identity crisis'.
- They may genuinely attempt to integrate into the new culture by acquiring a set of compatible and complementary value systems from their indigenous and from their adopted culture, which would lend meaning and significance to their lives. In other

words, they may acquire the rationality and the wisdom to appreciate the positive values of both cultures, and bring about a mentally and spiritually healthy integration of their identities.

Can one make any firm futuristic predictions? Will brothers and sisters of different faiths and religions, different skin colours, speaking different languages, holding different beliefs and values, different ways of living in the world, extend to one another the hand in friendship and learn to live together in centuries of peace, trust and harmony? Can one envisage the emergence of a genuine multicultural society? Who can tell? What will be will be.

Chapter 3

Cross-cultural differences in eastern and western cultures: a conceptual model

Introduction

One might argue that human beings are human beings are human beings, the world over. They all share a variety of common biological and psychological needs, which are necessary for their biological and their psychological survival. But having said that, it is also clear that human beings are different from one another, in terms of how they see themselves, how they perceive their own private world and the outside world around them, how they come to judge right and wrong, good and bad etc. In fact, when one thinks about this problem in depth, it would seem that human beings are separated more by their differences than they are united by their similarities. The differences in attitudes, beliefs and values tend to become accentuated when we observe and attempt to relate to people from different cultural backgrounds. What might seem a perfectly reasonable and appropriate behaviour to a person from one culture may seem completely unreasonable and inappropriate to a person from another.

Let us take a brief example to illustrate the point. Imagine a casual encounter between an Indian and an Englishman travelling on a train. Out of friendliness, the Indian enquires of the fellow traveller what he does for a living. Upon receiving a response, the Indian wishes to know what salary he earns, at which point the Englishman, put out by the Indian's impertinence, tells him to mind his own business; the curt response brings their encounter to an abrupt end. If we go a bit further we can see that both the parties involved have a right to feel angry and aggrieved. The Indian feels rejected and is unable to understand why his questions were treated with such scorn, and the Englishman feels angry at being asked questions which to him are personal, private and intrusive and of no concern to others. Similarly, for an English person to raise questions related to premarital sex in an Indian household would arouse acute embarrassment and hurt, for such topics are seldom discussed openly in Indian families.

How do these misunderstandings arise? The most obvious explanation that comes to mind is ignorance. People are often unaware or possess insufficient knowledge of the customs and the traditions, the norms and the rules, which guide the behaviours of people of other cultures. Rather than admit to ignorance, and tread cautiously, people 'rush in, where angels fear to tread'. It also seems fairly obvious that in the absence of firm knowledge, people tend to rely on stereotypes.

Stereotypes and their shortcomings

A stereotype is a short-handed way of categorizing any group or person – a hook on which to hang one's first impressions. There is hardly an object, an idea, a phenomenon, an experience or an event that is not open to stereotypic explanation. To arrive at value-laden judgements, which often tend to be negative, requires little imagination, no formal education and hardly any personal experience on the part of the person trading the stereotype. Stereotypes are the food which the ignorant feast on.

Stereotypes operate at all levels: individual, group, national and even international. Arundhati Roy (2001) gives a compelling example of an international stereotype. In order to offer humanitarian support, the US government air-dropped 37,000 packets of emergency rations into Afghanistan. This gesture was greatly publicized, and the contents of the food parcels were clearly recorded in the major newspapers. However, for reasons unknown, there was a false belief that Muslims were vegetarians, as per Muslim dietary law. In fact, while abstaining from eating pork, Muslims can and do eat other types of meat. Each yellow packet, 'decorated with an American flag, contained: rice, peanut butter, bean salad, strawberry jam, crackers, raisins, flat bread, an apple fruit bar, seasoning, matches, a set of plastic cutlery, a serviette and illustrated user instructions' (Roy 2001: 251).

Stereotypes, as Aronson (1992) and others have pointed out, often divide people into 'in-groups' and 'out-groups' where the in-groups are seen as possessing all kinds of positive and praiseworthy qualities and the out-groups as having vile and despicable attributes. Such attributions by members of the in-group, when translated into action, become hurtful and painful, and under certain conditions and in certain situations cause irreparable harm. Thus, any acts of violence and aggression perpetrated against members of the out-group carry their own self-justificatory labels – one is merely stamping out evil.

Let us flavour a few national stereotypes to understand their generalized nature and their negative, value-laden assumptions.

- Italians are operatic, romantic and quarrelsome.
- The French are rude, arrogant and untrustworthy.
- Germans are meticulous, precise, boring and militaristic.
- Americans are brash, aggressive and naïve.
- Indians are ignorant and superstitious.
- Afro-Caribbeans are dumb, athletic and musical.
- Bangladeshis are primitive and backward.
- Pakistanis are fierce fundamentalists.
- Swedes are dull and boring.
- The English are foul-mouthed, aggressive 'lager louts'.
- The Irish are lazy and intemperate alcoholics.

Persons subscribing to negative stereotypes are unable, incapable or unwilling to see the gross shortcomings in their evaluations. They tend to operate on the belief that all the negative characteristics attributed to a group are shared by each of the members of that group. There are no exceptions. Thus, all Muslims are seen as being fundamentalists, all Hindus as being deeply religious and superstitious, all Jews as being shrewd and mercenary, and so on.

A belief in the truth of stereotypes, according to Gordon Allport (1954) is the first step in the expression of national and racial prejudices. If unchecked, and when skilfully manipulated by political demagogues, such bigotry leads to acts of extreme violence, which past history reveals has often culminated in mass genocide of the most appalling kind. No country in the world – from times ancient to times present – has been free from the savagery arising out of such bigotry. All civilizations have been awash with blood.

However, it has been argued that not all stereotypes are negative and hurtful in their orientations. There is another side too – the creation of the 'positive' stereotype, which forms an integral part of the vast network of large multinational organizations anxious to promote their consumer goods and services across the world

(Taylor 1989; Aronson 1992). In addition to multinational organizations, such as the World Bank, the International Monetary Fund, the United Nations and its several organs, several governmental agencies, including non-governmental organizations, (NGOs) are all actively involved in promoting positive stereotypes related to a variety of issues, ranging from health and illness to education, family welfare, defence of human rights and the eradication of poverty.

Here one needs to add a word of caution. Even positive stereotypes can turn ugly. In the recent football World Cup in Japan one could not but witness the 'flag-waving', the 'tribal singing' and the 'tribal bonding' of each nation which supported its own team. Passions rose to dizzy heights of patriotism which, as has been wisely remarked, is the 'last refuge of scoundrels'! Little comfort can be derived from such 'positive' stereotypes for the simple reason that they often can and do lead to disastrous social, economic and political consequences (Stiglitz 2002).

Despite the inherent dangers of trading in stereotypes as a way of understanding people of different cultures (Allport 1954; Brown 1965; Aronson 1992) stereotypes remain as the main armoury of most people. Stereotypes appear to be an integral part of humanity, and like a deadly virus, most people tend to become infected by them. Sadly, there does not appear to be a way of stopping this. And although stereotypes may change from time to time, and negative stereotypes may get replaced by positive ones, the intervening harm they do is impossible to condone.

Since it is based on intuitions, first impressions, hearsay, unconscious negative evaluations and propaganda, stereotypic knowledge tends to be 'bitty'. It is impossible to piece stereotypes together and transform them into a rational and coherent whole. Thus the use of stereotypes in understanding people of other cultures (and indeed one's own) is not the best way forward.

Rationalist approaches to cross-cultural understanding

Is there another way forward? Could one, through the exercise of pure reason and rational argument, succeed in arriving at the 'truth'? In principle, it certainly sounds like a better approach than the one that involves the use of stereotypes. This line of thinking has a long pedigree. It is in keeping with the philosophies of Plato, who argued that it was through the exercise of pure reason uninfluenced by sensory perception that one was able to arrive at truth. But the later rationalist philosophers of the sixteenth and seventeenth centuries (with the exception of Descartes, but including Spinoza Leibniz and others) did not entirely rule out the value of sensory experiences (empirical approaches). They believed that it was the exercise of reason *combined with experience* that would enable an individual to arrive at 'truth', or in our case, an understanding of a given culture.

A rationalist approach certainly sounds superior to the earlier approach. But here too one runs into a serious difficulty. Experiences based on sensory perception, as we all know, vary. The planet Jupiter, when seen through the naked eye, appears very different to what is seen through a telescope. No two therapists are likely to perceive a client in identical terms. More importantly, it is not simply the experience or the encounter, but the *interpretation* which one puts on it that is likely to determine one's level of understanding of the encounter and the consequent attitudes one is likely to form.

There is little doubt that rationalist doctrines are exceedingly useful and have much to commend them; but they have built into them one fundamental weakness: they tend to disregard, if not eschew, empirical testing. Consequently there is the danger of a serious mismatch between their theoretical constructions and the social and empirical reality (or realities) which such constructions are designed to reflect.

The classical rationalist approach assumed that valid theories could be constructed in a social vacuum, without sensory experience, which, as it turns out, is a mistaken view. Knowledge, as Popper (1963, 1972) points out, does not grow and develop in a social vacuum. Sensory experience (empiricism) plays an exceedingly important role in our attempts to understand or arrive at truth. Ziman (1978) goes a step further. He argues that the credibility of science cannot be decided by formal logic, or by appeals to sophisticated computer programmes and the use of hardware. Ziman argues that the credibility of science often depends on intuitive human capabilities, such as problem solving abilities, consensual pattern recognition and the interpretation of language.

While rational and logical explanations may seem extremely plausible, there is no way of telling that they are also true. Truth, as Popper (1963) has argued, cannot be ascertained by reason alone. Reason clearly plays a fundamental part in helping us to formulate a theoretical proposition, but in the final analysis theoretical propositions need to be put to critical empirical tests to ascertain their validity.

A theory also needs to take into account its historical antecedents and its prevalent social, religious, economic (and other) conditions, including the objective and subjective states of knowledge which exist in a given society at a specific point in time. All these factors collectively influence the manner in which theories are conceptualized, formulated and tested. Failure to take account of these factors may impose severe constraints on rationalist theories and may render them meaningless (Laungani 2004).

The importance of theory in cross-cultural understanding

What one needs therefore is a conceptual framework, or a theoretical model from which hypotheses can be deduced and tested. Such models are by no means easy to construct. They cannot, as it were, be snapped out of thin air. One might even start with a hunch, a guess, an observation or a hypothesis. How one arrives at a hypothesis or a theory is immaterial. The history of science is replete with several fascinating and even bizarre examples of how scientists have arrived at theoretical formulations from which they have been able to deduce hypotheses, which they have then subjected to rigorous critical tests.

Over the years I have been involved in constructing and validating a conceptual model which attempts to explain similarities and differences between eastern cultures and western cultures in terms of the major value systems which guide and influence their behaviours. Our beliefs and behaviours, ranging from the trivial, the casual and the functional to the moral and the ethical do not arise in a social vacuum. What we consider to be right and wrong, proper and improper, good and bad, is to a large measure influenced by the dominant values prevalent in our culture (Triandis 1994; Laungani 1997a, 1997c).

Values are the currently held normative expectations that underlie individual and social conduct (Laungani 1995). They form the bases of familial, social, religious, legal and political order. The values we acquire are often the result of past religious and philosophical legacies that we inherit from our ancestors. Since these beliefs extend over centuries, they exercise a powerful hold over our lives and in that sense we are all prisoners of our own culture, handcuffed to it by past history. This is not to suggest that values do not change. The process of change – unless precipitated by cataclysmic political, religious, scientific or technological upheavals – tends, on the whole, to be slow, secretive and somnolent.

Let us now examine the theoretical model.

The proposed model argues that there are four interrelated core values or factors which distinguish western cultures from eastern cultures, or more specifically, *British* approaches from *Indian* approaches to the understanding of cultural differences. The four core values or factors are:

- Individualism—communalism (collectivism)
- Cognitivism—emotionalism
- Freewill—determinism
- Materialism—spiritualism

Before we go on to explain the relevance of each of the above factors, it is necessary to set a few ground rules in order to avoid any misinterpretation.

1. It is important to bear in mind that the two concepts underlying each factor are *not* dichotomous. They are to be understood as extending along a continuum, starting at, say, individualism at one end, and extending into communalism at the other. A dichotomous approach tends to classify people in 'either-or' terms. Such an approach is limited in its usefulness. People seldom fit into neat theoretically formulated and/or empirically derived categories. The sheer complexity and variability of human behaviours and responses within and between groups, even within a single culture, precludes serious attempts at such categorical classifications.
2. Categorical taxonomies may offer neat quantifiable numerical values, but their usefulness in understanding and explaining differences and similarities in core beliefs, attitudes and values between cultures remains problematic.
3. A dimensional approach on the other hand takes account of human variability. It has the advantage of allowing us to measure salient attitudes and behaviours at any given point in time and over time. It also enables us to hypothesize expected theoretical and empirical differences and changes in position along the continuum, both within and between cultural groups.

4 Each of the hypothesized dimensions subsumes within it a variety of attitudes and behaviours, which to a large extent are influenced by the norms and values operative within that culture.

The theoretical bases of these factors have been described at length elsewhere (see Laungani 1990, 1992b, 1993, 1995, 1997a, 1997c, 1999c, 2000b, 2001b, 2001d). Sachdev (1992) has provided an empirical validation of the four factors. In her research study, by means of specifically designed questionnaires, Sachdev compared the beliefs and values of the British-born Indian schoolchildren with those of Caucasian schoolchildren in West London. The two groups of children – although both born and socialized in a predominantly western culture – showed marked preferences in terms of their favoured value systems. Independent studies undertaken by Sookhoo (1995) and by Laungani and Sookhoo (1995) provide further empirical validity to the theoretical constructs.

Before discussing each factor, it needs to be pointed out that the constructs on the left are applicable more to British culture (and to western cultures in general) and those on the right to Indian culture (and to eastern cultures in general). Let us now discuss each of the core constructs.

Individualism—communalism

Individualism

One of the distinguishing features of contemporary western society is its increasing emphasis on individualism. From a theistic standpoint, the roots of individualistic philosophy can be traced in the writings of St Augustine in the fourth century. He asserted that one can and should be able to commune with God directly, without having to receive the sanctions of the clergy or the Church. However, theistic notions of individualism gave way to secular and humanistic notions as a result of a viable social and political philosophy which came into being during the sixteenth century. Individualism is recognized as being one of the dominant values in contemporary western society. In fact, this feature sets it apart from non-western societies, which are characterized by their emphasis on collectivism.

Over the years, much has been written on the concepts of individualism and collectivism (e.g. Hofstede 1980, 1991; Hui and

Triandis 1986; Schwartz 1990; Kim *et al.* 1992, 1994; Triandis 1994; Matsumoto 1996; Kagitcibasi 1997; Laungani 1998, 1999c) and they have come to mean different things to different people.

Main features of individualism

At an abstract level the concept itself has come to acquire several different meanings. It is the ability to exercise a degree of control over one's life, the ability to cope with one's problems, the ability to change for the better, rely upon oneself, be independent, autonomous and responsible for one's actions; to be self-fulfilled and realize one's internal resources. As Triandis (1994) points out, individualism, in essence, is concerned with giving priority to one's personal goals over the goals of one's in-group, or of one's family members.

Individualism has been the subject of considerable debate among western thinkers (e.g. Riesman 1954; Lukes 1973; Waterman 1981; Bellah 1985; Spence 1985; Schwartz 1990; Triandis 1994; Matsumoto 1996; Kagitcibasi 1997). Some writers have been unhappy with the concept of individualism and have argued that the notions of individualism are incompatible with, even antithetical to, communal and collective interests. The 'dog eat dog' philosophy is seen as being divisive and inimical in terms of the promotion of communal goals. In the long run, it alienates fellow beings from one another. The major downside of individualism is best epitomized by what can only be described as a gross egocentric phrase: 'each one of us must look after number one – to wit, oneself!'

But there are others – among them, Sampson (1977), an outspoken defender of individualism – who extols its virtues. Individualism, it is argued, is in keeping with the philosophy of humanism and secularism, which emphasizes among other things the notion of 'dignity of man/woman', a disentanglement from theology and religion and an espousal of scientific enterprise as the fundamental bases for understanding the universe (Cooper 1996). In recent years, the increasing popularity of individualism can also be attributed to the Weberian spirit of capitalism and free enterprise. Sampson (1977) sees no reason why the philosophy of individualism should not also nurture a spirit of cooperation and coexistence. Sampson's arguments are not without merit, but there is very little firm evidence which would lend further support to them.

Since the philosophy of individualism is not without its disadvantages, let us discuss some of the major ones.

Disadvantages of individualism

DEVELOPMENT OF IDENTITY

The philosophy of individualism, despite its merits, tends to create its own set of problems. The first is concerned with the development of one's identity. Identity, in western society, is generally seen in socio-psycho-cognitive-developmental terms. The process of identity formation starts in infancy and according to received wisdom passes through several critical stages, from childhood, to adolescence and into adulthood (Erikson 1963). To acquire an appropriate identity which asserts one's strengths, which is located in reality, which separates the individual from others and is thereby kept distinct from those of others, which reflects one's true inner being and which leads to the fulfilment or the realization of one's potential is by no means easy. It often results in conflict, which if unresolved, leads to severe stress and in extreme cases to an identity crisis (Rogers 1961, 1980; Erikson 1963; Maslow 1970, 1971; Camilleri *et al.* 1990).

EXISTENTIAL DREAD AND LONELINESS

Individualism often creates conditions and life situations which make it difficult for individuals to share their problems, fears, anxieties and dread with others. As several existential philosophers, from Kierkegaard and Nietzsche to Husserl to Heidegger pointed out several years ago, individualism creates in people an existential loneliness, which as Albert Camus (1955) pointed out in his famous book, *The Myth of Sisyphus* (1955), is an integral part of the human condition. Camus warned that there is no easy escape from this absurd state. The emphasis upon self-reliance – the expectation of being responsible for one's success or failure – imposes severe stress upon the individual and can lead to severe psychiatric disorders. Consequently, any failures with attendant feelings of guilt are explained in individualistic terms.

A similar theme of individualism runs through the writings of Jean-Paul Sartre, a contemporary of Camus. Sartre also believed that as human beings we are free – not only free, but *condemned to being free* in a world which is without meaning, other than that which we as free individuals bring to it by our actions. But to exist as a human being is inexplicable and wholly absurd. Blaise Pascal (1623–62), the

French mathematician and philosopher, describes the absurdity of the human condition in the following words:

> When I consider the short duration of my life, swallowed up in the eternity before and after, the little space I fill, and even can see, engulfed in the infinite immensity of space of which I am ignorant, and which knows me not, I am frightened, and am astonished at being here rather than there, why now, rather than then?
>
> (Quoted in Lavine 1984: 331)

Individualism and the freedom it entails does not come without a heavy price. The absurdity of the human condition creates a sense of dread, anxiety and anguish, and an acute fear of what Sartre refers to as 'nothingness', which becomes more acute when we contemplate the final nothingness: death.

MAINTENANCE OF 'BOUNDARIES' – PHYSICAL AND PSYCHOLOGICAL SPACE

One of the dominant features of individualism is its recognition of and respect for an individual's physical and psychological space. People do not normally touch one another for that is seen as an encroachment of one's physically defined boundaries. Physical contact, particularly between two males, may also be misconstrued. The taboos related to physical touch are so strong that even in times of grief they are not easily violated. Even eye-to-eye contact between two people is normally avoided. Several studies have shown that the effects of violating another person's physical space lead to severe stress and, in extreme cases, to neurosis (Rohner 1974; Greenberg and Firestone 1977).

Closely related to the concept of physical space is that of 'psychological space'. This is concerned with defining boundaries which separate the psychological self from others. It implies a recognition of and respect for another person's individuality. It is an idea of immense value in the West, respected in all social situations. It comes into play in virtually all social encounters, from the most casual to the most intimate. One hears of people feeling 'threatened', 'upset', 'angry', 'awkward', 'confused' etc. when they feel that their subjectively defined space is invaded. Even in the case of anxiety, grief, mourning and depression, people tend not to intrude and are reluctant to volunteer support for fear of invading the other person's 'psychological' space. Vine (1982) reviewed the major studies in the area related to crowding – the invasion of psychological space – and found that violating another person's 'psychological' space gives rise to stress and other forms of mental disorder. A separate study (Webb 1978) has shown that in extreme cases such invasion leads to neuroses and other psychosomatic disturbances. The need to define one's psychological and physical boundaries starts virtually from infancy.

Communalism

Although American psychologists prefer to use the word 'Collectivism' because of its neutrality, communalism is used here. The arguments for the retention of the word communalism have been discussed elsewhere (Laungani 2001b).

Family- and community-centred society

Indian society, not unlike other eastern societies, is family-based and community centred (Basham 1966; Zaehner 1966a; Mandelbaum 1972; Lannoy 1975; Kakar 1981; Koller 1982; Lipner 1994; Flood 1996; Laungani 1997, 1998; Klostermaier 1998; Sharma 2000). Most Indians grow up and live in extended family networks. The father, in most parts of India, is seen as head of the family. The extended family is often intergenerational. The family would normally include all the children, the unmarried sons and daughters, married sons and their wives, their children (if any), and other relatives, such as the father's younger brothers, their wives and children and the father's widowed sister, all living under the same roof. In such a family structure, incomes are often pooled and are redistributed according to the needs of the respective members within the family.

Indian society cannot be seen other than in familial, communal and caste-related terms. Consequently when a problem – financial, medical, psychiatric or whatever – affects an individual, it affects the entire family. In Indian family life, one's individuality is subordinated to collective solidarity, and one's ego is submerged into the collective ego of the family and one's community. It may be of passing interest to note here that Indians often use the collective pronoun 'we' in their everyday speech. The use of the pronoun we, or '*hum*' (in Hindi), signifies the suppression of one's individual ego into the collective ego of one's family and community. Thus one speaks with the collective voice of others, and in so doing gains their approbation.

A community in India is not just a collection of individuals gathered together for a common purpose, and has several common features. People within a group are united by a common caste and sub-caste rank (*jati*). The members within a community generally operate on a ranking or a hierarchical system. Elders are accorded special status and their important role is very clearly recognized. On important issues the members of a community may meet and confer with one another, and any decisions taken are often binding on the rest of the members of the community. In the event of a person being perceived as being mentally ill, it initially falls upon the individual's family to look after and support them. Should that become difficult, for financial or other reasons, it then becomes the responsibility of the community members, the family's sub-caste, to offer support.

However, it should be emphasized that for an individual to stay as an integral part of the family and of the community, it is expected that the individual will submit to familial and communal norms, and will not deviate to an extent where it becomes necessary for severe sanctions to be imposed or, as an extreme measure, for the deviant to be ostracized. The pressure to conform to family norms and expectations can and does cause acute stress in individual members of the family, leading in some instances to psychotic disorders and hysteria (Sethi and Manchanda 1978; Channabasavanna and Bhatti 1982).

The caste system

Although in many respects Indian society is similar to most other eastern societies, its unique distinguishing feature lies in its caste system. The caste system is construed in different ways by different scholars: it is seen as a form of institutionalized inequality, an instrument of social assimilation, as an extension of the joint family system, as a system of graded relationships etc. Its origin dates back over 3,500 years. The four castes in their hierarchical order are as follows:

- *Brahmins:* the learned and educated elite; the guardians of the *Vedas*; the priests.

- *Kshatriyas:* the noble warriors; defenders of the realm.
- *Vaishyas:* the traders, businessmen, farmers and moneylenders.
- *Sudras:* whose main function is to serve the needs of the other three.

Members of the upper three castes are known as 'twice born' because their male members have undergone an initiation, a rite of passage. It is after the 'sacred thread' ceremony that marks their 'second birth' that they are allowed to read and learn from the *Vedas* and participate in all religious ceremonies. This rite separates the three highest castes from the Sudras, who are not permitted such an initiation.

The Sudras are further subdivided into touchables and untouchables. The touchable Sudras engage in occupations, which are considered by the upper three castes to be demeaning and, to a certain degree, polluting: barber, masseur, cleaner, water carrier, cobbler, tanner, butcher etc. The untouchables, on the other hand, are expected to engage in what I refer to as permanently polluting activities: dealing with human and animal waste, working in crematoria and abattoirs. However, the line drawn between touchability and untouchability is by no means rigid.

What are the major consequences of the caste system?

Consequences of the caste system

The Indian caste system plays a vital role in understanding the nature of familial, communal, inter-communal and inter-religious relationships. There are several positive and negative consequences which can be attributed to the caste system, of which at least five are important:

- Hierarchy
- Purity and pollution
- Performance of rituals
- Notions of auspiciousness and purity
- Development of identity

HIERARCHY

Membership of a given caste is through birth only. One is born into a given caste and is destined to stay in it until death. It is virtually impossible to move from one caste into another, particularly from a lower caste into a higher caste. It is, however, possible to move downwards, from a higher caste into a lower caste, through actions which are caste-polluting. The sub-castes, within a given caste, also operate on a hierarchical model. Hierarchy consists of gradations and each sub-caste is graded from the lowest to the highest. Gradations of castes, to a large extent, are organized around degrees of purity and pollution, which include endogamy, commensality and vocational specialization. Brahmins who are at the top of the caste hierarchy wield spiritual and 'divine' power. The Kshatriyas come from the warrior caste. Most of the kings and noblemen of the past era came from the Kshatriya caste and despite their temporal power they deferred to the spiritual and divine power of the Brahmins. The Vaishyas, who constitute the bulk of Hindu society, belong to the trading caste and are normally in business, farming and a variety of other commercial activities.

As previously noted, the Sudras of the lowest caste are further subdivided into touchables and untouchables. The communities belonging to a particular sub-caste often attempt to have their own sub-caste upgraded by the performance of religious ceremonies, and also by ensuring that no member of their sub-caste engages in activities which would bring shame and ignominy upon their sub-caste.

PURITY AND POLLUTION

The day-to-day religious and secular behaviours of Hindus make sense when seen within the context of purity and pollution. Hindus view purity and pollution largely in spiritual terms and not in terms of hygiene (Fuller 1992; Filippi 1996). The status of a person in India is determined by his or her position on the caste hierarchy and by their degree of contact with the polluting agent. Proximity to a polluting agent may constitute a permanent pollution, and certain occupations are regarded as permanently polluting. Such a form of pollution is *collective* – the entire family remains polluted. It is also *hereditary*.

Pollution may be temporary and mild, severe or permanent. One is in a state of mild impurity upon waking up in the morning, prior to performing one's morning ablutions, when one has eaten food, when one has not prayed. Mild states of pollution are easily overcome by appropriate actions, such as baths, prayers, wearing clean, washed clothes and engaging in appropriate cleansing and purification rituals.

Severe pollution occurs when high-caste Hindus come into physical and/or social contact with persons of the lowest caste, or when they eat meat (particularly beef), or when the strict rules governing commensality are abrogated. Commensality is concerned with extending and receiving hospitality. To overcome this form of pollution it is necessary for the polluted individual (in some instances the entire family may get polluted) to perform a series of appropriate propitiation rites, rituals and religious ceremonies under the guidance of their family priest.

Permanent pollution occurs when a Hindu belonging to the highest caste (Brahmin) marries a person from the lowest caste, thereby breaking the principle of endogamy that has always been regarded as one of the cementing factors that has held the caste system together. Endogamy – marrying within one's own caste and sub-caste – is seen as a desired course of action in India. Historically, the Brahmins, in interpreting the *Vedas*, claimed that it was essential for persons to marry within their own caste. Such a form of marriage was considered to be sacred. An endogamous marriage enabled the parties involved in matrimony to retain the ritual purity of their caste and avoid any form of inter-caste contamination. It also ensured the perpetuation of the caste system.

It is notable that over the centuries, the principle of endogamy has not been swept aside; it has continued to retain its hold over Hindus all over India, particularly in the rural areas of the country, and to a large extent even in Britain. Marriages are still arranged and organized by the parents of prospective spouses. Although the style of arranged marriages has undergone a modest change within Indian society – particularly among the affluent members of society in the urban sectors of the country – arranged marriages are still the norm.

PERFORMANCE OF RITUALS

In western countries there is a clear distinction between the sacred and the secular, but in Hinduism there are no sharp distinctions between the two. The lines are blurred. This can be observed even in the most mundane day-to-day activities, such as washing one's hands, having a bath, carrying out one's morning ablutions, accepting drinking water or food from others, or offering it to others, and so on. Although seemingly trivial, these acts have deep-rooted religious connotations. To a westerner unversed in the day-to-day ritualistic practices of Hindus, such behaviours would seem strange and even quite bizarre. To a Hindu, however, they fall within the orbit of necessary religious ablutions, which she or he has internalized from childhood and performs automatically. So much of day-to-day Hindu behaviour is influenced by religious beliefs that it is virtually impossible to identify behaviours which might be seen as secular (Pandey 1969).

Since the majority of rituals, performed either privately or collectively, have a religious connotation it is clear that ritual activity is addressed to sacred beings, such as gods or ancestors. Ninian Smart (1996) refers to such rituals as focused rituals, where the focus is on worship. Rituals are therefore forms of personal communication with the gods. Communication itself may serve different purposes: worship, giving thanks, asking for favours, expiation and atonement. Smart adds that a variant of the religious ritual is the yogic ritual where the performance of yogic exercises is seen as a means by which a person seeks to attain a higher state of consciousness.

The efficacy of rituals is believed to rest on their repetition; their meticulous performance provides a source of comfort to those practising them. Failure to perform the rituals leads to a form of spiritual pollution. Flood (1996) points out that it is ritual action which anchors people in a sense of deeper identity and belonging.

Although there are varying numbers of rituals recorded in different texts, the rituals appear to be organized in a sequence which expresses the Hindu social order, or *dharma*. The most important rituals are those related to birth, the initiation ceremony, marriage (which signals the beginning of the householder's life) and the final funeral rites and after-death rites.

NOTIONS OF AUSPICIOUSNESS AND PURITY

In western thinking, the notion of auspiciousness does not hold the same meaning as it does for Hindus all over the world. In the West there are a few events which might be construed as being auspicious: baptisms, christenings, church weddings, sacramental rites etc. To a large extent they are seen as vestiges from the past, of no great consequence to people's day-to-day lives. Equally meaningless to a westerner is the concept of an 'auspicious time' or an 'auspicious place'. The nearest that one comes to understanding the notion of auspicious time from a western point of view is this classic quotation from Shakespeare's *Julius Caesar* (IV, iii, 217):

> There is a tide in the affairs of men
> Which, taken at the flood, leads on to fortune;
> Omitted, all the voyage of their life
> Is bound in shallows and in miseries.

But even this glorious statement is less concerned with the idea of auspicious time than with 'seizing the moment'. This is akin to a speculator who 'knows' intuitively when to buy or when to dump his stocks and shares, or a skilled poker player who 'knows' when to raise the stakes or throw in her hand. But as a concept, auspiciousness, with its important religious connotations, has little or no meaning for westerners.

In Indian philosophy the two words 'auspiciousness' and 'purity' are interrelated. In Sanskrit, auspiciousness is referred to as *shub* and purity as *shudh*. In ordinary, everyday language auspiciousness refers directly to time and temporal events (Madan 1987). To Hindus there is an auspicious time for most activities: starting a journey, undertaking a pilgrimage, starting a new business, buying a new house, moving into the house, time of birth, marriage, cremation, and other activities. (It might interest readers to know that Mrs Gandhi, prior to travelling abroad, consulted astrologers, who after studying the almanac would specify the auspicious time of her travel; whether she heeded their advice remains unknown.) Apart from time, auspiciousness is also associated with places, objects or persons. Varanasi (or Benaras) is regarded as a holy city and a pilgrimage there is seen as being auspicious. Similarly, some metals (silver, gold, copper, brass) are also considered to be auspicious.

In contrast to auspiciousness, the term, purity (*shudh*) is not used in everyday speech (Madan 1987). Purity and its opposite, impurity (*ashudh*), are seen as attributes of persons, objects and places. For instance, an infant, *ghee* (clarified butter), unboiled milk, a temple and a consecrated area of land are seen as being pure. On the other hand, contact with certain kinds of human being (low-caste Hindus or non-Hindus) is seen as being impure. So are certain places, such as abattoirs, cremation grounds and brothels. Contact leads to pollution. It is therefore in the interest of a Hindu to avoid such impurities and pursue those actions and eat those foods that ensure purity.

By now it is beginning to become clear that the daily life of an orthodox Hindu is beset with all kinds of polluting agents. But what protects a devout Hindu from pollution is the detailed attention that she or he pays to performing the required rituals during the course of the day. As was stated earlier, the performance of all the daily rituals is internalized at an early age and become functionally autonomous.

The meticulous and precise performance of rites and rituals to avoid pollution and spiritual contamination is seen as being desirable for Hindus. It binds and preserves the caste system, which in turn provides a sense of continuity and belonging. Rites and rituals legitimize social order and uphold social institutions.

Rituals also enable Hindus to earn merit, which leads to their own spiritual development. Their importance cannot be overstated. Despite the fact that over the centuries many ancient rituals have lost their functional value and are interpreted in different ways by Hindus in different regions, they have not been abandoned.

It is worth pointing out here that the majority of Hindus living in Britain tend to abide by their caste-related norms on matters which are of importance to them, (e.g. births, betrothals, marriages, funerals, visits to temples, pilgrimages etc.).

DEVELOPMENT OF IDENTITY

Identity in Indians, to a large extent, is *ascribed* and, to a lesser extent, *achieved*. By virtue of being born into one of the four hereditary castes (this applies mainly to the Hindus who comprise over 82 per cent of the total population of India), one's identity is ascribed at birth. There are advantages and disadvantages in such a traditional arrangement. On the one hand the individual in an Indian family set-up does not have to pass through the critical stages in the process of developing an identity, as is normally the case with children in western individualistic cultures. On the other hand, an ascribed identity tends to restrict the choices open to the individual. While personal choice is central to an individualistic society, it is seen as an exception in a communalistic society.

One's identity, to a large extent, tends to be a reflection of familial and social norms and expectations. For instance, a female, when she is born, is seen as a daughter; after marriage she is seen as someone's wife; then as a mother; when her children get married, she is seen as a mother-in-law. Finally, she may become a grandmother. She has no individual identity of her own.

With the exception of the caste system, which is a singularly unique feature of Indian society, other collectivist cultures including

China, Taiwan, Korea, Hong Kong, the Philippines, Thailand, Nepal, Pakistan, Iran, Turkey, Portugal, Mexico, Peru, Venezuela and Colombia also share most of the features described above (Hofstede 1980; Cheng 1996; Gulerce 1996; Matsumoto 1996; Ward and Kennedy 1996; Jing and Wan 1997; Kim 1997; Yang 1997). For instance, Kuo-Shu Yang (1997) in his excellent analyses of the traditional Chinese personality, refers to the tight, close-knit bond between the individual and his or her family. He points out that 'Chinese familism disposes the Chinese to subordinate their personal interests, goals, glory, and welfare to their family's interests, goals, glory, and welfare to the extent that the family is primary and its members secondary' (p. 245). Kuo-Shu Yang (1997) also points out that in order to attain harmony within the family it is essential for an individual to 'surrender or merge into his or her family, and as a result, lose his or her individuality and idiosyncrasies as an independent actor' (p. 245).

The ubiquitous power of the caste system

It is important to emphasize here that one's caste origins are so strongly ingrained in the Hindu psyche that it is difficult for many people to renounce them. Some do attempt it, as a cosmetic exercise or because they want to appear more 'modern', educated, rational and westernized; but more often than not, it tends to remain intact.

Hinduism, unlike Islam and Christianity, is not a proselytizing religion. But such is the awesome power of the caste system that variants of it have spread to other religious groups, including Muslims, Catholics and Sikhs, in certain parts of India. Although in theory these religious groups would consider the very idea of caste as anathema to their own religious beliefs, caste and caste relations creep into social practices and relationships in extremely subtle ways. In India, it is not uncommon to notice that many Catholics, in addition to their own Christian names, also have Hindu names, and operate a *de facto* caste system. Many Muslims also operate on a similar basis and their names are often indistinguishable from Hindu names. A person unacquainted with Indian names would find it difficult to tell from surnames such as Bahadur, Bhat, Bhatti, Bhimji, Chamar, Choudhary, Darzi, Ghani, Kamal, Mistry, Nawab, Raja, Ramji, Sutaria and Shah (to name but a few) whether the persons concerned are Hindus or Muslims. Even within Sikhism, which is a caste-free religion, many Sikhs operate on a caste basis in certain parts of India, and in Britain.

Despite the inequities of the caste system, the heavy burden it imposes on people and the appalling prejudices it engenders in terms of occupations, areas of residence, social and marital relationships, it has survived. Why? To examine this question is beyond the scope of this chapter – it would need a separate book.

The major features of individualism and communalism are shown in Table 3.1.

Cognitivism—emotionalism

Cognitivism

This is concerned with the way in which the British (the English in particular) construe their private and social worlds and the ways in which they form and sustain social relationships. In broad terms

Table 3.1 Features of individualism and communalism

Individualism	*Communalism*
Emphasis on personal responsibility and self-achievement	Emphasis on collective responsibility and collective achievement
Identity achieved	Identity ascribed
Anxiety is related to the acquisition of identity	Anxiety may be related to the 'imposition' of a familial and caste-related identity
Family life operates on a horizontal model	Family life runs on a hierarchical model
Emphasis on nuclear (and one-parent) families	Emphasis on extended families
Social behaviours 'class related'	Social behaviours caste and religion related
Pollution and purification seen in terms of hygiene	Pollution and purification seen in spiritual and caste-related terms
Religion tends to be less important; secularism important	Religion plays a dominant role in everyday life
Rituals, if any, tend to be secular	Religious rituals play a dominant role in day-to-day behaviours

it has been suggested by Pande (1968) that western society is a work- and activity-centred society and in contradistinction, eastern societies in general and Indian society in particular are relationship centred. At this point, the reader might well inquire why this is the case.

It should be emphasized that these different constructions of social worlds are not accidental cultural developments. They stem from their inheritance of different philosophical legacies (Laungani 2000b).

Rationality and logic

In a work- and activity-centred society, people are more likely to operate on a cognitive mode, where the emphasis is on rationality, logic and control. Within a cognitivist framework, there is a cultural expectation that people in most social situations will exercise a high degree of self-control in day-to-day behaviours and also in their display of feelings and emotions. Public expression of feelings and emotions – particularly among the middle classes in England – is often frowned upon. It causes mutual embarrassment and is often construed as being vulgar. It is not as though negative feelings and emotions are never expressed, but they are expressed in a subtle way. Even in situations where it would seem legitimate to express feelings openly, without inhibition (at funerals, for instance) the English are guided by control, which suggests that one must not cry in public, one must at all times put on a 'brave' face, one must, above all, never lose one's dignity. Dignity lies in restraint. If one has to cry, one must do so in the solitude and privacy of one's home, away from prying eyes and ears. The unwillingness or the inability to express emotions openly is a theme that has caused some worry to other writers in the field (Gorer 1965; Hockey 1993).

Relationships

In such a society, relationships outside the family are formed through shared commonalities. One does not take a relationship 'for granted'; one is expected to 'work at a relationship', in a marriage, in a family situation, with friends, with colleagues at work, and even with one's children. In a work and activity society, one's identity, one's self-image and self-esteem grow out of one's work and one's attitude to work. Work defines one's sense of worth. Given the overarching ideology of individualism, one's work and one's attitudes to work have a far greater impact on one's life than relationships.

As was stated at the start of this chapter, to enquire of a person's age, marital status, income, religious beliefs and practices, might seem reasonable and innocuous questions when put to people from eastern cultures, but the same questions when put to people from western cultures would in all likelihood arouse suspicion and hostility. Such questions are considered too private and personal for people in western countries. However, questions related to work tend not to arouse any misgivings or objections.

Conception of time

Work and its relation to self-esteem acquire meaning only when seen against the background of time. Our conception of time is both objective and subjective. At an objective level, time is seen in terms of an Einsteinian dimension, where each hour is divided into its fixed moments of minutes, seconds and milliseconds. Each moment (at least on earth) expires at the same speed – an hour passes not a moment sooner, not a moment later. At a subjective level, however, there are variations in our perceptions of time. In a work- and activity-centred society, one's working life, including one's private life, is organized around time. To ensure the judicious use of time, one resorts to keeping appointment books and computer-assisted diaries; one works to fixed time schedules; one sets deadlines; one tries to keep within one's time limits. One is constantly aware of the swift passage of time, and to fritter it away is often frowned upon. Time therefore comes to acquire a significant meaning in a work- and activity-centred society. McClelland (1961) has shown that people in general (and high achievers in particular) use metaphors such as 'a dashing waterfall', 'a speeding train', etc. to describe time. The fear of running out of time, the fear of not being able to accomplish one's short-term and long-term goals on time, is seen as one of the greatest stressors in western society. Even casual encounters between friends and between colleagues at work operate on covert agendas. Meeting people is seldom construed as an end in itself; it is a means to an end, with time playing a significant role.

Emotionalism

The close physical proximity in which people continuously live and share their lives with one another forces a relationship-centred society to operate on an emotional dimension, where feelings and emotions are not easily repressed and their expression in general is not frowned upon. However, it should be stressed that relationships are also organized around hierarchical lines, and tend to be 'tight', 'closed' and rigid.

Relationships

In such a society crying, dependence on others, excessive emotionality, volatility, even verbal hostility, both in males and females, are not in any way considered as signs of weakness or ill-breeding. Since feelings and emotions – both positive and negative – are expressed easily, there is little danger of treading incautiously on others' sensibilities and vulnerabilities, such as might be the case in work- and activity-centred societies. Given the extended family structure of relationships, emotional outbursts are taken on board by the family members. Quite often the emotional outbursts are of a symbolic nature – even highly stylized and ritualistic. Given the extreme closeness of life, the paucity of amenities, the absence of privacy, the inertia evoked by the overpowering heat and dust, the awesome feeling of claustrophobia, it is not at all surprising that families do often quarrel, fight and swear at one another and from time to time assault one another too. But their quarrels and outbursts are often of a symbolic nature – otherwise such quarrels would lead to a permanent rift, the consequences of which would be far more traumatic than those of living together. There is in such outbursts a surrealistic quality: at one level they are alarmingly real and at another bewilderingly unreal. They serve an important function – cathartic relief.

However, caution needs to be exercised here. In a hierarchical family structure, feelings and emotions are not expressed indiscriminately. Each member within the family soon becomes aware of his or her own position within the hierarchy, and in the process of familial adjustment learns the normative expressions of emotionality permissible to them. Even in emotionally charged situations, the internalized familial norms often prevent the younger members of the family from openly expressing negative emotions towards their elders. In other words, who can say what to whom, how and with what effect is guided by a familial pecking order which the members of the family learn to internalize quite early on in their lives.

However, in a relationship-centred society, one is forced into relationships from which one cannot or is unable to opt out without severe sanctions being imposed upon the individual. Several studies have shown that one's inability to break away, or even sever enforced relationships based on birth and caste, often leads to severe stress and neurosis (Channabasavanna and Bhatti 1982).

Concept of time

Although at an objective level, time is construed in virtually the same way as it is in the West, at a subjective level time in India is seen in more flexible and relaxed terms. Time, in Indian metaphysics, is not conceptualized in linear terms. A linear model of time signifies a beginning, a middle and an end, or a past, a present and a future. Time, in Indian philosophy, is conceptualized in circular terms, which means that time has no beginning (or its beginnings remain unknown), no middle and no end. Taking this philosophical consideration into account, it follows that one can no more talk of the 'big bang' theory of time than one can of the end of the universe. These different conceptualizations have serious implications for our understanding of the nature of private and social behaviours.

For instance, at a day-to-day observational level, one does not notice among Indians the same sense of urgency which has become the hallmark of western society. Time in India is often viewed as 'a quiet, motionless ocean', 'a vast expanse of sky'. It therefore comes as no surprise to learn that in Hindi there is only one word – *kal* – which stands both for 'yesterday' and 'tomorrow'. One gleans the meaning of the word from its context.

To use a popular phrase, there is a laid back attitude towards time and work within Indian culture. The only exceptions to this flexible construction of time are to be found in those situations which are considered auspicious: undertaking an important journey, fixing the time of christenings, betrothals, weddings and funerals etc. In these situations one is expected to consult the family Brahmin priest, who then consults an almanac from which he calculates the most auspicious time for the commencement of that particular activity. Because of their religious significance such events are seldom left to chance; one seeks divine guidance in their planning and execution.

The major features of cognitivism and emotionalism are summarized in Table 3.2.

Freewill—determinism

All cultures, the world over, subscribe to ideas underlying freewill and determinism. Logically the two sets of beliefs are incompatible, but this has never prevented people from subscribing to both in varying degrees, to the extent that the same behaviour can be regarded as determined on one occasion and voluntary on another. From time to time the emphasis shifts and a given culture may move from one set of beliefs to the other. This would suggest that certain beliefs and behaviours, which in the past may have been seen as being voluntary and freely executed, may subsequently be construed as being determined by other 'forces', ranging from the divine, the theological and the religious, to the genetic, the biological and the environmental. Let us examine the ideas underlying freewill and determinism first in western cultures and then in Asian cultures.

Freewill and determinism in the West

Freewill and determinism are complex philosophical issues, which incorporate within them a variety of other constructs (Russell 1961; Dilman 1999). Until about the sixteenth century, notions of freewill and determinism were entangled largely in their religious connotations. God was the creator of the universe and was seen

Table 3.2 Features of cognitivism and emotionalism

Cognitivism	*Emotionalism*
Emphasis on rationality and logic	Emphasis on feelings and intuition
Feelings and emotions tend to be kept in check	Feelings and emotions tend to be expressed freely
Emphasis on work and activity	Emphasis on relationships
Relationships are often a byproduct of work	Work is often a byproduct of relationships
Relations based on shared interests	Relations based on caste and family
'Rigid' attitude to time	'Flexible' attitude to time

as being omnipotent and omniscient – 'all-knowing'. Thus, God had knowledge of the past, the present and of course our future. The fact that God had knowledge of our future indicated that it was fixed, much in the same way as our past is 'fixed' in our memories. Thus, the idea of freewill becomes an illusion, and the idea that God has created us free becomes a contradiction in Christian theology. Needless to say, philosophers through the ages, from St Augustine and St Aquinas to Descartes, Spinoza, Hume and Kant, have worried over this problem and each in his own way has endeavoured to find an acceptable solution.

However, it was not until after the publication of Newton's *Principia* in 1687 that the concept of determinism was partially freed from its theistic connotations and a non-theistic and mechanistic view of determinism in science (and indeed in the universe) gained prominence. A scientific notion of determinism with its emphasis on causality, or conversely its denial of non-causal events, found favour among the rationalist philosophers who embraced it with great fervour (Popper 1972). With the emergence of quantum mechanics in the early twentieth century, determinism in science, if not in human affairs, once again came to be seriously questioned. In keeping with his own views on the subject, Popper (1988) avoids the terms 'determinism' and 'freewill' altogether and proposes the term 'indeterminism', which he argues is not the opposite of determinism and nor is it the same as freewill.

Despite the advances in science and quantum mechanics, the arguments related to freewill and determinism have not been resolved. They keep re-emerging in different forms and guises among philosophers such as Schopenhauer, Nietzsche, Heidegger, Sartre, Camus and others (Dilman 1999; Honderich 1999).

Notwithstanding the unresolved debates in philosophy, there is a strange form of dualism in western thinking on this subject. Scientific research in medicine, psychiatry, biology and other related disciplines, including psychology, is based on the acceptance of a deterministic framework – hence the concern with seeking causal explanations and with predictability in accordance with rational, scientific procedures of prediction. The emphasis on evidence-based empirical research, on complex multivariate research designs, on proof and on probability values is evidence of the increasing concern among scientists with the rational and logical search for causality.

On the other hand, the notion of freewill becomes evident at a social, psychological and common-sense level. This manifests itself in the constant use of proverbs, homilies, poems and popular advice offered freely to children and adults – occasionally by the very people who adopt a deterministic model in the course of their professional and scientific work (Laungani 1992a).

The question is what do we mean by freewill? Freewill might be defined as a non-causal, voluntary action. However, at a common-sense level it is defined as exercising voluntary control over one's actions. Thus, freewill allows an individual to do what she or he wills, and in so doing take 'credit' for his or her successes and accept blame for his or her failures and mishaps.

When one turns to counselling and psychotherapy, the situation becomes more complex. Determinism played a major role within the Freudian framework. Every event, Freud argued, had a cause. There were no chance events. Freud was at pains to point out that 'free associations', reaction formations, 'slips of the tongue', temporary amnesia and all other 'defence mechanisms' are not really free. They arise out of past connections, which are located in the unconscious. One might in this context recall Freud's notion of psychic determinism (or psychological determinism) which suggested that chance factors could not explain these patterns of behaviour. They were a result of (or determined by) unconscious psychological processes. But although he posited very serious limitations on the *notion* of freewill, Freud managed to escape from a tyrannical deterministic model by arguing that these issues have little bearing on the *question* of freewill. It is within our 'character' to initiate desirable changes within our psyche and acquire a strong, rational ego, which is firmly located in reality.

Western therapists hardly ever attempt to find 'solutions' to the problems presented by their clients. They make it clear in subtle and even in not-so-subtle ways that if the clients 'choose' to exercise their freewill, they will succeed in bringing about the desired changes in their psyche, their values, their feelings, emotions and behaviours.

Such contradictory ways of thinking are also to be found in other psychotherapeutic frameworks, including those of neo-Freudians, behaviourists and person-centred therapists. It would seem therefore that at an abstract, philosophical, scientific and theological level, serious consideration is given to the importance of determinism in 'shaping' our lives; but at a personal, social, private, day-to-day level, freewill tends to be favoured over determinism.

Freewill and determinism in eastern cultures

Similar contradictions with regard to notions of freewill and determinism are also to be found in eastern cultures. Indian thinking, for instance, is dominated by the belief in the law of karma, which is an integral part of the Hindu psyche.

The law of karma

The law of karma, in its simplest form, states that all human actions lead to consequences. Right actions produce good consequences and wrong actions produce bad consequences. At first sight, the law of karma seems to be identical with the law of universal causation, which asserts that every event has a cause, or that nothing is uncaused. Though seemingly identical, there are significant differences between the two laws. Unlike the law of universal causation, the law of karma is not concerned with universal consequences but with consequences which affect the individual – the doer of the action. Second, the law of karma applies specifically to the moral sphere. It is therefore not concerned with the general relation between actions and their consequences but 'rather with the moral quality of the actions and their consequences' (Reichenbach 1990: 1). Third, what gives the law of karma its supreme moral quality is the assertion that the doer not only deserves the consequences of his or her actions but is unable to *avoid* experiencing them (Prasad 1989). It should be made clear that the actions of the doer may have occurred in his or her present life *or in his or her past life*. Similarly, the consequences of the doer's actions may occur during the person's present life or in his or her *future life*. The main point is that it is impossible to avoid the consequences of one's actions. In his analysis of the law of karma, Hiriyanna (1949) explains that the events of our lives are determined by their antecedent causes. Since all actions lead to consequences, which are related to the nature and the type of the actions, there is absolute justice, in the sense that good actions lead to happiness and bad actions to unhappiness.

The doctrine of karma is extremely significant because it offers explanations not only for pain, suffering and misfortune, but also for pleasure, happiness and good fortune. Each of us receives the results of our own actions and not another's. Thus, the sins of our fathers are *not* visited upon us. The deterministic belief that one's present life is shaped by one's actions in one's past life (or lives) allows

Hindus to explain and accept a variety of misfortunes (and good fortunes) which befall them through the course of their journey through life. It engenders within their psyche a spirit of passive, if not resigned, acceptance of misfortunes.

Paradoxically, the law of karma does not negate the notion of freewill. As Christoph von Furer-Haimendorf (1974) has pointed out, in an important sense karma is based on the assumption of freewill. The theory of karma rests on the idea that an individual has the final moral responsibility for each of his or her actions and hence the freedom of moral choice. The law of karma stands out as the most significant feature of Hinduism. Although there is no basis for establishing its empirical validity, Hindus in general have an unswerving faith in the workings of the law of karma. It has shaped the Indian view of life over centuries. One might even go so far as to say that the Hindu psyche is built around the notion of karma (Zaehner 1966; O'Flaherty 1976, 1980; Sinari 1984; Reichenbach 1990; Sharma 2000). The influence of the law of karma manifests itself at every stage in a Hindu's life: at birth, in childhood, during adolescence and adulthood, in marriage, in illness and health, in good fortune and misfortune, in death, and bereavement, and *after death*.

Let us summarize the main advantages and disadvantages of subscribing to the law of karma:

- A belief in determinism is likely to engender in the Indian psyche a spirit of passive, if not resigned, acceptance of the vicissitudes of life. This prevents a person from experiencing feelings of guilt – a state from which westerners, because of their fundamental belief in the doctrine of freewill, cannot be protected.
- It often leads to a state of existential, and in certain instances, moral resignation, compounded by a profound sense of inertia. One does not take immediate proactive measures; one merely accepts the vicissitudes of life without qualm. While this may prevent a person from experiencing stress, it does not allow the same person to make individual attempts to alleviate his or her unbearable condition.
- A belief in the unending cycle of birth and rebirth, a belief that one's life does not end at death but leads to a new beginning, and that one's moral actions in one's present life or past lives will lead to consequences in one's future life, may create in the

Hindu psyche a set of psychologically protective mechanisms in the face of death. A belief in an afterlife helps to reduce the terror of death and the fear of extinction.

- The acceptance of the doctrine of karma instils in one the idea that, in the final analysis, no one but we ourselves are ultimately responsible for the consequences of our actions. This brings the notion of individualism to its highest level.
- The belief in the cycle of birth and rebirth creates an aspiration of hope. Hindus 'know' that they need to engage in meritorious acts of piety because in so doing they will reap the rewards of their actions in their present life or in their future life.

The major features of freewill and determinism are shown in Table 3.3.

Materialism—spiritualism

Materialism

Materialism refers to a belief in the existence of a material world, or a world composed of matter. What constitutes matter is debatable; this question has never been satisfactorily answered (Trefil 1980). If matter consists of atoms, it appears that atoms are made of nuclei and electrons. Nuclei in turn are made up of protons and neutrons. What are protons and neutrons made of? Gell-Mann (see Davies

Table 3.3 Features of freewill and determinism

Freewill	*Determinism*
Emphasis on freedom of choice	Freedom of choice limited
Proactive	Reactive
Success or failure due largely to effort	Although effort is important, success or failure is related to one's karma
Self-blame or guilt is a residual consequence of failure	No guilt is attached to failure
Failure may lead to victim-blaming	No blame is attached to victim
Lukewarm beliefs in birth, rebirth and afterlife	Very strong beliefs in the cycle of birth, rebirth and afterlife

1990) coined the word 'quarks'. But quarks, it appears, have their own quirks. In other words, the assumed solidity of matter may indeed turn out to be an abstraction, if not a myth (Davies 1990). Heisenberg (1930) also questioned the assumed solidity of matter in his famous research paper on indeterminacy principle in quantum theory, which he formulated in 1927.

The idea that there is an external reality, an external world, which is 'out there' and that human beings by the exercise of their intellect and reason can attempt to unravel, runs through the entire history of western philosophy. This theme, in its many variants, reached its apogee during the spectacular rise of the Renaissance and post-Renaissance period which, given its adherence to the philosophy of humanism also managed to a certain extent to disentangle western philosophy from its religious dogmas (Cooper 1996). But such debates have in the main been confined to journals of philosophy and science. Nonetheless these philosophies have had a profound influence on the shaping of the western mind and of course on dominant western values, which, to a large extent, guide, sustain and regulate private and public behaviour.

At a practical, day-to-day level, however, one accepts the assumed solidity of the world which one inhabits. But one pays a heavy price for such acceptance, which gives rise to the popular myth that all explanations of phenomena, ranging from lunar cycles to lunacy, need to be sought within the (assumed) materialist framework. This is evidenced by the profound reluctance among psychiatrists, medical practitioners and psychologists in general to entertain explanations which are of a non-material or supernatural nature. Non-material explanations are treated at best with scepticism, and at worst with scorn.

A materialist philosophy also tends to engender in its subscribers the belief that our knowledge of the world is external to ourselves; reality is 'out there', and it is only through objective scientific enterprise that one will acquire an understanding of the external world and with it an understanding of 'reality'.

The few psychiatrists and psychologists who have steered away from materialistic explanations, or have shown a willingness to consider alternative, non-material explanations, comprise a very small minority. Most of them are painfully aware that anyone offering non-material explanations of phenomena is in danger of incurring the wrath of the scientific community. Non-material explanations fall within the purview of the pre-scientific communities, or in other words superstitious and backward societies, to be found mainly in underdeveloped countries and, by implication, in collectivist societies.

Let us take an example to illustrate such forms of thinking in western society. For over 2,000 years yogis in India have made claims about their abilities to alter their states of consciousness at will, thereby bringing their autonomic nervous system under voluntary control. Western scientists dismissed these claims as unsubstantiated exaggerations. It was not until 1969 that Neal Miller successfully trained his laboratory rats to lower and raise their blood pressure levels by selective reinforcement (Miller 1969). It was then that it began to dawn on the western mind that there might after all be some substance in the claims made by yoga. Using a similar selective reinforcement strategy, Miller found that he could train his students to exercise voluntary control over their autonomic responses. Suddenly the claims made by the yogis began to acquire credibility. Miller's performing rats did the trick! His findings opened the doors to yoga in American universities, and research into altered states of consciousness was followed by its applications into techniques of bio-feedback. It is therefore hardly an accident that classes and training courses in yoga have become a thriving business both in Britain and in other western countries. The philosophical and spiritual underpinnings of yoga, the variations within different forms of yoga, the teleological purposes in yoga, have to a large extent been ignored. Yoga has been put on a business footing. Commercialism has replaced spiritualism.

Spiritualism

In striking contrast to the philosophies in the West, Indian philosophy has been concerned not with information but with transformation (Radhakrishnan [1929] 1989; Zimmer [1951] 1989; de Riencourt 1980a; Embree 1988). It is not concerned with exploring, describing and understanding the visible world, as is as evident with western philosophy. The reason for this neglect is due to the strong Hindu belief that the world is illusory, and although bound by time and space, it is subject to change and decay. Therefore, nothing is to be gained by studying and exploring this changing, transient, illusory world. Thus, the notion of materialism is a relatively unimportant concept in Indian thinking. The external world to Indians is not composed of matter, it is *maya* (Zimmer [1951] 1989). The concept of *maya*, as Zimmer points out, 'holds a key position in Vedantic thought and teaching' (p. 19). Since the external world is illusory, reality, or its perception, lies *within* the individual, and not, as westerners believe, *outside* the individual.

The supreme concern of the Indian mind is therefore on the discovery of the self, wherein lies 'ultimate reality' or ultimate truth (Radhakrishnan [1929] 1989; Zaehner 1966a; de Riencourt 1980a; Sinari 1984). The ultimate purpose of human existence is to transcend one's illusory physical existence, renounce the world of material aspirations, attain a heightened state of spiritual awareness, and finally liberate oneself from the bondage of the cycle of birth and rebirth, thereby attaining *moksha*. It is then that one's soul (*atman*) merges with the ultimate *brahman*. Any activity that is likely to promote such a state is to be encouraged.

But how is such transcendence – inward-seeking spiritual consciousness – to be achieved? *Moksha* (or *nirvana*, according to Buddhist philosophy) cannot be achieved overnight. It can only be achieved through continuous effort and adopting a meditative perspective. The search for *moksha* is long and arduous and may involve a series of lives and deaths in the process.

It is only through the discovery of the self that transformation becomes possible. Everything that we normally know and express about ourselves is subject to change and decay. But the discovered self, as Zimmer points out, is forever changeless, beyond time and space, beyond the normal (scientific) methods of human understanding. It transcends intellectual and rational understanding. Thus the main goal of Indian philosophy has been to know and understand this self, which leads to a total transformation of the individual: a *transmutation of the soul*. The main object of Indian philosophy is to bring about a radical change in human nature, a change that eventually leads to human perfection, a divine God-like state. This, according to Zimmer ([1951] 1989) tends to make Indians more inward-looking and westerners more outward-looking.

Also, given the illusory nature of the external world, the Indian mind remains unfettered by materialistic boundaries. It resorts to explanations where material and spiritual, physical and metaphysical, natural and supernatural explanations of phenomena, coexist with one another. What to a western mind, weaned on Aristotelian logic, nourished on a scientific diet, socialized on materialism, empiricism and positivism might seem an irreconcilable contradiction, leaves an Indian mind relatively unperturbed. To a westerner if A is A, A cannot then be not-A. If dysentery is caused by certain forms of bacteria, it cannot then be due to the influence of the 'evil eye'. The two are logically and rationally incompatible. But contradictions to Indians are a way of life. A is not only A, but *under certain conditions*, may be not-A. This differential construction of one's physical world has an important bearing on the development of identity and patterns of social relationships.

The major features of materialism and spiritualism are shown in Table 3.4.

Conclusion

We have travelled a long, long way. It was necessary to undertake such a long journey because of the complexities involved in the correct understanding of the differences and similarities between eastern and western culture. As has already been mentioned in the first chapter, one needs to avoid trading in stereotypes and/or offering simplistic and ill-founded explanations of different cultures. Such explanations are ill-conceived and potentially dangerous. Instead of ushering in an era of genuine multicultural understanding and coexistence, they may act as divisive forces among cultures.

Cultures exercise a powerful influence on the development of one's identity, one's worldview. The normative prescriptions of a culture help in initiating, sustaining and controlling private, familial and social behaviours. Behaviours which fall outside the established conventional norms may be seen as deviations, and depending on the importance and the functional value of the behaviour concerned, pressures (from mild to severe) may be brought to bear upon the individual to conform to the norms. And when that fails, sanctions

Table 3.4 Features of materialism and spiritualism

Materialism	*Spiritualism*
The world is 'real', physical	The world is illusory
Rejection of contradictory explanations of phenomena	Coexistence of contradictory explanations of phenomena
Reality is external to the individual	Reality is internal to the individual
Reality is perceived through scientific enterprise	Reality is perceived through contemplation and inner reflection

may be imposed upon the deviant individual, ranging from confinement to ostracism. Certain forms of deviation in certain instances may be construed as forms of mental aberration and once identified are dealt with in culturally appropriate ways (e.g. confinement, medication, exorcism, yogic exercises etc.) by a culturally accepted 'expert' who is trained in such practices.

Thus each culture devises its own internally consistent sets of rules. To understand a given pattern of behaviour in another culture, it is necessary to understand the system of rules and the assumptions which guide the private and social behaviours of people in that culture.

This would suggest that a 'wise' and informed therapist to a significant extent would do well to adopt a *relativistic position* when dealing with his or her clients. However, a relativistic stance cuts both ways. It contains its own dangers to which a therapist needs to be alerted. It is very important that we discuss this here so that practising or trainee therapists are aware of this issue and take it into very serious consideration in the course of their work.

Let us first consider the obvious advantages. It is reasonable to assume that the adoption of a relativistic position would put an end to any form of pejorative (or racist) judgements of other cultures – because one is attempting to understand a culture from within the client's frame of reference and not from the investigator's cultural standpoint. The system of norms and rules followed by the client doubtless originate from the client's culture; they would need to be taken and accepted for what they are. Thus there would be no need to 'order' cultures on a measurable scale of superiority or inferiority. Such an approach would also help to dilute, if not dissolve altogether, the oft-voiced accusations of scientific, educational and economic imperialism which have been levelled against western countries by the developing countries.

So far so good.

But let us go a bit further and consider the downside to this argument. Let us paint a scenario to highlight the problems involved. We see a white (Caucasian, for want of a better word) therapist offering therapy to a black client or a client of Asian or Middle-Eastern origin. Let us assume that the therapist is free of bigotry and prejudices and is even prepared to bend over backwards to understand and construe the world from the client's point of view. In such a situation, the therapist's behaviour would tend to be non-judgemental, politically correct and accepting. But the question is this: how far would the therapist go in adopting such a stance if some of the attitudes and values of the client were totally incompatible and irreconcilable with those of the therapist? Such a situation, one can see, could easily become exacerbated in cases where moral and ethical issues are concerned (e.g. a client who has had a past history of being a child abuser, a wife-beater, a swindler, or a client who is a staunch supporter of a fascist or a neo-fascist group). The list of moral issues involved in therapy is almost without limit. What is the therapist expected to do in such a situation? Turn a blind eye? Refuse to continue with the therapy? Attempt to 'change' the client in a manner in keeping with the therapist's personal values? The incompatibility of values, if left unresolved, may become a source of acute psychological distress for the therapist.

Ethical and moral values are what most reasonable and rational people order their lives by. But whether ethical and moral values have universality and an eternal permanence about them is a point that has been debated for over 4,000 years. Whether one adopts a Christian ethic or a secular ethic, a rational ethic or an idiosyncratic ethic, a consensual ethic or a singular ethic, there does not appear to be a perfect solution to this bewildering human problem of paramount proportions. For every ethical principle or 'stricture' one would, if one reflected strongly and deeply, find extenuating circumstances which would challenge the principle's claim to universality and permanence.

What advice one might wish to offer therapists, who in the course of their work are unlikely to acquire any immunity from these soul-searching problems, one cannot say. But it is professionally and morally incumbent upon therapists to take these issues on board, reflect upon them and perhaps find satisfactory ways of dealing with them in a manner which serves the long-term interests of the client and society.

Chapter 4

Western models of counselling and therapy: historical and contemporary perspectives

Introduction

Marcus Aurelius, one of the great Roman emperors, wrote his *Meditations* during the last phase of his life (around AD 170). A remarkable fact, which has remained almost unknown, is that Aurelius chose to write his *Meditations* in Greek, instead of in Latin. But then, Marcus Aurelius *was* a classical scholar. Even to the uninitiated reader, the writings of Marcus Aurelius offer clear, succinct and profound insights into a variety of fields, which, among others, include ethics, politics, psychology, cosmology, theology, the nature of human relationships and spirituality. One is dazzled, awed, by his classical scholarship. Upon reading the book one experiences the excitement at discovering what, in contemporary terms, would be referred to as an extraordinary book on counselling. Marcus Aurelius does not attempt to counsel anyone in particular. He counsels himself. The book is written in the form of aphorisms, a style which has found several imitators, notable among them being Nietzsche in the nineteenth century. Aurelius, through an exchange of letters, also seeks counsel from Fronto, who was 25 years older than he and whom he looked upon as his master (Rutherford 1990).

Let us sample a few pearls of wisdom. As counsellors and therapists we might acquire profound insights from the emperor.

- Do things from outside break in to distract you? Give yourself a time of quiet to learn some new good thing and cease to wander out of your course (Book II, 7).
- Never value as an advantage to yourself what will force you one day to break your word, to abandon self-respect, to hate, to

suspect . . . to act a part, to cover anything that calls for walls or coverings to conceal it (Book III, 7).

- Run always the short road, and Nature's road is short. Therefore say and do everything in the soundest way, because a purpose like this delivers a man from troubles and warfare, from every care and superfluity (Book IV, 51).
- To pursue the impossible is madness: but it is impossible for evil men not to do things of this sort (Book V, 17).
- There was a time when I was fortune's favourite, wherever and whenever she visited me. Yes, but to be fortune's favourite meant assigning good fortune to yourself; and good fortune means good dispositions of the soul, good impulses, good actions (Book V, 37).
- The noblest kind of retribution is not to become like your enemy (Book VI, 6).
- Do not, because a thing is hard for you yourself to accomplish, imagine that it is humanly impossible; but if a thing is humanly possible and appropriate, consider it also to be within your own reach (Book VI, 19).
- Habituate yourself not to be inattentive to what another has to say and, so far as possible, be in the mind of the speaker (Book VI, 53).
- How many praises have been loudly sung are now committed to oblivion: how many who sang their praises are long departed (Book VII, 6).

The above meditations are self-explanatory. The moral rectitude, combined with endearing humility, forms an integral part of the emperor's psyche. His inner being appears to be in perfect harmony with his intrinsic nature, which rests on the premise of rationality, self-reliance, perseverance, a sense of forgiveness and an unswerving commitment to one's duty, regardless of the consequences.

The roots of counselling, as one can see from the foregoing, run long and deep. Marcus Aurelius could not be called a professional counsellor in the modern sense of the word, yet the advice he offers in his *Meditations* has significant relevance for counsellors (and for clients) even today. Many of the problems which clients bring into the consulting rooms of counsellors and psychotherapists are problems of living, or, in other words, relational, sexual, existential, moral, and spiritual problems. The above concerns were first expressed by Socrates in or around 400 BC. He asked, 'What constitutes a good life?' or, 'How shall we lead our lives?' These questions are as relevant today as they were almost 3,000 years ago.

Several philosophers, theologians, scientists, psychiatrists, psychologists and scholars from other related disciplines concerned with these fundamental questions have attempted to provide answers, and the quest continues today.

A brief history of counselling

Professional counsellors and therapists are to a large extent a mid-twentieth-century phenomenon. Therapy, in all its forms, has now grown into a large industry. In the distant past, one turned to one's aged aunt or granny, one's friends and relatives or one's neighbours and associates for guidance and help. The communal structure of social life fostered its own network of interdependence. It was not at all difficult to find the kind of person to whom one could turn for guidance and help. One had faith and confidence in the ability of one's helpers and relied on their experience, knowledge and wisdom.

Religion too, acted as glue. It united societies. It brought communities together. The medieval superstructure of Christianity provided by St Thomas Aquinas enshrined custom, guided behaviour, promoted ritual, perpetuated tradition and assailed doubts. All this created a certain degree of stability in society. Influenced by the teachings of religion, people remained unperturbed by some of the questions that torment us today. They were as certain of heaven and hell as one is of one's hands held in front of one's eyes. The world in which they lived did not seem devoid of meaning. The purposelessness of human existence about which Albert Camus, Jean Paul Sartre and several other existentialists have written, had no place in the scheme of things. Religion formed an integral part of daily life within a community.

The demonological model of mental disturbance

Although sheltered by religion, people were also frightened by it. The Catholic confessional was a double-edged sword. It did not require a great feat of imagination for people to experience the stark terrors of the different layers of hell, as portrayed by Dante Alighieri in *The Divine Comedy*. Disease, illness and suffering, both physical and mental, were not chance events which befell upon the hapless individual. Nor were illnesses and diseases explained in terms of social and environmental deprivation. Since people lived in small communities, where face-to-face interaction was the norm, bizarre, irrational behaviours could not be kept concealed for long from the rest of the members of the community. A concerned parent could no more protect his child than a husband his wife. Malicious gossip often polluted the communal atmosphere, and it was not long before the Church came to hear of it. To protect its orthodoxy, the Church reacted swiftly and decisively. The afflicted individuals were interrogated and found to be 'possessed' by evil, demonic, malevolent forces, and in many instances were seen to be in 'league' with the devil, and were accused of being witches. More often than not, the accused were found to be guilty and were then subjected to barbaric forms of torture and execution, which included drowning and burning. Such was the awesome power of the Church that virtually all disturbances of a psychological nature were explained in terms of the demonological model. The burning of witches in Europe and America reached epidemic proportions during the medieval period, with the greatest excesses being committed in the seventeenth and eighteenth centuries by the Church in its attempts to wipe out witchcraft and heresy (Summers 1994).

Here we must pause and ask ourselves a question. Is there firm, incontrovertible evidence to support the diagnosis of witchcraft? Several scholars have attempted a rational reconstruction of events to piece together what transpired at a witch trial, even though such an analysis often creates serious methodological and interpretative problems. However, the problems are not insuperable. One can take an imaginative leap, as many scholars have done, and present an alternative model which would explain the afflictions of the accused more accurately and with greater reliability than the demonological model. It would then become possible to derive several sets of hypotheses from the alternative or competing model(s) and find ingenious ways of testing them. Such methods have been fairly successfully used in the testing of intelligence of people who lived in the past (e.g. Francis Galton, Charles Darwin, Beethoven, Mozart, Newton and others). In the final analysis one is looking for the most plausible explanation of the phenomena being investigated. Modern-day psychiatrists and psychologists have argued that the victims who were diagnosed as witches may in fact have been suffering from a variety of psychiatric disorders, such as hallucinations, delusions, schizoid tendencies and other symptoms of hysteria and paranoia. Even if such explanations had been made available at the time, it is doubtful that the Church, in its attempts to preserve its hegemony, would have given them any serious consideration.

The theme of witchcraft, witches and evil, affected and even attracted large sections of European society. Witches were not fantasies drummed up by silly little girls with feverish minds, or the results of unresolved sexual urges. They were seen as being *real* and as being evil. Closely related to the belief in witches was the belief that one could sell one's soul to Satan for infinite knowledge and absolute power. This started around the sixth century, became crystallized in the Middle Ages and started to decline around the beginning of the nineteenth century. People from a variety of scholastic, literary and dramatic persuasions were affected by the prevalent beliefs.

As a result, fascinating changes took place in the English theatre, which had a religious, or more appropriately, a *liturgical* origin. Major themes of witches, devils, witchcraft and black magic began to appear in plays. Witchcraft had a very important part in many of the plays of Shakespeare, including *The Tempest*, *Macbeth*, *King Henry VI*, *Part II*, and *The Comedy of Errors*, as it did in Christopher Marlowe's *The Tragical History of Dr Faustus* and Goethe's *Faust*. Such plays are too well known to merit further discussion.

However, there were exceptions. Although the burning of witches became a commonplace event, not all afflicted individuals were tortured, drowned or burnt at the stake. In the case of those whose innocence was established, attempts were made to remove and exorcise the evil, demonic forces that had taken temporary refuge in their bodies. Although they escaped the 'final solution', the 'treatment' methods used were harsh and barbaric, being totally devoid of any humane considerations. It might, in passing, be pointed out that exorcism itself has not been exorcised in the present century. It is still practised by several members of the clergy in England and elsewhere in Europe and America.

The impact of science on religion and therapy

The sixteenth century witnessed a spectacular rise in the growth of science. Copernicus, as it were, 'cast the first stone', and Galileo threw down the gauntlet! A thousand-year unquestioning belief in Ptolemy's geocentric model of the universe was challenged and shown to be false by Copernicus, Galileo and others. It was replaced by the heliocentric theory, which argued that the sun, and not the earth, was the centre of the universe. The earth was merely a small planet, one of many, which revolved round the sun. Thus, the truthfulness of divine revelations came under serious attack.

Despite pressures by the Catholic orthodoxy on dissenters and heretics, doubts concerning the literal veracity of the teachings of the Bible began to creep into the changing European psyche. The indisputable power which religion had exercised over the lives of people in Europe began to be questioned. Religion was excommunicated by the scientific papacy. In the prophetic words of Arthur Koestler, religion was the God that failed. However, despite growing disenchantment with religion, the power of the Catholic Church remained supreme.

Developments in other fields, such as biology, medicine, anatomy and cosmology added to the growing disenchantment with religion and with the demonological model of mental illness. The Industrial Revolution brought about its own metamorphosis. The growth of capitalism dramatically transformed the existing structures of societies and rural communities of the past, where people knew and lived close to one another, gradually gave way to large faceless towns, where the pattern of life differed significantly. Gone was the sense of bonhomie, which in the past had joined communities together. People were left to their own devices, and had to learn to fend for themselves in most situations. Capitalism also placed great emphasis on frugality, deferred gratification and the work ethic. Societies, which in the past had been 'tradition-directed' (Riesman 1950, 1954) were giving way to 'inner-directed' societies, which emphasized a high degree of self-reliance and the utilization of one's inner resources, which, in turn, imposed severe psychological pressures upon people. Riesman has argued that the pressures of living in an inner-directed society often led to feelings of loneliness, isolation and alienation.

The gradual alienation of people from other people within their own community was also hastened by the rising tide of individualism, humanism and secularism. These are extremely important issues that strike at the very root of our understanding of the nature, type and process of counselling and therapy in European countries today. We shall discuss them at length in later chapters. All these factors had a powerful impact on the way in which neurotic disorders and other forms of mental illness came to be defined. Mental illness was no longer seen as a result of the influence of evil and malevolent forces. The harsh, cruel and inhuman forms of treatment which were used to incarcerate the mentally ill started to give way to more humane forms of care and treatment. New ways of conceptualizing mental illness came into being and new methods of treating mental patients were implemented. Pinel, in response to the brutal treatment which was meted out to mental patients, insisted that madness had nothing to do with demon possession, but was a response to severe stresses and inhumane conditions. The work pursued by Pinel, Mesmer, Charcot and several others who followed in their wake brought about a much-needed paradigm shift. Mental illness came to be seen as a form of illness, no different from physical illness.

The demonological model of mental illness gave way to the medical model. The medical model, to this day, continues to exercise a powerful influence in the understanding, diagnosis and treatment of mental illness (Laungani 2002b).

Counselling in England: contemporary perspectives

Phase I: The British Association of Counselling (BAC)

This organization was formally established in 1977, prior to which it was possible for any enterprising entrepreneur to 'set up shop' as a counsellor. To work as a counsellor all one needed was an office located in a reasonably prestigious area, a scattering of seemingly relevant books and journals, and the accoutrements that went with running a flourishing 'practice'. There were no checks, no guidelines, no registration with recognized organizations and no accreditations of any kind. In 1977, the BAC had about 1,000 members on its register (McLeod 1998). Over the years, the membership has grown, and according to McLeod there were 8,556 members in 1992.

More recently, membership was in excess of 17,000. In order to meet with the diverse needs of the client group, the BAC formed seven divisions, each different from the other, each with a different focus, each attempting to meet the specialized needs of people living in a complex, multiethnic, multicultural, multilingual, British society (Dryden *et al.* 1996).

Phase 2: The British Association of Counselling and Psychotherapy (BACP)

As time went on, more and more trained psychotherapists joined the BAC, with the result that the Association was renamed in September 2000 and became the BACP.

The key issue of concern to the BACP is public protection through regulation by the Health Professions Council. Such regulation has several advantages including the safeguarding of the rights of clients, ensuring that clients are not abused in any way and ensuring the best possible services to clients in need of counselling and therapy. To achieve this end, there are continuing debates with the Department of Health and other professional bodies.

The annual research conferences organized by the BACP are always extremely well attended, with delegates from all over the world. At the last conference there were over 80 presentations by experts from several countries, including Australia, New Zealand and America. The BACP also funds reviews of research into counselling at work, counselling old people and student counselling. The BACP journal, *Counselling and Psychotherapy Research* has been a major development since April 2001 and has a circulation of over 20,000, each article submitted being peer reviewed. The journal is innovative, practice-based and a major addition to the other British journals in counselling and psychotherapy.

Counselling, thanks to the efforts by dedicated officers within the BACP, has become one of the biggest growth industries. One is impressed by and appreciative of the efforts of the BACP in attempting to place the entire field of counselling on a sound professional footing.

However, there is also a downside to counselling. For in addition to the qualified and accredited counsellors, the field is awash with unqualified and non-accredited counsellors. To quote from an issue of *The Times* (17 July 2000), 'Britain now has more counsellors than soldiers, with an army of at least 30,000 paid, full-time, 270,000 volunteers, and 2.5 million with counselling as part of their work' (p. 10).

Membership to the BACP, at present, is virtually open to any person. Anyone who displays an interest in counselling and is prepared to pay the required fees is entitled to become a member of the BACP. However, being a member does not mean that a person is automatically able to work as a counsellor. The BACP has created six categories of professional training. To work as a bona fide counsellor, one is obliged to undergo the required training courses, approved and/or recognized and accredited by the BACP.

Sadly, the BACP does not possess any legal or statutory powers which it could exercise to prevent any non-qualified, non-accredited person from offering his or her services as a counsellor. In that sense, therefore, the situation has remained unchanged over the last 20 years. Such a state of affairs is undesirable. A client in search of a counsellor may not be able to distinguish between a professionally trained and accredited counsellor and an unqualified one. Or even more seriously, how can the client distinguish between a genuine counsellor and a fraudulent one? The fact that the BACP maintains a register of counsellors is the first step in safeguarding the interests of the client, but this places the onus on the client. Many clients may be unaware of the existence of the BACP, let alone of the register. Given the fact that a client would be anxious to find a counsellor as quickly as possible, it is hardly likely that they will attempt to check the credentials of the potential counsellor. Unless serious and concerted attempts are made to close these loopholes in the system, the client is likely to remain in a vulnerable position, which may expose them to being exploited.

Defining counselling

Intuitively, we all know what counselling means, and many of us may have had the occasion to counsel others or be counselled by others. Many of us, at some point in our lives, may have experienced pain, sorrow, distress, illness, mourning, depression and other forms of suffering, including psychological disorders, irrational fears, phobias, panic attacks, phases of depression and crippling anxieties. Such an experience is unnerving, intense and terrifying. The world closes in on us and we feel that we will never be able to break out. The pain, the hurt, the suffering, the terror, suffocates us. Our silent screams, our sleepless wanderings in the night, our private agonies remain unheard and unheeded. The world, we soon realize, doesn't care. It is indifferent, hostile. We may even feel that we are being blamed for our own misfortunes. The sympathy that we expected turns to antipathy. Under such circumstances, we may feel impelled to approach a friend, partner, spouse, elderly family member or relative, even a stranger in a pub – whoever we feel will lend a sympathetic ear, in the hope that talking and unburdening our heart and soul may lead to an understanding of our innermost conflicts and torments. The religious among us may go to church, synagogue, mosque or temple, burn incense, light candles, meet with our local vicar, rabbi, mullah, imam, priest or guru, and pray for succour.

This form of counselling may be referred to as subjective, non-professional and to a certain extent spontaneous. Whether the unburdening of our innermost torments proves to be beneficial, and whether the benefit is short-term or more enduring, or counter-productive, one cannot say. It is for the person concerned to judge. Let us now take a few well-known definitions of counselling and see if they can clarify our understanding.

McLeod (1998) points out that the term counselling in its modern sense is a recent phenomenon. The simplest definition of counselling is as follows: 'Counselling is helping people to help themselves' (Laungani 1994). Davis and Fallowfield (1991) define counselling as 'a means of assisting people to understand and cope more effectively with their problems'. Burks and Stefflre (1979) define counselling as a professional relationship between a trained counsellor and a client. The relationship is usually person-to-person, although it may sometimes involve more than two people. Burks and Stefflre point out that the counselling situation is designed to help clients understand and clarify their views of their 'life space', and to learn to reach their self-determined goals through meaningful, well-informed choices and through resolution of problems of an emotional or interpersonal nature. The BACP introduced the notion of an *explicit agreement* by the counsellor to help the client. This suggests that there is a contractual relationship between the client and the counsellor and that the relationship is of a professional nature.

There is an obvious need for such a professional relationship and in that sense the work undertaken by the members of the BACP needs to be commended (Woolfe and Dryden 1996). In theory, it might be argued that the 'contract' is designed to safeguard the position of both client and counsellor. Whether this works out in practice is open to conjecture. It is possible that a few clients, in the course of the agreed number of counselling sessions with their counsellor, may feel that their condition has actually worsened. Instead of gaining the insights which would eventually enable them to make positive changes in their lives, they might come to view the entire enterprise not only as a waste of time and money, but as injurious to their sense of psychological well-being. The counsellor, on the other hand, may feel aggrieved about a particular client. In either case, it is imperative that the misunderstandings between the client and the counsellor are satisfactorily resolved.

Such misgivings may arise for a variety of reasons. Szymanska and Palmer (1997) present a comprehensive catalogue of situations where the client may feel that, they have been exploited, let down, abused (psychologically and even sexually), humiliated and even cheated morally and financially by their counsellors. The interested reader is referred to Jehu (1994b); Gonsiorek (1995); Bisbing *et al.* (1996); and Szymanska and Palmer (1997) for clear, rational and comprehensive discussions of the issues surrounding this problem. Szymanska and Palmer (1997) discuss ways and means by which this extremely serious and delicate issue ought to be handled, if the entire field of counselling in England is to remain, like Caesar's wife, beyond reproach.

Despite the variations in the definitions, which we have examined, it is clear that the differences are 'cosmetic' rather than structural. One counsellor may talk about a client 'working' towards 'self-determined' goals. Another counsellor may refer to their client's attempts to bring about the kind of positive changes which they are able to recognize and appreciate. A third counsellor may feel that their client, through the process of counselling, may arrive at a deeper understanding of his or her existential predicament. A fourth counsellor, subscribing to a different theoretical orientation, might aim to create conditions that will lead to positive observable behavioural changes in the client. The terms used by one counsellor may well be different from those used by another, but most counsellors are agreed that counselling is a process of interpersonal influence. The counsellor plays a role which is aimed at helping the client to arrive at a deeper and better understanding of his or her conundrums, dilemmas, worries and anxieties.

Roles that counsellors play

The question that arises here is this: what role *ought* a counsellor to play? It need hardly be stressed that the counsellor is not an actor who is expected to play a carefully rehearsed role on the stage. Is there a specific counselling role into which counsellors are initiated? Given the multi-theoretical and multicultural nature of counselling, such an expectation may be untenable and even undesirable. At its most fundamental level, a counsellor is involved in a process of interaction with the client. In a close encounter, which can often become emotionally charged, carefully rehearsed roles are unlikely to remain rigid and static – although Freud wanted us to believe otherwise. One might recall the copious writings of Freud on the subject of 'transference' and 'countertransference', arguing that a fully trained and experienced psychoanalyst learned to cope with these potentially explosive situations by maintaining the same detached demeanour to his clients (Freud [1953] 1976). Despite what Freud wrote on the subject, it is hard to imagine that a counsellor will remain totally unaffected by his or her encounter with the client. There are counsellors who claim that they maintain the same 'face', preserve the same 'demeanour', use the same tone of voice, display the same facial expressions, from one occasion to another. One wonders whether this is possible. Clients are not assembly-line products. Each client brings into the counselling situation his or her own unique, inimitable history, of which he or she is a product. To treat each client in an identical manner, as some counsellors might wish to do, is not only to insult the intelligence of the client but also to misconstrue the very basis of a counselling encounter. It also displays a basic ignorance of the fundamental principles underlying the psychology of individual differences. Yet one often hears many counsellors talking about their ability to treat all clients in an identical manner, including those from non-western cultures.

Let us return to our original question: what role ought a counsellor to play? The short and swift answer is that there is no prescribed role which all counsellors, regardless of their theoretical orientation, are expected to play. No doubt there are general recommendations and suggestions, a list of 'dos' and 'don'ts', including directions offered by experienced counsellors to novices under their tutelage. There are sets of expectations that apply to all counsellors. A 'good' counsellor would need to be objective, rational, empathetic, caring, dispassionate, and a good listener. At a practical level, therefore, it is reasonable to suggest that counsellors normally play the kind of roles which they have played in the past and with which they have had a significant measure of success. Thus, one would expect a counsellor with a person-centred orientation to play the role which, to a large extent is in keeping with his or her theoretical orientation: objective, caring, dispassionate, empathetic, non-directive and person centred. Whereas a counsellor subscribing to a cognitive-behavioural model may choose to play his or her role as counsellor differently, adopting a prescriptive, directive and perhaps even a didactic approach to the client's perceived problems.

Continuing with the theatrical analogy for a moment, it might be true to say that there are certain sets of essential requirements for any form of role-playing on the stage. However, within those sets of requirements there are significant variations in performance by different actors playing the same role. No two Shakespearean actors play Hamlet in an identical manner. Similarly, it is impossible to expect a counsellor to play an identical role with all his or her clients. Nor is it possible for two counsellors from the same counselling 'stable' (e.g. Rogerian) to play their roles in an identical manner.

Counselling and psychotherapy

An unsettling debate which keeps raising its ugly head is that related to counselling and psychotherapy. Are counselling and psychotherapy merely different terms which stand for the same therapeutic process, or are they two distinct therapeutic processes? Is one superior to the other? Does one deal with more 'severe' psychological disorders than the other? Is one more prestigious than the other? Does one begin where the other ends? Do counsellors and psychotherapists undergo different forms of training, acquire different types of qualification, earn different levels of income and achieve different levels of prestige and recognition? Do they collaborate and work together, or do they deliberately keep themselves apart, jealously safeguarding their own area of work and expertise? What adds to the difficulty is the entrance of a third group of health professionals who refer to themselves as 'counselling psychologists'.

Counselling psychologists are professional counsellors who have also acquired a professional qualification in psychology. Given their understanding of academic psychology, aware of the diverse theoretical models of intervention, aided by their knowledge of statistics, research design and scientific methods of investigation, they may employ sophisticated methods of intervention in the course of their therapeutic work. Whether the growing number of counselling psychologists will pose a serious threat to counsellors remains an issue for the future.

Let us try and answer some of the above questions. Some health professionals have argued that there really is very little difference between counselling and psychotherapy. Both groups of professionals are engaged in the same kind of work, they use similar techniques, employ similar strategies and hope for similar, if not identical, outcomes from their clients after the required number of sessions. Since the two obviously are interrelated, any distinction between counselling and psychotherapy, as Tyler (1960) has argued, is bound to be arbitrary and therefore, false. The difference, according to McLeod (1998) lies in the titles used. But the reason why they use different titles, according to McLeod, is because of the different 'demands of the agencies who employ them' (p. 4). In the past, counselling was associated with the field of education and student counselling centres, whereas psychotherapy, given its medical and psychiatric historical associations, was concerned with care and treatment.

However, the above arguments are far from convincing. Although in many respects counsellors and psychotherapists are both involved in a similar enterprise and may employ similar therapeutic techniques, there are fundamental differences that separate the two groups from one another, particularly that related to *severity*. Counsellors in general deal with problems which are considered to be less severe than the ones which fall within the remit of psychotherapists. (But then, it is not always clear how one distinguishes severe problems from mild problems.)

The differences between the two groups also become manifest when one examines the range of areas in which counsellors have spread their activities over the years. Counselling is now on offer to a variety of client groups: AIDS counselling, bereavement counselling, cancer counselling, child abuse counselling, drug-related counselling, Holocaust victim counselling, IVF counselling, marital counselling, palliative care counselling, rape counselling, redundancy- and unemployment-related counselling, stress-related counselling, sudden infant death (SID) counselling, terminal care counselling, trauma counselling and victim support counselling to name but a few.

More recently many entrepreneurial counsellors, realizing the immense financial potential, have started to offer their counselling services on the internet. There are, it would appear, more than 200,000 websites offering counselling services around the world. More are spawned each day. There are now thousands upon thousands of counsellors, ready to help individuals with all kinds of real, imagined, trivial, absurd, silly and, of course, genuine problems. There is hardly a problem which a dedicated counsellor will not accept. It should be recognized that the increase in counselling services offered by the counselling fraternity is also a reflection of our times. Why has it become desirable, if not necessary, for people to seek counselling *en masse*? Are the increasing needs for counselling symptomatic of some deep-rooted malaise which faces the western world? These are serious issues, which we shall discuss in a later chapter, when we concern ourselves with cross-cultural differences in counselling needs.

Let us now return to the argument that counsellors, in general, deal with less severe cases and psychotherapists with more severe ones. This argument gains substance only when we are able to learn objectively how severity is defined and measured. How do health professionals know when a given problem falls within their area of expertise? How do they arrive at the conclusion that the problem is one which would benefit from counselling and not from psychotherapy, or from psychotherapy and not from counselling, or from both, or indeed from neither?

Even a moment's reflection tells us that human problems cannot be arbitrarily dichotomized into severe and non-severe. The judgement of severity or non-severity, more often than not, is based on the experience of the health professional involved. Nor have human problems been objectively and precisely graded (like temperature readings in a clinical thermometer), ranging from the least severe to the most severe. Although temperature readings in a clinical thermometer serve an extremely useful and practical function, such a gradation has been artificially created, and does not conform to standards of objective reality. Ask a physicist, and they will tell you that water neither freezes at zero degrees, not does it reach boiling point at 100 degrees centigrade. Stevens (1951), in his brilliant paper 'Mathematics, measurement and psychophysics', explained that the arbitrary gradations in a clinical thermometer conform to the interval level of measurement and not to the ratio level of measurement, which is a measure of true objective reality (e.g. length, weight, density, tone, etc.). In other words, the numerical values which are assigned to the scale are a matter of convenience or convention because they continue to serve a useful and practical function – as indeed the thermometer continues to do.

No such gradations or distinctions have been formulated which would allow us to classify human problems along an objective scale of measurement. Therefore, for health professionals to decide on the severity of a problem, they would need to rely on their subjective judgement – which of course, despite one's vast experience, is fallible.

At any rate, to arrive at a clinical judgement concerning the severity or otherwise of a given client's 'problems', 'disorders', 'conflicts', 'emotional crises' or whatever, a counsellor or psychotherapist would need to be experienced and, more importantly, competent. Who one would classify as a 'competent counsellor' is not an easy question to answer. (One might have years of experience and still remain hopelessly muddled and incompetent.) The competence of a counsellor is related to several factors, one of which is the ability of the counsellor to get to the root of the client's problem – the diagnostic problem.

Diagnostic considerations: the health professional's perspective

Given the growth in the number of people seeking counselling and psychotherapy (Howard 1996), how far would one be correct in saying that the diagnostic strategies used by contemporary psychotherapists and counsellors are more robust and superior to those used in the past? And how far are their current methods of diagnosis reliable and valid? The answer to both these questions is that they are not. The diagnostic problem is a very real and a very important one in any therapeutic enterprise. In fact, correctly diagnosing the nature of the problem is one of the major obstacles which confronts modern psychiatry, clinical psychology, psychotherapy and counselling. Many counsellors appear to shy away from the problem of diagnosis altogether, regarding it as irrelevant. Their role, as many of them see it, is concerned with 'empowering' the client to deal effectively with his or her problems. The word 'empowerment' is often uttered in hushed and reverential undertones, almost as a religious mantra which through repetition acquires the aura of mysticism. This, it seems to me, is an extremely naïve and short-sighted view to adopt. Unlike Banquo's ghost, diagnosis is *not* an ephemeral problem, which can be made to disappear in the blink of an eye. The longer counsellors keep avoiding the problem of diagnosis, the longer they continue to offer naïve rationalizations and the longer they continue to offer fanciful and phantasmagoric explanations of the work they do, the more difficult they will make it for themselves to establish their professional credibility. In the years to come, they may come to be associated with hundreds of 'fringe' therapists, healers and caregivers, about which Howard (1996) has written with barely restrained anger.

To give the reader a flavour of how difficult it is to arrive at a correct diagnosis of a psychological disorder, let us recall the well-known study undertaken by Rosenhan in 1973. As part of the study, he sent eight pseudo-patients (including himself) to different American psychiatric hospitals, where they presented to the psychiatrist who interviewed them a single set of symptoms, such as, 'I feel empty', 'I hear a thud', 'I feel hollow' etc. All the pseudo-patients, without exception, were diagnosed as suffering from schizophrenia and were admitted to hospital. The pseudo-patients fooled the doctors, the psychiatrists and the psychiatric nurses on the ward. But what was even more remarkable was the fact that they were instantly recognized as being pseudo-patients by 35 out of a total of 118 real patients. The genuine patients were convinced that the pseudo-patients were journalists, professors or some such type of person, in search of a story. It is clear that the reliability and validity of a variety of diagnostic techniques remains an unresolved issue (Rosenhan 1973; World Health Organization 1973, 1979; Laungani 1999c). Notwithstanding the devastating findings of the above study, psychiatrists have always claimed that their methods of diagnosis are more precise and more accurate than the methods used by other groups of therapists, including clinical psychologists. But whether their claims are justified remains a debatable point.

Diagnostic considerations: the client's perspective

So far we have been considering the problem of diagnosis from the health professional's perspective. Let us consider the problem from the point of view of the client. The client's initial concern is to find out as quickly and as clearly as possible the nature of his or her problem. Obviously there are some clients who are blessed with a deep and penetrating insight into their own problems, but are unable to find ways of dealing with them. It is important therefore that the counsellor is able to arrive at a tentative diagnosis, after a careful interview, aided by a detailed case history and, in some instances, by the client's performance on a battery of standardized psychological tests. The clients must be careful not to allow themselves to be duped by their counsellors into believing that they are 'such complex, deep and sensitive souls that it would be impossible for them to arrive at an understanding of their deep-rooted, innermost, existential and psychological problems within a few interviews'. Such honeyed words often turn out to be a cover-up for ignorance and a crude attempt at flattery. They may keep the counsellor's cash register ringing and singing, but will do little for the client's personal welfare. A genuinely knowledgeable counsellor ought to be able to arrive at a reasonably clear diagnosis with a minimum of fuss and should also be able to explain all this to the client in a language free from obfuscating jargon. It makes very little sense for the counsellor to talk about the client's 'anal explicative or anal retentive psychic tendencies, which manifest themselves in overtly hostile but covertly passive unconscious oedipal relationships with his or her significant others'. This is high-sounding nonsense on a grand scale!

Clients need to be assured that had they gone to another counsellor, the nature of their problem would have remained unchanged. If the diagnosis changes from counsellor to counsellor, it is impossible to know if the first diagnosis was accurate, or indeed, any other diagnosis. They could, of course, all be wrong! A high degree of consensus among counsellors would be quite heartening. Even under those relatively secure conditions, the client needs to be a bit wary, as a high degree of consensus is nothing more than a statement of reliability. It is not a measure of validity.

In an ideal situation, one would expect to find a high degree of reliability (or consistency) of diagnosis across counsellors, psychotherapists and counselling psychologists. However, in reality, this does not happen. It would be a miracle if it did. This is because counsellors subscribe to different theoretical models, which define the basis of their work. Each theoretical model makes a different set of assumptions and offers different guidelines for understanding a client's problem. Thus, a high degree of consensus, although desirable, both from a practical and from a scientific point of view, is seldom or never achieved.

What is equally important from the client's point of view is the 'effectiveness' of the therapeutic procedures implemented by the health professional. It is only natural that clients undergoing counselling should want some indication about how soon or how late they might expect some positive results. The counsellor in turn may attempt to disabuse their clients of such false optimistic expectations, arguing that positive results, however one might care to define them, can only be brought about by the clients themselves – thus throwing the therapeutic ball back into their clients' court. And so the 'game' proceeds, with most (if not all) the rules being set by the counsellor. While the counselling game is being played, the very serious problem of validity or effectiveness of treatment gets sidestepped, or is ruled out of court.

It is important to know whether a given form of therapy works or not. To many practitioners such a question might seem irrelevant and even absurd. But ignoring the problem is a form of defensive avoidance. It needs to be stressed that without informed, objective and valid answers to such questions, the present-day psychotherapies will be subjected to the same kind of attack and ridicule that their proponents have, until now, levelled against the theories and therapies of the past.

It needs to be stressed that all psychotherapeutic and counselling practices explicitly or implicitly spring from their respective theoretical framework. Of this fundamental fact many counsellors appear to be blissfully unaware. A close examination of the literature shows that the theoretical underpinnings of present-day psychotherapies and counselling techniques, to a large measure, are in a state of 'epistemological anarchy'. It is not at all clear how therapies work, and under what conditions. Nor is it always clear what counsellors and psychotherapists mean when they use the word 'work' with reference to the effectiveness of psychotherapy. Some rely on the client's subjective reports, some on the disappearance of symptoms, some on changes in test scores and behavioural measures in the predicted direction, and others rely on the holistic changes manifested in the client's attitudes and values concerning his or her mental health, work and interpersonal relationships.

What makes it worse is that in many cases there is not even a faint resemblance between theory and practice. A theory may be valid, but there is no exact way of telling. Nor can one know why a theory is valid. And in the absence of such objective knowledge, we face the moral issue of whether or not we ought to recommend a theory-based approach to a given client. It might help the client or it might be doing the client an injustice, or even an injury.

Let us now examine the major theoretical models which form the basis of the work of all counsellors, psychotherapists and counselling psychologists.

Theories of counselling

To offer a clear, systematic and articulate record of the contemporary theories of counselling is like picking multi-coloured mushrooms growing wild on a hillside, with each mushroom representing a 'theory'. By the time one has examined a mushroom picked at random, noted its colour, shape and form, and determined whether it is edible or poisonous, other mushrooms have started to surface from the ground and demand our attention. It therefore comes as no surprise to read that according to Herink (1980) there are more than 250 theories of counselling in America! This seems a conservative estimate to Howard (1996) who points out that Karasu (1986) discovered more than 400 models of counselling and psychotherapy. Over the last 18 years, the number of theories can only have increased.

Most of the so-called theories of counselling do not merit being called theories. They may best be construed as the personal, private 'ramblings' of a counsellor who has come to believe that she or he has finally discovered the elixir of counselling, and with more haste and less prudence rushes to promote and propagate the astounding discovery. For a theory to be accepted as good and sound, it must satisfy most, if not all, of the following criteria:

- The theory needs to be clearly and explicitly stated.
- It must be logically consistent.
- It should become possible to deduce a set of hypotheses arising out of the theory, which should be actually or potentially testable.
- The theory should be capable of being disconfirmed (or falsified).
- Its acceptance or rejection should be unrelated to the number of people subscribing to the theory.
- The theory's popularity should not be regarded as a legitimate criterion of its acceptance.
- Psychological factors such as beliefs, attitudes and values concerning the theory have nothing to do with the validity (or otherwise) of that theory.
- The theory may be true (valid) even if no one believes in it, and conversely it may be false even if everyone believes in it.
- Confirming evidence of a hypothesis does not establish a causal relationship between the theory and the hypothesis. (Logically, the confirming evidence could have been obtained by an infinite number of hypotheses.)
- The relationship between the theory and therapy needs to be clearly and unambiguously explicated.

As has already been pointed out, most of the so-called theories of counselling and therapy do not meet many of the above requirements. Many such theories, like attractive but ephemeral rainbows in the sky, make their dazzling appearance and disappear in a flash. They need not concern us here. Since a moment's amusement will not go amiss, let me quote a few eye-catching names, which I have gleaned from Howard's book, *Challenges to Counselling and Psychotherapy* (1996). Here they are: vita-erg therapy, zaraleya psychoenergetic technique, elavil sleep therapy, psychobiological psychotherapy, psychedelic therapy, mythosynthesis, C1C2 project psychotherapy, bio scream psychotherapy, logotherapy, pharmacotherapy, soap opera therapy, puppet therapy, neurotone therapy, mandala therapy, senoi dream group therapy, anti expectation psychotherapy, rebirthing – the list goes on and on. As the Scottish philosopher David Hume would have remarked a couple of centuries ago, such theories are best consigned to the flames. This of course raises an important question: are there any theories in counselling and psychotherapy which merit serious consideration? The answer, luckily, is yes.

Major theoretical orientations in counselling and psychotherapy

There are at least three theories that need serious consideration. Their origins can be traced to the Freudian, the behaviourist and the humanist schools of psychology. The three schools developed three refreshingly different and diverse approaches to psychotherapy and reflect fundamentally different ways of viewing, construing and understanding human behaviour and the emotional, cognitive, behavioural and existential problems which form an integral part of humanity.

The three forms of psychotherapy from which counselling theories have developed are best described as follows:

- Therapies as *intrapsychic processes* (Freudian theory and its variants).
- Therapies as *cognitive and behavioural changes* (behaviour therapy and its variants).
- Therapies as *growth movements* (humanistic psychology and its variants).

Freudian and post-Freudian theories

No person, in the entire history of psychology and psychiatry, has been written about, quoted and referred to more than Sigmund Freud (Boring 1950). Until very recently, Freud was the most quoted person in psychology (Eysenck 1998). His writings have always aroused strong, deep and even hostile feelings among his critics. On the other hand, his protégés and admirers have taken him to their hearts, and have been unable to find sufficient superlatives to garland him with. It is perhaps a sign of greatness to engender in others such a wide range of feelings and emotions.

His theory of personality, which he kept changing and amending from time to time, is too well known to warrant a detailed exposition. Suffice it to say that Freud's study of the human mind offered a new and fascinating insight into the workings of the human psyche. Although he was not a philosopher in the strictest sense of the word, his writings on the unconscious, subconscious and conscious mind, on the id, the ego and the superego, on the psychosexual stages of identity development, offered a formidable challenge, if not a solution, to the mind-body dualism dilemma posed by Descartes in the seventeenth century.

Freud's theory arose out of his clinical work, and his clinical work gave him new and fresh insights into the problems of the human psyche, which were then fed back into his theory. Whether he 'forced' his clinical observations to fit in with his theorizing, or amended his theory to fit in with his clinical observations, is an issue which even today is seen by many as being quite contentious.

Neurosis, according to Freud, comes about when a patient has no conscious awareness of the intrapsychic conflicts which rage within his or her unconscious mind. Under such conditions, the distressed patient may acquire a variety of incapacitating physical and psychological symptoms which underlie the disorder. It is here that the unique skill of the psychoanalyst comes into play. Through therapeutic sessions, the analyst attempts to recreate the conditions which will bring the unconscious problems to the surface of the patient's consciousness, thus providing the patient with much-needed insight into his or her innermost traumas, conflicts and defences, which, unknown to the patient may have occurred during the patient's infancy.

Freud's clinical work attracted a large number of brilliant minds that came from different parts of Europe and even America to learn from him and eventually work with him. It was not long before psychoanalysis became a major therapeutic enterprise in western Europe. Some psychoanalysts such as Karl Abraham, Sandor Ferenczi and Ernest Jones stayed loyal to their master, following in his footsteps, whereas many others, including Carl Jung, Alfred Adler and Otto Rank, broke rank and started their own 'schools' of psychoanalysis. The parting with Adler was perhaps the most bitter.

Many counsellors, therapists and psychotherapists in Britain have 'appropriated' psychoanalysis into their own work. Most counsellors have abandoned 'classical' Freudian psychoanalysis altogether, and have instead espoused a shortened version of Freudian psychoanalysis. Others have moved into Jungian, Adlerian and other psychoanalytical orientations. Many have launched their own brands of psychoanalysis or psychotherapy.

A few, seeing some virtue or merit in each and every form of psychotherapy, in their brazen naïvety and misplaced enthusiasm, have adopted an eclectic approach to psychotherapy. Eclecticism is nothing but a euphemism for poverty of the imagination, for even a moment's reflection would alert one to the potential dangers of eclecticism. If there is some merit in each and every form of psychotherapy, how does one decide which of the bits and pieces are meritorious and which are not, and how do they all cohere together in their own eclectic recipe? To subscribe to the philosophy of eclecticism is like trying to cook a grand meal from the random leftovers of yesterday's dinner party.

Other changes of a practical nature have also taken place in the therapeutic work of counsellors. Most counsellors and therapists do not see their patients – now referred to as clients – four or five times a week, as Freud often did. Clients are seen on not more than one or two sessions a week and the total number of sessions is also kept to a bare minimum.

The Freudian model of therapy is the oldest. Even in the twenty-first century it has not lost its attractive power. But despite its attractiveness and its extensive following, the validity of the model still remains an open issue. Does the Freudian model (or its variants) work? If so, how? Do clients get the expected insight into their problems? Does this 'cathartic' insight enable them to make the necessary positive adjustments in their lives? Do clients come to terms with their unconscious complexes? Is there any truth in the assertion that if you leave your neurotic tensions and your existential dilemmas well alone, there is a 66 per cent chance that your problems will disappear within two to three years (Eysenck 1953)? Answers to these important questions have been fought over bitterly by adherents and adversaries alike for nearly 50 years. It was Eysenck who drew first blood when he first published his devastating critique of psychoanalysis, *Uses and Abuses of Psychology* (1953). But most psychotherapies, be they Freudian or Jungian, behavioural or humanistic, are seldom 'killed' by contradictory scientific findings. They may sink for a while, or go out of fashion. But sooner or later, they tend to resurface, like corked wine in new bottles.

Behaviour and cognitive therapies

Unlike psychoanalysis, which owes its origins to the genius of one man, Freud, the growth and development of behaviour therapy and cognitive behaviour therapy cannot be attributed to any one person in particular. Several innovative psychologists from round the world have had a hand in the evolution and development of behaviourism. The main impetus was provided by the pioneering work of Ivan Pavlov during the late nineteenth century at the University of St Petersburg, in Russia. On the basis of his carefully controlled experimental studies on dogs, Pavlov claimed to have discovered laws of higher nervous activity. That Pavlov was wrong in his assertions need not concern us here – the point is that his research paved the way for a much-needed paradigm shift.

In the USA, John B. Watson ushered in a new era of psychology and the year 1913 saw the birth of behaviourism (Boring 1950; Cohen 1979). Watson's pioneering research provided an impetus for further research in the area. His formulations were quite naïve and it was not long before his model of behaviourism was replaced by the controversial model of radical behaviourism, founded by the late B.F. Skinner in the 1940s.

At a general level, the behaviourists argued that all human behaviour is learned. Environmental factors play a crucial role in both animal and human learning. Learning in its simplest form involves responding to perceived stimuli and responses to stimuli are capable of being modified by the careful and selective use of reinforcement contingencies, positive and negative. This means that human behaviour can be changed, altered and modified. Socially undesirable behaviour, such as violence, fear, phobias etc. can be extinguished and desirable and adaptable social behaviours such as compassion, love and affection can be initiated and implemented by a systematic programming of reinforcement contingencies. There was thus, in behaviourist philosophy, little need to invoke concepts of mental processes, consciousness, introspection and of course the mind. These were seen as antiquated concepts, which had little place in the 'science of human behaviour'. Just as Faust sold his soul to Mephistopheles for infinite power and wealth, psychology too surrendered its soul to 'science'; and as Sir Cyril Burt was reputed to have remarked, it then lost all 'awareness', abandoned its 'consciousness' and with the rise of behaviourism finally lost its 'mind'. The behaviourists were eager to apply the principles of learning to solving human problems and the term 'behaviour therapy' was introduced by Eysenck in 1968, and by Arnold Lazarus in the same year, independently of one other.

But behaviour therapy, which pointedly paid no attention to mental processes, began to arouse disquiet and hostility towards those psychologists working within and outside behaviourist paradigms. This hostility stemmed partly from the value orientations of the critics, who seriously questioned the implicit theoretical acceptance of the 'black box' model, and all that it subsumed. The 'black box' model, although on the surface appearing to be scientific, had serious limitations and raised fundamental epistemological questions which were not easy to answer. To some critics it was totally unacceptable. Behaviour therapy also aroused unease among psychologists because of the implicit 'manipulative' aspects of the theory, thus raising several serious ethical questions. This unease, in many instances, was transformed into a sense of fear, bordering on paranoia, among professionals in allied disciplines – social work, psychotherapy and counselling in particular. The fear was fanned by the media; lurid and terrifying images of Huxley's *Brave New World* and Orwell's *Nineteen Eighty Four* began to appear in popular magazines and the tabloid newspapers.

But the strongest objection to the widespread acceptance of behaviourist theories – and particularly their application – lay in the fact that they were seen as being out of step with the fundamental humanist value systems of contemporary western society. Humanist values were seen as being incompatible with behaviourist paradigms. The influence of humanist psychologists such as Maslow, Rogers and others on the growth of what came to be called the 'Third Force' in psychology also had an impact on behaviourist theories. The concept of mind, which the behaviour therapists had discarded, was reintroduced into behaviour therapy through the back door. The word 'mind' was replaced by the word 'cognition', and behaviour therapy came to be referred to as cognitive behaviour therapy.

The use of the word 'cognitive', to precede 'behaviour therapy', could not have been more appropriate. Given the great importance that is currently placed on the study of cognition in all its aspects, and given the complex investigations in neuropsychology and neurolinguistics, the behaviour therapists were able to use the term cognitive behaviour therapy without losing face.

Cognitive behaviour therapy is a term that is here to stay. As is well known, within cognitive behaviour therapy there are several variants and a detailed case study highlighting the essential features will be presented in a later chapter.

Therapies as growth movements

Humanistic psychology, also known as the Third Force in psychology, came into prominence during the 1960s in America. Its growth was partly accelerated by the sociopolitical climate in America during that period. America had got involved in the Vietnam War and young Americans, many of whom did not even know where Vietnam was, let alone why America had got embroiled in a war which was not of their making, were being drafted into the army and sent to Vietnam. They were being forced to fight a war which was not their war. Not surprisingly, this was a period of acute unrest, uncertainty, dissension and disenchantment among American youth (Gold *et al.* 1976). Disenchantment led to the rejection of prevailing value systems which were found to be false. But having abandoned one set of values, young Americans needed to acquire another if they were not to plunge into a state of nihilism. Humanistic psychology provided the required value shift.

The growth of humanistic psychology can be attributed to the work of several psychologists, psychotherapists and counsellors during the 1960s in America. The most prominent among them were Carl Rogers and Abraham Maslow. Others, such as Fritz Perls, Eric Berne, Sidney Jourard and Rollo May soon followed. Humanistic psychology, at various times, has been referred to as 'non-directive', 'person-centred', client-centred' or 'Rogerian counselling'. Its theoretical underpinnings, to a large extent, arise out of the European tradition of existential and phenomenological philosophy. Humanistic psychology posed a challenge, even a threat, to the major 'schools' of psychology. They were critical of the Freudian school and also of the behaviourist brand of psychology. To them the Freudian school portrayed human beings in extremely pessimistic and negative terms. They were seen as being victims of their own unconscious intrapsychic conflicts, which they neither understood nor had any control over. Such an approach offered no room to individuals for their own personal growth and development and for the realization of their personality.

Humanistic psychology was also critical of the 'behaviourist' school of psychology. In adopting a mechanistic model of human behaviour which had no place in it for the concept of mind, the behaviourists portrayed a sterile and distorted view of human nature. In their enthusiasm to place psychology on a scientific footing, the behaviourists took away from psychology the very essence of humanity – which has to do with the manner in which we construe our private world, our own existential place in it, and the manner in which we grow, develop and relate both to ourselves and to others. The development of our identity, the humanists emphasized, is an ongoing process; it cannot, as the behaviourists believed, be fashioned by a series of reinforcement contingencies.

Humanistic psychology offered its own brand of 'hope', and attracted a large following. Its message was simple and clear. Human beings, it argued, are evolving, growing, changing creatures. All human beings move towards growth and fulfilment and the realization of their personality. This is facilitated by our ability to reflect on our life experiences, to be aware of the choices in our life and take authentic decisions which take account of the moral and ethical considerations that constantly impinge upon us in the course of our day-to-day life.

Here it should be pointed out that the fundamental assumptions which underlie humanistic psychology are by no means of an original nature. It was not as though Carl Rogers or Abraham Maslow had made these startling discoveries themselves. Ideas of a similar nature have been propounded by several philosophers over the centuries, including Marcus Aurelius, with whom we started this chapter. For instance, the Kantian concept of the 'categorical imperative', Sartre's notions of authentic and inauthentic living, and the Vedic concepts of *dharma*, bear a striking similarity to many of the ideas propounded by the humanistic psychologists. They also incorporated within their own domain the theoretical formulations and the therapeutic work of the Gestalt psychologists, led by Fritz Perls, and of the existential psychologists, ably represented by

Rollo May and Moustakas. Despite the differences among these three schools, they are united in their major philosophical assumptions.

The interesting question that we need to raise here is this: given the fact that there was nothing of any great originality in humanistic psychology, why did it, along with humanistic counselling, capture the imagination of the people and gain ascendance over other forms of therapy?

The answer lies partly in understanding the social, political, economic and historical factors which have an influence on theory construction. Regardless of *how* one gets an idea for a theory, all theories, in the final analysis, are social constructions (Popper 1972; Ziman 1978). Theories are not constructed in a social vacuum, but are rooted in social reality. They are part of the social milieu and reflect the norms and dominant values of society. As we noted earlier, the demonological model of mental illness gained acceptance only because the dominant values of society during that period lent legitimacy to the belief in the existence of witches and demons and their malevolent power over the minds and actions of people. As has been argued elsewhere:

> a theory also needs to take into account its historical antecedants, its prevalent social, religious, economic (and other) conditions, including the objective and subjective states of knowledge which exist in a given society at a specific point in time. All these factors collectively influence the manner in which theories are conceptualized, formulated, and tested. Failure to take account of these factors may impose severe constraints on rationalist theories and may even render them meaningless.
>
> (Laungani 1997c: 2)

You might recall that Riesman wrote about the changes that had taken place in American society; the 'tradition-directed' person of the nineteenth century was replaced by the 'inner-directed' person at the turn of the century. He then went on to argue that in the 1940s and the 1950s, the 'inner-directed' person gave way to the 'other-directed' person: a conformist who had lost his or her sense of inner direction, and depended on the media, on his or her peers, neighbours, friends, work colleagues and acquaintances to give him or her a sense of meaning, direction and purpose. This period was referred to as the 'age of conformity'. Within academic psychology, this can be evidenced by the prolific and sustained research that took place in the field of social conformity around that time (see Asch 1952, 1955; Crutchfield 1954, 1955, 1962; Deutsch and Gerrard 1955; Milgram 1974).

Unable to find satisfactory solutions to their life problems, people sought outside help, and humanistic counselling and humanistic psychology, which embodied in their own theoretical frameworks the dominant values of individualism and humanism, provided the necessary support. Being non-directive, humanistic psychology provided the necessary 'space' to individuals to explore their own confusions, conundrums and conflicts, in an atmosphere of trust and acceptance (which is an integral part of the therapeutic process in humanistic counselling). Unlike Freudian forms of therapy, the emphasis of humanistic psychology has always been on the present, on the here and now. Rogers (1961) believed that present tensions and present needs are the only ones which a person is anxious to reduce or satisfy. This is not to suggest that past experiences do not matter or are of no significance; they merely serve to modify the manner in which an individual might perceive those experiences in the present (Rychlak 1973).

One of the startling features of client-centred therapy is to dismiss any attempt at systematic diagnosis. Therapists argue that little purpose is served in categorizing disorders since all categories are arbitrary and therefore unnecessary. The client, according to them, is the only person who is aware of his or her subjective reality and the dynamics of his or her behaviour.

This of course creates a serious problem in terms of assessing the effectiveness of client-centered therapy; in other words, its validity as a therapeutic enterprise. A few controlled studies were undertaken in the 1950s (Rogers and Dymond 1954) which provided some evidence for the success of client-centred therapy. Greenberg *et al.* (1994) reviewed some more recent outcome studies and their findings provide some supportive evidence for the success of humanistic counselling and psychotherapy.

But a few isolated studies do not necessarily settle this argument. Instead of undertaking carefully designed, carefully controlled, large-scale empirical studies to determine the efficacy (or otherwise) of the therapeutic enterprise, practitioners appear to have abandoned such attempts altogether. They have argued that what constitutes success is difficult to define and operationalize. This is because counsellors and therapists tend to have their own subjective views about what constitutes success. To operationalize a concept and to devise empirically robust ways of measuring that concept, requires a solid and sophisticated grounding in research design and statistics. A significant number of practitioners lack such expertise; sadly, it does not form part of their training, and not surprisingly they tend to disregard its importance. Their indifference to research methods, and their unwillingness to undertake sustained research, is an indication of a serious weakness. Given the growing emphasis on accountability and evidence-based interventions, counsellors and psychotherapists can ill-afford to remain complacent. In the years to come, many well-informed and litigious clients, dissatisfied with their counsellors and their psychotherapists, may attempt to seek redress through the courts.

Instead of treating the whole field of effectiveness as an integral part of their work, many practitioners appear to have opted out of it altogether, and have instead concerned themselves with the *process* of therapy or the *process* of counselling, rather than with the *outcome* of their counselling and therapeutic endeavours.

Conclusion

It is time to take stock. Let us pause and list some of the major points which have emerged from this chapter:

- Counselling is fast becoming a gigantic industry.
- There are few formal and stringent qualifications required to *practise* as a counsellor.
- Non-accredited counsellors exceed the recognized, accredited counsellors by a ratio of 3:1. This ratio is likely to increase in the years to come.
- Despite efforts by the BACP to put counselling on a professional footing, these have not met with a great deal of success.
- The BACP does not have any powers to impose any legal sanction on 'rogue' counsellors.
- The felt need for counselling in western societies appears to be increasing at an exponential rate.
- Most counsellors do not concern themselves with issues related to the diagnosis of their clients' problems.
- Many counsellors are virtually unaware of the theoretical orientations of their work.
- In counselling practice, there does not appear to be a close match between theory and practice.

- The word 'cure' or a successful outcome, or evidence-based interventions, do not hold an important position in counsellors' own frames of reference. Consequently, most counsellors do not concern themselves with 'successful outcomes'.
- The variety of training courses in counselling are divided more by their differences than united by their similarities.

It is clear from the above points that all is not well with the state of counselling in Britain. Unless some radical measures are implemented, the situation is unlikely to improve. It may even get worse over time. One is aware of the concerted efforts by the BACP to improve and polish up its image of counselling, but such efforts, unless supported and promoted by an act of Parliament, are unlikely in the long run to prove successful.

My own fears are that the area of counselling may be taken over by what I can only describe as mercenary pseudo-therapists. What the consequences of such an appropriation of power might be, one cannot even begin to comprehend.

A second disturbing feature of counselling lies in the fact that the major counselling approaches adopted in Britain tend to be European and American 'products', which reflect European and American value systems. Very little attention is paid to the counselling needs of the members of ethnic minorities who may or may not share or subscribe to the dominant value systems of western society. This shows an unwillingness on the part of counsellors to concern themselves with the needs of ethnic minorities from the Indian sub-continent, from the Afro-Caribbean countries, from the Middle East, from South-East Asia, China and elsewhere. Whether this unique form of 'cultural blindness' among many counsellors is due to arrogance or naïvety one cannot say. The arrogance may be the result of the unfounded assumption that European and American models of counselling and therapy currently in use have 'universal' applicability, and therefore there is little or no need to search for culturally relevant counselling approaches. In other words, European counselling is seen as the gold standard. All other counselling strategies must take their lead from the gold standard. Such an attitude leads to a form of cultural blindness. One fails to, one is unable to, one does not want to, one cannot be bothered to perceive any differences between the mainstream and members of ethnic minorities – at least for the purposes of counselling. This form of cultural (and colour) blindness has been so beautifully described by the black American writer Ralph Ellison, in his classic novel *The Invisible Man* (1965) that I would like to have him end my chapter for me. As a black man in America, he believes that he is invisible. This is how he starts his prologue:

> I am an invisible man. No, I am not a spook like those who haunted Edgar Allan Poe; nor am I one of your Hollywood ectoplasms. I am a man of substance, of flesh and bone, fibre and liquids – and I might even be said to possess a mind. I am invisible, understand, simply because people refuse to see me . . . When they approach me they see only my surroundings, themselves, or figments of their imagination – indeed, everything and anything except me.
>
> (Ellison 1965: 7)

Chapter 5

When therapists and clients meet: Asian and western perspectives

Introduction

This chapter is divided into two parts. The first will examine the means by which potential clients locate or find their therapist. We shall discuss this first with reference to India. This will enable us to understand the culture-specific means by which therapists and clients are brought together in India, Pakistan, Bangladesh and Sri Lanka. We shall then turn to England and see how indigenous white clients and Asian clients get to meet their therapists.

The second part is concerned with what transpires between the client and the therapist when they meet for the first time. How do they perceive one another? What impressions do they form of one another? What impact do such impressions have on the course of therapy? Do they in any way influence the course of therapy? Once again, we will 'switch' from India to England so that the reader gets a clearer picture of the differences and similarities in the two countries.

A client in search of a therapist in urban centres in India

The above heading sounds a little like the title of Luigi Pirandello's famous play, *Six Characters in Search of An Author*, and a parallel between the two can be drawn. Just as the characters in the play had what they believed was a dramatic life history which needed to be revealed, similarly Indian clients often experience the same feeling. And since an Indian client, as we shall see, is often accompanied by his or her family members when they meet with the therapist, the analogy is not as far-fetched as it might appear at first sight.

But let us first examine how a client gets to meet a professionally qualified therapist in India. This question, straightforward though it seems, is by no means easy to answer. To a very large extent, a one-to-one meeting between a client and a therapist is an extremely rare event. It is not as though clients *never* get to meet a therapist on a one-to-one basis. They do. However, in India such one-to-one meetings are best seen as a recent development, to be found mainly in large, metropolitan cities such as Bombay (now referred to as Mumbai), Calcutta (now referred to as Kolkata), Madras (now referred to as Chennai) and Delhi. The clients who meet professionally trained and qualified therapists tend to come from westernized, educated, affluent backgrounds. Such westernized clients have considerable knowledge and awareness of psychological therapies and their potential advantages. Moreover, they are also in a position to afford the fees of therapists (which by western standards are ludicrously low). To take themselves or one of their family members to a psychotherapist is seen as being 'progressive' – in keeping with the modern trends of living in a 'stressful' society.

But despite the 'progressive' views which many clients hold concerning the value of psychotherapy, they still display an initial reluctance to meet with the therapist. When they do consent to meet, they ensure that the meeting takes place in the privacy of the therapist's office, away from the prying eyes and wagging tongues of their neighbours and relatives.

It should be pointed out that the number of professionally qualified counsellors, psychotherapists, psychiatrists and clinical psychologists in India is far less than would adequately meet the needs of the population. Sadly, they do not have a high profile. This is due largely to the fact that the entire area of mental health is not high on the list of health-related government agendas; it is not given the same degree of priority as, for example, physical communicable diseases. Notwithstanding the difficulties that stand in their way, professionally qualified therapists in India undertake dedicated and rewarding work in a variety of child guidance clinics. Such work, again, is undertaken mainly in large, metropolitan cities. Some therapists of course engage in private practice, but in small towns and in the rural areas of the country, for a variety of political, social, financial, religious and caste-related reasons, they have made hardly any impact.

How do clients choose their therapist? Private consultation comes about mainly through personal acquaintance and through the recommendations of friends. Indians, as was pointed out in Chapter 3, operate on the basis of large social, familial and caste-related networks. Asking favours of friends or seeking information from friends and acquaintances causes no embarrassment. It is through this network of interlocking relationships (one person knows another, who in turn may know a third, and so on) that they are able to get the necessary information and arrange to meet the recommended therapist. But let us understand this.

There is an interesting paradox here. On the one hand the clients are eager to meet the most competent therapist, which they can only do by asking friends, acquaintances and relatives. On the other hand, they are loath to disclose the true purpose of their enquiries, and may resort to a variety of subterfuges when making them. A great deal of caution is exercised in case the friend or the acquaintance starts to suspect that all is not well within the family. The need to protect the family from any ignominy takes precedence over all other considerations. As far as possible, any problem arising within a family is kept within the confines of that family.

But when a psychological problem of a more grave and serious nature is detected (it is astonishing and humbling how even a lay person in the family is often able to diagnose a serious psychotic disturbance) the family members may resort to several strategies. As stated above, their first ploy would be to conceal the problem from the outside world because of the fear of social stigma befalling the entire family. Among other things, such a social stigma could have long-term adverse effects on the marital prospects of the children. Few families would be willing to entertain a marital proposal where one of the members was suspected of or known to suffer from a mental disorder. And given the close-knit nature of Indian society, such news spreads, leading to all sorts of genetic, religious, karmic and demonological explanations of illness within the family. From a cultural point of view the fear of social stigma often cripples action. Many parents have been known to keep a severely disturbed member of the family in hiding, concealed from the outside world, confined to a room.

I have painted a slightly exaggerated and grim picture here, but I have done so with a purpose. It is to show that on the one hand each Indian family is an extended family unit with its extended, interlocking and interdependent network of social relationships; yet on the other, in situations such as the one described above, the family concerned will go to great lengths to conceal a problem in case it is discovered and leads to social censure, if not rejection. Safety lies in concealment.

Let me illustrate this with an example. A few years ago, I had gone to India for a holiday. One of my distant relatives who lived in Poona (now referred to as Pune) on hearing of my arrival (through a network of interconnected relationships) came to see me in Bombay. I had not met him for over two decades and had had no contact with him whatever during that period. His keenness to invite me to his home to meet his family, which included his wife, their two teenaged daughters and their two sons, surprised me intensely. Not wishing to seem churlish, I accepted his invitation – not without some reservations, which I kept to myself. We drove down to Pune, which is a lovely little town about 120 miles to the south of Bombay and I was introduced to the family. Their friendliness and hospitality, to say the least, was overwhelming. Nothing, it would appear, was too good for me!

Eventually, I was taken to a room, which was locked. Inside it lay a young man, in his mid-twenties, on a stringed cot. He was dressed in a pair of cotton pyjamas and a stained sleeveless vest. I noticed a few bruises on his arms and around his neck. He paid no attention to me or to his father. He lay there, staring vacantly into space, rubbing his fingernails against his unshaven cheeks, which were lacerated, doubtless due to the constant rubbing.

Without going into any elaborate details, it was clear that the young man lying in the cot was quite severely disturbed. It transpired that he had been kept concealed in the room for over a year. His parents had kept his concealment a closely guarded secret and had let it be known that their son had been offered a lucrative job in Lagos, and had been living there for over a year. In the meantime, the parents had often called in a priest who also claimed to be a demonologist. The priest had involved the entire family in a series of ritualistic prayers, fasts and sacrifices in order to placate the gods, who may have brought this illness upon their son. When such attempts failed to bring about the required recovery, the priest claimed that it was not the gods but a demon (*shaitaan*) who had taken refuge in the boy's body and was forcing him to behave in this crazy manner. In an attempt to drive out the demon, the priest, from time to time, wielded a stout and hefty stick to beat the demon; this explained the bruises.

For over a year, the son had been locked away in the room, shut off from the rest of the world. The family's logic in approaching me was based on two considerations: they had some awareness of the kind of work I did; and I lived abroad, and would be returning soon. And that, as far as their assessment was concerned, ensured my integrity. They were certain that I would not betray their confidences. Lest you believe that in recounting this story I have already done so, let me hasten to add that what you have just read is a heavily disguised account of the family and where they lived.

To my great sense of shame I was unable to offer any help other than suggesting that I could arrange for the son to be seen professionally by persons whose expertise and integrity I commended highly. But my offer went unheeded. I can only surmise that their fears of 'discovery' and the ensuing social stigma overrode all other considerations. I returned to Bombay saddened and disappointed.

A client in search of a therapist in villages and rural areas in India

While we now have some idea as to how affluent and educated clients living in large metropolitan cities get to meet with their therapists, we still need to know what happens in the rest of the country, particularly in the rural areas.

The Indian government has established primary health care centres which operate both in the rural and urban areas of the country. To a considerable extent the bulk of the work on mental health problems in India (particularly in the rural areas) is undertaken by groups of indigenous workers, referred to as multi-purpose workers, in primary health care centres. But sadly, these workers are inadequately trained. They receive very low wages and have very high workloads. They are expected to travel vast distances in harsh weather with no adequate means of transport. Blessed is the worker who manages to get a bicycle! Generally, they are expected to walk long distances from one village to another; occasionally they may find a ramshackle bus service or beg a ride in a farmer's cart. They have little or no access to medical supplies, even of the most basic kind. The nearest municipal hospital may be over 200 miles away from their area of work. What adds to their problems is the fact that they often deal with clients who are ignorant, uneducated, suspicious, hostile and steeped in their own ancient superstitious beliefs, rites and rituals.

What compounds the problem even further is unbelievable governmental indifference to the problems of mental health. For a variety of reasons, mental illness and its treatment is not seen as a major priority in India. The fact that in a country with a population of over 1 billion people there are less than 5,000 qualified and registered psychiatrists bears testimony to the government's lack of concern for this vital problem (Murthy *et al.* 1992; Krishnamurthy *et al.* 2000). To this, one must add inadequate resources, staggering levels of corruption and a sub-standard if not non-existent infrastructure. Although in theory the valuable role of the multi-purpose worker cannot be overstated, in practice it does not meet the needs of people in rural areas of India, which constitute over 75 per cent of the total Indian population. Given that the population of India is just over 1 billion (Manorama 2002) the total rural population comes to over 750 million people. This is over 13 times the population of Great Britain!

The one group of people in India that appears to thrive is the increasing number of religious therapists. They are the gurus, saints, bhagats, shamans, spiritual healers, demonologists, pirs, astrologers, palmists, fortune-tellers and mystics who publicize their 'saintly', 'godlike' 'miraculous', 'mystical' and 'heavenly' healing powers, which they are prepared to use in order to alleviate human pain, misery and suffering. Many such 'therapists' stay confined to a particular village in which they have settled. This makes it easier for people from neighbouring and surrounding villages to come and visit them. Others, not unlike wandering minstrels, move around from village to village, offering their miraculous cures.

During my recent visit to India (2001–2), I attended lectures and religious sermons preached by several 'healers' in and around Bombay. They extolled the virtues of yoga and yogic exercises, they preached dietary practices based on Ayurvedic theories, they offered homeopathic advice related to a variety of health-related problems, including diabetes, coronary heart disease, asthma and hypertension. Such was their confidence that there was hardly a health-related problem they were not prepared to tackle!

During the course of their work, a few of them manage to acquire great fame (and great fortune too). Word spreads, leading to a vast following. Whether the work they do leads to positive results and the clients return home 'satisfied' customers, remains an unanswered question. When seen from an Indian context, such empirical questions, although of extreme importance from a theoretical point of view, are often seen as redundant. The fact that hundreds, if not thousands, of people flock to see the mystic healer is seen as proof enough of the person's efficacy in dealing with human unhappiness and misery in all forms.

In India, a healer who commands a large following is imbued with all sorts of magico-religious and supernatural powers. His clients soon become devotees, and eventually turn into worshippers – such is their faith and reverence. Short of raising the dead, the healer is reputed to be able to perform miracles, cure incurable diseases, make the impotent potent and the unhappy happy. In some instances the fame of the healer spreads to western countries. This is evidenced by the massive following which Mahesh Maharishi Yogi, Sai Baba and Bhagwan Rajneesh (three names which immediately spring to mind) have had over the last 40 years and more. Although Rajneesh died several years ago, his mantle has passed on to one of his European disciples and his *ashram* in Pune continues to thrive and be flooded with foreign worshippers from Australia, Britain, Denmark, Germany, New Zealand, Sweden and, of course, the USA. To describe and record the interviews that I have had over the years with many such foreigners in India would require a separate book. Suffice it to say that it is impossible to place them into any definable categories: they are at all ages and cut across all social classes, levels of education and levels of affluence. But what they do have in common is what I can only describe as their 'search', their 'spiritual quest', or what Carl Jung referred to as 'modern man in search of his soul'.

It would seem therefore that a western client is no more 'sophisticated' than an Asian client in their choice of a therapist. The difference, if any, may merely be in numbers. While in the past western clients may have been unwilling to consider indigenous (eastern) therapies, they now seem less hostile to the idea. For in the West too, alternative, complementary and integrated medicine is beginning to acquire a certain degree of credibility; western clients no longer rule such therapies out of court as they might have in the past. If this trend continues, it is possible that the twain – the East and the West – contrary to Rudyard Kipling's grim foreboding, *shall* meet.

A white client in search of a therapist in England

In England the situation tends to be different. The well-known avenue through which a client gets to meet a therapist is through referral by one's general practitioner (GP). However, this is not as easy as it sounds. First, given the inordinate pressures on the National Health Service, the waiting period may extend to several weeks, if not months, before one gets a first appointment. Second, one may have little or no choice in the therapist to whom one is referred. One might consider one's problem to be serious, requiring urgent attention, and consequently be unwilling to wait. One might therefore wish to exercise choice and arrange to see a therapist privately.

The question that then arises is, how to choose a therapist? In the West too, there is an increasing number of therapists who advertise their skills and offer their services through their customized websites on the internet. Astonishingly, some of the more technologically intrepid therapists even offer treatment *via* the internet – or e-therapy, as I prefer to call it. The fact that therapists of all sorts – from fakes and fraudsters, herbalists and homeopaths, mystics and masseurs, spiritualists and shamans, to counsellors and psychotherapists – have set up their 'stalls' in western countries must make one wonder as to the mental health of people in the West. One must also wonder whether the demand for therapists is consumer-led or therapist-driven.

When you look around you find an exciting world opens before your disbelieving eyes: you are in a consumer's paradise! Every conceivable type of therapy, treatment and counselling is on offer: bespoke therapies, exclusive therapies, individual therapies, group therapies, long, elaborate residential therapies, transcendental therapies and yogic therapies. Everything is on offer. You can, if you choose, engage in primal screams, get shouted at, even abused, massage, get massaged, sing and dance, watch others do the same, work yourself into a frenzy, throw tantrums, rest, sleep, dream, have nightmares – all is permitted. You are bound to be confused, even quite bewildered. There are so many types of therapy to choose from. Bewildered, if not intimidated, by the variety of 'treatments' on offer, how does a client go about locating an appropriate therapist?

The sharp and astute client may wish to ascertain the qualifications, experience and professional reputation of the therapist and even meet with them before making a decision. There are other avenues too that are open to the client. A friend may recommend a particular therapist. One may have a chance encounter with a 'satisfied' client; one may obtain information from the BACP, the British Psychological Society (BPS) or a variety of other similar organizations which maintain updated directories of qualified therapists. One may also be concerned about the fees charged by the therapist, the time spent in travelling to meet with the therapist and the number of sessions in a week. A more knowledgeable client may also take into serious consideration the theoretical leanings of the therapist. The client may wish to know whether the therapist subscribes to a humanistic model, a cognitive-behavioural model, a psychoanalytical model, a transactional model, a Gestalt model, or whether the therapist pursues his or her 'own brand' of counselling or psychotherapy.

One can see that finding an appropriate therapist is not as straightforward as it might seem. What complicates the matter even further is the issue of ethnic matching of clients with therapists and vice versa. There is a strong belief voiced by many therapists (both black and white) and by clients (both black and white) that the process of therapy is likely to move more easily and smoothly if clients and therapists are 'matched' in terms of their ethnic background, their age and their gender. Several reasons have been offered as to why this is likely to be the case. Since 'matching' in all its forms appears to have a strong bearing on the process of monocultural, multicultural or cross-cultural therapy, and perhaps even on the outcome of therapy, we shall examine this very important issue in some depth in a later chapter.

Let us now turn to what transpires when clients and therapists meet for the first time.

When western clients and therapists meet in England

Let us visualize and reflect upon what happens when a client and therapist meet for the first time. The first meeting is obviously when each is engaged in forming impressions of the other. What impressions do they form?

In certain ways, a counselling and/or therapeutic interview is like a game with its own set of rules. It is, however, a game with a difference. For in a game, the rules are overt and can, on demand, be made explicit; and the parties concerned may agree to abide by the rules, amend them, or even flaunt them. But in a therapeutic interview some rules are covert and remain unknown to the client. And therapists, for reasons which will become clear may prefer to let them remain unknown. This may place the client at a certain disadvantage.

The first interview is quite crucial. It provides an opportunity for the therapist and the client to learn something about each another. Each is involved in assessing the other. The outcome of the first interview often sets the scene or creates a 'template' for all subsequent therapeutic sessions. For instance, inexperienced clients who have never before met a therapist may be quite anxious about their initial interview. They may not know what is expected of them or what to expect. Each client will tend to perceive the therapist in his or her own way. Some may see the therapist as an expert who will solve their problems, and some may even come to look upon the therapist as a friend, or as a benevolent benefactor. The impression the therapist creates on the client may be related to a variety of factors, including the age, gender, ethnicity and demeanour of the therapist. Seasoned therapists learn to cultivate a 'professional face' when dealing with their clients, and this professional face contains several interesting features. There are three which are of concern to us:

- neutrality and objectivity;
- cognitive control;
- empathy.

Let us discuss each of these features in turn.

Neutrality and objectivity

The idea of being neutral and objective seems to be the hallmark of a professional therapist. It has undeniable merits. To sit back and listen to one's client without making any overt (or covert) judgements, to suspend one's biases, prejudices, one's preconceived notions, is the stuff of which good and competent therapists are made. Neutrality and objectivity are considered to be the prerequisites of good therapy. Most textbooks on counselling and psychotherapy emphasize this point. But does this really happen? Is this what most experienced therapists do?

Let us turn the clock back to the seventeenth century and see where this idea of neutrality came from. This attractive and popular idea of neutrality of perceptions, to a large measure, can be traced to the inductive writings of Francis Bacon (1561–1626). Bacon argued that the reason why we do not correctly 'read of the book of Nature' is due to our inherent biases and prejudices. Truth has no guises.

It is our own prejudices which impede us from perceiving truth. He suggested that we should 'purge' our minds of such prejudices: then and only then shall truth become manifest. René Descartes (1596–1650), the great rationalist philosopher, also argued in a similar manner. He believed that by adopting a method of 'systematic doubt' one would be able to destroy all false prejudices of the mind, 'in order to arrive at the unshakable basis of self-evident truth' (Popper 1963: 16). The belief in the neutrality of perceptions has filtered down through the ages and has come to acquire the status of a myth. But the idea, as we shall see, is mistaken.

Karl Popper (1963) has argued that the perception of any phenomenon is *never* neutral. He explains that all perception is theory-laden or theory-saturated. This is because to perceive involves a hunch, a guess, a conjecture, or an unverified hypothesis. This holds true at all levels, from the trivial to the complex. Let's say you see a black dot against a white background. You might point out that this is a perfectly neutral perception: it involves no predispositions, no hunches, no guesses whatever on your part. Moreover, you add triumphantly, everyone else would see it the same way: a black dot against a white background. 'Wrong!' says Popper. For you to perceive black against white, you would have had to imbibe the concept of colour. You would need to have some understanding of colours, the ability to distinguish between colours, and some understanding of the concept of the superimposition of figure against background. It is this prior knowledge that enables you to perceive correctly. One can see that perception of even the most simple and trivial phenomena rests on complex theoretical structures.

When one turns to perceiving people, the problem becomes even more complex. One is forever constructing 'theories', ideas and hunches about people, and one uses those hunches (which of course may turn out to be totally false and misplaced) in the course of one's interactions with others. The hunches may be acquired stereotypes. Although we may try not to, we cannot avoid assigning meanings (or even stereotypes) to all our observations. They may be based on our past experiences, our learning, our level of education, or whatever. We may modify them in the light of new experiences but it is impossible to get rid of them.

They act as our guides. The therapist can no more give up assessing the client than the client the therapist. Both are engaged in mutual assessments, regardless of whether they operate at an overt or covert level. Consider the number of observable variables to which both the therapist and the client are exposed in the first interview: age, gender, ethnicity, height, weight, level of education, clothes, type of speech, tone of voice, gestures, facial expression etc. To these, add all the covert variables that also come into play during the interview: nervousness, fidgety behaviour, feelings of sorrow and sadness, anger – to name but a few.

Which of the multiple sets of variables we respond to and which we ignore is not necessarily, as is assumed, a chance event. It is often related to a personal set pattern (Popper 1963), which we may have acquired early in life. Such a personal set pattern is not easily given up. It may be maintained throughout one's life, allowing every new experience to be interpreted in terms of the pattern. Such an approach tends to create a dogmatic pattern that is resistant to any critical assessment or modification. Neither the client nor the therapist is immune from acquiring such rigid pattern reactions in their own constructions of the world around them.

Let us move from philosophy to psychology and see if similar arguments hold. Evidence from research on the primacy factor, or first impressions, does *not* support a stance of neutrality. The pioneering experiments by Asch (1946), Heider (1946), Brown (1965, 1987), Bem (1972) and Higgins *et al.* (1976) have demonstrated clearly that first impressions allow us to integrate and synthesize information into a meaningful pattern – even reconciling conflicting and contradictory information. What is not very clear is whether first impressions are enduring or transient, accurate or inaccurate, and whether they influence the observer in making accurate long-term assessments. But the impact of first impressions is a well-established finding. There is further evidence to show that positive and negative first impressions create their own positive and negative haloes. A person judged favourably tends to be seen in favourable terms despite objective evidence to the contrary – and vice versa.

No honest therapist can remain unaffected by the power of his or her own first impressions. There is no point in pretending that one's perceptions of a client are objective and neutral. They aren't. Although one cannot avoid the power of first impressions, it would do therapists good to take on board all their prejudices and biases, all their preconceptions and predilections, accept them as part of their being, and use them as assumptions or working models in the interview situation. That would be a far more honest and just way of dealing with first impressions instead of denying their existence, as many tend to do. To assert, as some therapists do, that they are perfectly objective and neutral in their assessments of their clients, and that this ojectivity and neutrality remains constant, is a mistaken view.

Cognitive control

'The professional needs always to be in control' appears to be the guiding philosophy of most therapists. The client may weep and cry, have emotional outbursts, betray tensions, display wild swings of mood, but the therapist needs to remain calm and rational even under the most trying conditions.

Why is the therapist expected to exercise such a high degree of cognitive control in a therapeutic situation? There is a well-founded belief that it is through the judicious exercise of one's cognitive processes – the exclusive powers of reason – that one can uncover the nature and structure of reality and acquire knowledge of the external world and of the human mind. The origins of the cognitive model can be traced to the writings of Descartes, who was one of the greatest rationalist philosophers of the seventeenth century. The advantages of using a rationalist approach cannot be overstated. It allows the therapist to exercise some degree of control over the interview; the therapist can remain calm and unperturbed in the face of emotional outbursts by the client and such an approach also permits the therapist to continue, change, alter and even terminate the interview, if it threatens to get out of hand.

The exercise of cognitive control is facilitated by the fact that western society tends to be 'work and activity centred'. This has already been discussed in Chapter 3 (see p. 73). In such a society, people tend to operate in a cognitive mode, where the emphasis is on rationality, logic and control. Given the cultural moratorium on the public expression of feelings and emotions, whom does a person in distress turn to? It is evident that in such a society a need arises for the creation of professional therapeutic and/or counselling settings, which permit the legitimate expression of feelings and emotions by clients and their handling by experts trained in that area. (One of my postgraduate students in years gone by was so terrified of expressing her anger, her rage and all her aggressive sentiments in public that she used to drive down a motorway, lower the window of her car and shout and scream until she was completely drained. I was never able to determine how often and how many miles she drove on each occasion to achieve this unusual but dramatic state of catharsis. Without sounding flippant one wonders if she might not have fared better had she used the same strategy on her therapist!)

There is one danger to which a therapist needs to be alerted. In the process of exercising cognitive control, there is a strong likelihood that the client may come to perceive the therapist as being cold and uncaring. 'Here I am, crying my heart out, and he (or she) just sits there, doing nothing!' might become the client's lament. Contemporary research on therapeutic outcomes points out that the one important factor which influences outcomes positively is the perceived warmth of the therapist. The personality characteristics of the therapist have an important bearing on therapeutic outcomes (Barnlund and Araki 1985; Garfield and Bergin 1986). To put it very simply, we like people who are warm and reciprocate our feelings, and we are indifferent, if not hostile, to people we see as being cold. Warmth, you will agree, is an emotional dimension, *not* a cognitive one.

Empathy

Closely related to warmth is empathy. Empathy is a complex process. It is regulated by both cognitive and affective (emotional) components, which interact in a systematic manner to produce an emotional understanding (Bhandari and Parathi 2000). To be truly empathetic, you would need to be sensitive to your client's feelings, you would need to have the ability to share your client's emotions, and you should be able to identify with your client's present position or status. If you were a psychoanalytically oriented therapist, you would see empathy as an affective understanding of another person's emotional state reached through momentary identification. In other words, empathy involves the ability of an individual to 'crawl' into the 'skin' of another person and construe the world from their perspective. To feel what the other person feels, to see the world as the other person sees it, to experience in a symbiotic way the emotional experiences of the other person may be defined as empathy. It should however be emphasized that for a given emotional or affective response to be seen as empathic, it needs to be perceived as such by the recipient. Unlike virtue, empathy is not its own reward. It has to be acknowledged by the beneficiary.

Several research workers have proposed that the notion of empathy is best understood in developmental terms; consequently, a variety of developmental models of empathy have been proposed (e.g. Hoffman 1976, 1982; Elizur 1985; Markowitz 1987; Kozeki & Berghammer 1992).

It is clear that no one is born with an inexhaustible reservoir of empathy. It is a learned emotional response which develops in conditions where a child's parents are supportive, responsive, warm and accepting of the child's emotional reactions. Hoffman (1976, 1982) argued that parents should allow their children to be exposed to a broad range of experiences and emotions so as to enable them to develop their sensitivity to the feelings of others. To shield children from distressing experiences, such as a serious illness, or death in the family, under the mistaken belief that such experiences might traumatize them may turn out to be counterproductive (Hoffman 1976; Laungani 1997c, 1999b, 2001c). The child will have serious difficulties in acquiring the psychic maturity to empathize with others.

Where does this finding leave those therapists who have not had the good fortune of having been socialized in conditions which are ideal for the development of genuine empathy? And since empathy has been identified as a necessary condition for effective therapy – particularly of the Rogerian mould – how is such empathy to be achieved by those who have failed to acquire it? And furthermore, given that therapists in general are expected to exercise a high degree of cognitive control, how do they reconcile reasoned calm with emotional turbulence? This question remains unanswered.

A few therapists might have cause to feel aggrieved and even angry at the seemingly negative tone of the discussion so far, and experienced therapists may take exception to some of the criticisms offered. In expressing their concern they might argue that what I have portrayed is a grossly exaggerated caricature of the initial therapeutic interview session. If that is the case (and I cannot deny the possibility that that may well be), it would give me considerable pleasure (not unmixed with pain) to read and learn from any counter arguments that I may have missed in the course of my own work.

My purpose here has been to raise awareness of some vital issues related to counselling and therapy. It is hoped that my comments will promote serious and sustained discussions and constructive criticisms in the area, which will lead to a better and more objective understanding of the problems with which we are all so deeply concerned.

When Indian clients and therapists meet in England

The question of a one-to-one interview between a potential client and the therapist seems almost redundant when seen from an Indian context. Such formal client-therapist relationships are largely a western phenomenon. They rest on the ideology of individualism, which has been discussed at length in Chapter 3. Such a formal relationship acquires legitimacy only when both parties respect and accept the fundamental notions arising out of an ideology of individualism. In simple terms, the one-to-one meeting between the client and the therapist rests on following mutually shared assumptions: 'I have a problem. It is my problem. It may be of concern to my family and even to my friends. But despite their concern, it is essentially my problem – and not my family's problem. The therapist too accepts this. I meet the therapist so that with his or her help I may be able to find a solution to my problem.' Such mutually shared assumptions have very little meaning within an Indian context. Eastern value systems, as was explained in Chapter 3, to a large extent rest on the ideology of communalism (or collectivism). Thus, in India, and among Indians living in the West, the above scenario would read differently: 'Our son (or our daughter, or whoever) has a serious problem, which has affected the entire family. Everyone in the family is deeply concerned and deeply worried. We need to find a satisfactory solution to the problem. If the problem remains unresolved, it will have a serious adverse effect on the entire family.' Notice the change in pronouns in the two scenarios. The first person singular pronoun 'I' is replaced by the collective term 'our' in the second scenario. In the first scenario, the psychological problem, whatever it might be, is the sole concern of the afflicted individual. The concern of others may no doubt be important, but is often seen as being peripheral. In the second scenario, the 'afflicted' person has no voice, or hardly any; his or her problems are spoken for and discussed by the patriarch – the head of the family. (In certain parts of India, particularly in Kerala, families operate on a matrilineal structure and the major decisions tend to be taken by the mother, the head of the family.) Even the solutions to the problem – i.e. whether to take the afflicted person to a therapist, to a guru, a spiritualist or on a pilgrimage etc. are offered by the patriarch in consultation with the rest of the members of the family.

In eastern cultures, individual problems, as has already been pointed out, are transformed into family problems and individual egos are 'submerged' into the collective family ego. Under such conditions, it is unlikely that a one-to-one meeting between client and therapist would even seem appropriate. Several therapists who have worked with Asian clients in Britain have testified to this kind of arrangement. The elders in the family may accompany the client and may even take an active, if not a leading, part in the discussions, consultations and the proposed therapeutic strategies.

The role of the therapist under such conditions shifts significantly. The three features discussed in the preceding section (neutrality and objectivity, cognitive control, and empathy) are of far less concern within an Indian setting than in the West. The qualities which the parents of the afflicted person expect the therapist to possess are often vague and not easily definable – wisdom, sagacity and a feeling of spiritual, mystical and magical powers, plus decisiveness. While in the West the client, after a few sessions, may come to place a high degree of confidence in the ability of the therapist, the situation among Indian clients tends to be different. The parents of the afflicted person come seeking solutions; they operate on an article of faith, and it is important therefore that the therapist, if she or he is to succeed, arouses the desired faith in the client.

Even the nature of the relationship between the client and the therapist follows its own cultural course. In the West, the relationship is based on a 'horizontal' structure, where the therapist and the client relate to one another on an 'equal status' basis. (Whether this actually works out in practice is debatable.) In eastern cultures, however, the relationship is based on a 'vertical' structure, where the therapist is not only seen to be in a superior position but is also accepted as such. After all, when a therapist is seen as the help-giver, a purveyor of wisdom and learning, a spiritual healer, a mystic, a learned sage, it is understandable that they be accorded deference, respect and reverence from their clients. In fact, it may be in the interests of the therapist to 'cultivate' such an image. The therapeutic approach tends more often than not to be didactic. The therapist leads and the client follows.

Even the goals in terms of therapeutic outcomes may differ. In a western setting the emphasis, as we have seen, is often on self-realization, self-actualization, empowerment, freedom to do, to achieve, to realize one's potential etc. 'Freedom to' is the key phrase. This idea is also in keeping with western ideological notions of individualism, liberalism, individual liberty and freedom. In eastern cultures, however, the key phrase is 'freedom from'. One needs to be free from, rid oneself of, escape from, overcome, treat, cure, get better etc. Concepts such as self-actualization, realization of one's potential etc. may not be seen as the desired goals which a client is expected (doubtless with the non-directive help of the therapist) to work through. One of the major goals is to ensure that in the process of 'treating' the client, the therapist is able to restore harmony and balance within the family network so that the family once again operates as a unified and integrated family unit. It is obvious that such a culture-specific construction is likely to call for a variety of different therapeutic approaches. All these issues will be discussed in depth in the next chapter.

A word of caution

It is extremely important to bear in mind – I cannot stress this enough – that not all Indians or Asians and South-East Asians from Pakistan, Bangladesh, Sri Lanka, East and South Africa, Kuala Lumpur, Indonesia, and from other parts of the world who live in Britain will or are likely to construe mental and psychological distress in the manner described above. As was pointed out in Chapter 2, the Asian population has been living in Britain for over 80 years. The children, the grandchildren and the great-grandchildren (and perhaps even the fourth generation) of the pioneering immigrants who first came to Britain have been socialized in ways quite different from what they would have experienced within their own cultural settings. They have been the recipients of diverse cultural norms and values, which have had a significant impact on shaping their identities and their own construction of their subjective worlds. Many of them of course, over the years, have acquired a western 'identity' or persona, retaining only a few remnant vestiges of their cultural ancestry.

What kinds of problems or issues (if any) are likely to arise when a therapist of Indian, West Indian or African ancestry working in the West has clients from different ethnic groups, including white? Several therapists, including Atkinson (1983), D'Ardenne and Mahtani (1989), Carter (1995), Laungani (1999b), Jewel (2001) and Johnson and Nadirshaw (2001) have reviewed this problem from different ethnic and racial perspectives and Fernando (1988) has considered the issue from a psychiatric perspective.

The situation can also be reversed when a white therapist has 'mixed' clients, both white and Asians. Would the therapist be expected to, and above all have the skill and the ability to, 'switch' from one cultural mode to another, depending on the client's ethnicity and perceived values? Even if the therapist were blessed with such a skill, there are several other factors which would need serious consideration – the gender, the age, the educational background, the occupation of the client, among others. Or would each therapist prefer to 'play safe' and elect to work with clients from his or her own cultural and ethnic background? This leads us into the extremely sensitive, serious, and important problems of matching clients and therapists, which we shall examine in Chapter 7.

Chapter 6

Asian models of counselling and therapy: historical and contemporary perspectives

In the preceding chapter we examined the means by which clients get to meet their therapists both in India and in England, the major assumptions which they bring to bear during their initial meetings, and the manner in which they perceive one another – all of which have an important bearing on the type, the course and perhaps even the outcome of therapy. In this chapter we shall examine the therapeutic options that are available to Asian clients living in England.

What the reader must bear in mind is the fact that Asian clients (from the Indian sub-continent) living in Britain 'span' three if not four generations. As we saw in the earlier chapters, Asians from the Indian sub-continent have been living in England for many years, due largely to historical associations between India and Britain. Given the unprecedented changes that have occurred in western countries (and indeed in eastern cultures) during the last hundred years or so, it is virtually impossible for people – regardless of the culture and the country of their origin – to remain unaffected by such changes. One would have to search far and wide to find a person or a group of people living, so to speak, in a 'time-warped' Victorian Britain; not impossible, but unlikely. Since change, as the pre-Socratic philosopher Heraclitis argued, is the only form of permanence one can ever be certain of, one would rationally expect to observe vast intergenerational changes among the Asians and also among the Britons in Britain. It is not just a question of a hansom cab giving way to a black cab, a steamer to a cruiser, a calculator to a computer, a letter to an email – the changes have been staggering and wide-reaching.

However, one needs to remember that the past is never completely swept aside; parts of it remain. Literature, poetry, art, music, philosophy, significant patterns of human behaviour (both desirable and reprehensible) and a large number of our salient attitudes, values and beliefs which guide our lives, survive the onslaught of such changes. With minor modifications, they remain intact. It is these enduring consistencies and characteristics, unwashed by time, which allow us to talk in terms of our inherited cultural legacies, which to a large extent account for differences and similarities between cultures.

The point being made is this: although at one level the observed differences between say a third-generation Indian and a first-generation Indian living in Britain might appear to outweigh any similarities, were one to observe closely with a trained eye, the similarities would become manifest in certain attitudes, beliefs, values and behaviours shared by people in all cultures.

The close delineation of cultural similarities and differences explicated in Chapter 3 should now allow us to put into perspective the Asian models of counselling and therapy to which Asian clients might turn in times of emotional and psychological distress. It should be made clear that in using the phrase 'models of counselling' the term 'model' must not be interpreted in its strict scientific and/or philosophical sense. It is a loosely coined phrase used as a convenient form of classification. It serves the purpose of distinguishing one therapeutic approach from another.

Most eastern therapeutic approaches, as the readers will no doubt have worked out for themselves, are centred round the deeply-rooted religious beliefs of both Hindus and Muslims living in western countries. As was made clear in Chapter 3, in Asian thinking there have seldom been sharp distinctions between the sacred and the secular. Even the most natural events such as disease, illness (physical and psychological), mishaps, 'misfortunes', death, disasters, etc. are explained not in scientific and/or medico-legal terms, but in religious and supernatural terms. People are 'victims' of sorcery, bewitchments and evil spirits (Kakar 1982; Laungani 1988, 1999a; Fuller 1992). People are 'victims' of God's wrath. For instance, belief in the evil eye – commonly referred to as *najar* or *dishti* – is quite strong and widespread among Indians. A child who meets with an accident or falls seriously ill might be the victim of an evil eye. In addition to wearing charms and amulets and sacred threads (the symbol of the 'twice-born' high caste Hindu), parents might symbolically blacken the child's face with ash or coal dust or even kohl to ward off the dangers of the evil eye. A plain and 'ugly' child is less likely to become a victim of the evil eye than a pretty child (Laungani 1990).

Social acceptance of such attributions has served to legitimize the belief in the evil eye, in other evil spirits and their malevolent variants. All over India one finds an army of shamans, faith healers, mystics, gurus, astrologers and yogis who are accorded greater respect and reverence than medically trained doctors and psychiatrists.

What about Asians living in western countries? Is the situation any different? Although responsive to and appreciative of the services offered by the National Health Service, they have not completely abandoned their own centuries-old indigenous therapeutic approaches, to which many of them turn in times of need and stress. The kind of indigenous remedies and the type of 'experts' the Asians are likely to turn to is related to several factors: the manner in which they construe the nature and the severity of the affliction, the available social and financial resources, past practices, the perceived severity of the disorder etc. What must also be taken into account by the therapist uninitiated into the intricacies of Asian culture is the fact that Asians, whether in the East or in the West, do not 'shy away' from seeking succour from more than one therapist at any one time. To use an apt cliché, they tend to hedge their bets. 'Since God,' they might argue, 'works in mysterious ways, it is best to see as many healers and therapists as possible. How can one be sure that any one particular person turns out to be the right person?' Such a belief also tends to carry over into organic disorders and it is not at all unusual for Asian patients to attempt to meet with several consultants without abandoning their search for a 'magical' cure, which they hope they might miraculously receive from their gurus, religious leaders, mystics, astrologers and the like.

While Asian clients (Hindus, Muslims or Sikhs) may have no qualms about consulting a variety of professionals and semi-professionals for help, European clients might. But with the increasing interest in complementary therapies related to health, diet, illness, stress, cardiovascular disorders, etc. shown in western countries, this situation appears to be undergoing a subtle change. The two approaches, the eastern and the western, appear to be less divided now than they were a couple of decades ago.

Let us now examine the major therapeutic options open to Asians.

Demonological therapies

Shamanism (and its variants) is a form of treatment commonly found in several parts of the world, including Africa, Haiti, the West Indies, India, Pakistan, Malaysia, Indonesia and several other Third World countries. Shamans, in certain instances, are often accorded a far greater respect and veneration than the medically trained psychiatrists in western countries. It is not uncommon to find the concerned relatives of a distressed person consulting some, if not all, of these specialists for effective treatment. There are variations in styles and techniques of treatment, but the main object is to 'cure' a person of any serious psychological and/or psychotic disorder, the underlying basis of which may be 'possession' of the afflicted person by a devil, a malevolent, demonic spirit or a *shaitaan*. Why a demonic spirit should take possession of one individual and not another is attributed to a variety of factors: the envy of neighbours at the visible affluence, success and good health of the afflicted person, serious quarrels between the family members, disputes over wealth and inheritance within the family, sexual misdemeanours, alcoholism and drug addiction. The result may be unexplained illnesses, depression, impotence, rashes, raging temperatures and even smallpox. The patient afflicted by these disorders is considered blameless because the illness is seen as the work of demons and other malevolent spirits that have taken possession of the patient's mind and body (Chandrashekar 1989).

Western psychiatrists and psychologists subscribing to the natural science model tend to be at best sceptical and at worst scathing and dismissive about the efficacy of eastern indigenous therapies – in particular exorcism and shamanism. While scepticism and rational doubt are the prerequisites of an enquiring, scientific mind, the prejudgement of a theory or a technique without any genuine attempts to seek objective, empirical evidence, is not in keeping with an open mind.

In this context, I should like to describe an experience I once had several years ago when I was invited to present a paper at an international conference in England on mental illness across cultures. I had only just returned from India, where I had had the unique opportunity of meeting a shaman and seeing him at work. I had assumed that the delegates, psychiatrists and psychologists, would find my account of meeting the shaman fascinating and that we would even set up a small study group to take the ideas further.

Nothing of the kind happened. Hardly did I finish narrating the story of my meeting when I was subjected to a barrage of ridicule and the collective wrath of a large group of psychiatrists and psychologists. The supercilious arrogance displayed by one or two of the delegates took one's breath away!

This is the story. I had just returned from India where I had stayed for a few days in a small village in Gujarat in connection with a research project on infant weaning and feeding practices. The villagers with whom I stayed often spoke of the shamans who visited their village and 'cured' them of their ailments, which ranged from snakebites and malaria, aches and pains to paranoid delusions and being possessed by demons. They swore by the amazing skills and the success rate of the shamans. My curiosity aroused, I waited to meet one.

Shamans, I had learnt, were like passing minstrels, who wandered from village to village exercising their healing powers on those who needed their help. A few days later, my wish was granted. A shaman, who was passing through another village, was hastily summoned to 'treat' a villager (a woodcutter) who had been stung by a scorpion on his calf. Like the rest of the villagers, I rushed out to see the shaman at work.

Although I had no conscious stereotypes of what a shaman would look like, I was not surprised when I saw him. He seemed ageless. With his thick, matted hair, his coarse, sun-blackened skin and an ankle-length gown (like the *jaleba* worn by Arabs), over which he wore a multi-coloured waistcoat, he cut an impressive but forbidding figure! He was dirty, unkempt and even quite coarse, both in his speech and his demeanour. But it was his eyes that held my attention. His large penetrating eyeballs protruded from their sockets and one could not meet them without flinching. Although aware of my presence, he ignored me completely and turned to the woodcutter, who lay on the ground, writhing in agony.

The shaman spoke with the woodcutter in a mixture of dialects and languages, a couple of which I was unable to follow; but it was not difficult to get the gist of what was happening. Flailing his arms, he looked heavenwards and cursed all the devils and the *shitans*. And then, within a few minutes, he started to sway, his shoulders moving to their own rhythm, at first gently, and then gaining momentum. He muttered sounds, looked heavenwards, then at the woodcutter writhing on the ground, raised his hands and swirled round and round for several minutes. We all stood mesmerized, unable to take our eyes off him. He then articulated invocations to Allah, and then suddenly after several athletic leaps in the air, dropped onto his knees in front of the woodcutter. From the folds of his gown he removed a large shiny polished slab – it might have been marble – and placed it over the spot where the woodcutter said he had been stung. The swelling on his calf appeared to grow larger by the minute. He explained to the woodcutter (and of course for all to hear) that he had acquired the smooth, shiny, black stone from South Africa, and, combined with his own mystical skills that it had indisputable healing powers. He placed the stone over the swelling, and said that he would lower the stone in gradual stages until it reached the tip of the woodcutter's toes, assuring him all the while that his pain would also shift with the movement of the stone. After about half an hour or so, the stone reached the tip of the woodcutter's toes. 'Son!' the shaman said to the woodcutter, 'as soon as I take away the stone from your toes you will swoon and become unconscious. But don't worry! So long as I have the powers which Allah has bestowed upon me, you do not have to worry.' After a few more invocations the shaman, with a flamboyant flourish, moved the stone away from the toes of the woodcutter. The woodcutter swooned, his head lolled and he became unconscious. The villagers revived him by sprinkling water over his face. Someone fetched an earthenware bowl of milk, which he drank, and soon afterwards he rose to his feet, bowed down at the feet of the shaman (who looked fazed himself) and hobbled away.

For a moment, there was stunned silence when I narrated this episode to the delegates at the conference. And then, some of them roared with laughter. A few of them 'honoured' me with slow handclaps. One of them turned to me and remarked: 'Dr Laungani, for an intelligent man, it is astonishing how you could have become a victim of your own self-delusion!' I paused, took a deep breath and turned to the 200-odd delegates and asked if it wasn't one of the cardinal principles in science that one suspended judgement when one came across an anomalous observation? Yet, not only had they passed judgement on my observation but they had made me a victim of my own self-deception! I shall pass over what transpired subsequently, other than to say that the apology, which my accuser offered me, was given with bad grace. All this however is unrelated to the main theme under discussion, which is to consider the above problem from a scientific perspective. There are several points to be made:

- It is plausible to assume that the woodcutter had *not* been stung by a scorpion. He could have been stung by a bee, a wasp or another insect.
- It is also possible that the woodcutter's swelling may have been due to the sting of a scorpion.
- Other unknown factors may have been at work. Using a psychoanalytical framework, it is possible to hypothesize that the swelling may have been a symptom of a deep-rooted hysterical disorder.
- It is also possible that it was an old wound, which for some unknown reason had begun to reappear.
- An alternative hypothesis is that the woodcutter *was* cured by hypnosis and faith in the healing powers of the shaman.
- The most plausible hypothesis is to look upon the success of the 'treatment' as a result of a culturally shared and accepted form of treatment.

Given such a state of uncertainty, one would expect a scientist to suspend judgement while seeking more plausible, verifiable and alternative explanations. But it was clear that many of the psychologists, therapists and psychiatrists at the conference, wedded as they were to a natural science paradigm, had abandoned the much-valued stance of Socratic purity and had passed judgement with more haste and less caution. To be fair to them, during the coffee break, several psychiatrists and psychologists came to see me, eager to learn more of the episode that I had narrated to them.

The point which is being underlined here is that in the East there is no conflict whatever between fact and faith. As de Riencourt (1980b: 67) points out, 'Eastern faith (*sraddha*) aims basically at subjective cognition rather than the objective "believing to be true" of the Westerner.'

Indigenous Ayurvedic therapies

Ayurveda is a traditional Indian system of medicine. Its fundamental goal is to bring about and maintain a harmonious balance between the person, the person's body and the person's psyche (Leslie 1976; Larson 1987; Bhavasar and Kiem 1989). In modern western terminology it might be construed as a form of holistic medicine. However, its roots run deeper. There is a shared belief among Indians and people from South Asia that Ayurvedic medicine has no beginning since it reflects 'the laws of nature inherent in life and living beings and thus mirrors their unchanging essence' (Kakar 1982: 221). Since it is the person who has an illness (mental or physical) Ayurvedic medicine is focused more on treating the person rather than the disease. (This philosophy to a certain extent is also in keeping with the Hippocratic oath of treating the person who suffers from a disease and not the disease independent of the person.) It is believed that illness occurs when there is a humoral imbalance between the psyche-soma identity. Such an imbalance is likely to lead to different types of insanities. For effective treatment therefore it is as important to understand the person as the disease which is to be treated.

In Ayurveda, the emphasis of treatment is on purification, which may often consist of purges, emetics, enemas and bleeding. However, these practices appear to have fallen into disuse, even though they are still practised in certain parts of south India. They have been replaced by other traditional herbal remedies. Since the Ayurvedic goal is to restore a harmonious balance, the treatment procedures tend to be diverse. The patient is also encouraged to undertake regular physical exercise, including breathing exercises or *pranayamas*. Closely related to the emphasis on breathing exercises is an emphasis on the acquisition of desirable personal and social habits, which include ways of relating to oneself (not 'abusing' one's body by not engaging in excess) and to others, and the imbibing of those thoughts, attitudes, beliefs and values which promote a harmonious balance between the person, the soma and the psyche. There is a strong emphasis on rigid dietary practices, in keeping with the belief that certain types of food produce certain mental states (both desirable and undesirable) and therefore can only be eaten at certain times of the day.

Ayurvedic dietary prohibitions and prescriptions

Restrictions and prohibitions on diet play an extremely important role in the day-to-day lives of both Hindus and Muslims (Paranjpe *et al.* 1988; Sivaraman 1989). In Hindu tradition, foods are considered to possess certain characteristics. The first one is concerned with degrees of pollution. Cooked food is more polluting than uncooked food and cooked foods offered by persons of a lower caste to persons of a higher caste are also polluting, since any contact with members of lower castes is polluting. (Although such a case of caste contamination with its negative consequences for the person concerned is unlikely to occur among Hindus living in England, it would serve the therapist well to be aware of such a possibility.) Hindus do not normally touch food eaten by others, nor will they eat off a plate shared by others, for that is considered to be polluting, or *jutha*. To bring one's lips to a glass from which another person has had a drink is polluting. To eat before one has washed is polluting; not to wash after one has eaten is polluting. The list is endless. As Lannoy 1975: 150 points out, among Hindus, 'the most important quality of food is the degree to which it is pollution free'.

Some foods, by definition, are polluting, of which beef is the most polluting because of the survival of the ancient tradition among Hindus to look upon the cow as sacred. To eat beef is to commit a sacrilege. Although Hindus in general tend to be vegetarians, there are regional differences. Hindus from the Punjab eat meat, whereas Gujaratis in general tend to be vegetarians. A Gujarati family might occasionally eat eggs, but meat in any form is not likely to find its way into the home. If within the home there is a conflict in dietary preferences, allowances may be made for the carnivorous member of the family to engage in culinary misdemeanours – provided they do so outside and not in the home. Among orthodox Hindus not only meat, and to a lesser extent eggs, but also some vegetables (in particular root vegetables such as radishes and garlic) are seen as being polluting.

Hindus also tend to divide their foods into three categories: cold, hot and foods which are considered to be sour. Cold foods, such as rice, yoghurt, oranges, buttermilk etc. are considered to have a cooling effect on the body; hot foods, such as meat, eggs, mangoes and certain vegetables are considered to have a heating effect on the body; and sour foods such as lemons and tamarind, tend to create gases and stomach upsets in the body. What adds to the complexity of these restrictions is the fact that certain foods can be eaten only during the day, some only at night, some after prayers, and others only during particular seasons and festivals. There are also concerns related to the mixing of foods. Chutneys and sweets, for instance, do not mix. In many Indian homes one is not allowed to drink after one has eaten sweets prepared in ghee; one is not allowed to eat ice cream or have a cold drink if one has a cold; no chutney should be given to a person who has been coughing. Milk products are not usually mixed with savoury products, and so on and so on.

Yet another characteristic of foods is their inherent capacity to convey certain qualities to the eater. Some foods, known as *rajas*, are deemed to increase passion and lust, and are therefore to be avoided at certain times in one's life. Other foods, such as meat, are known to create inertia and dullness; these are referred to as *tamas*. Finally, there are foods known as *sattvic* foods. These include milk products, sugar, rice, wheat, pulses and many vegetables. Such foods are known to produce harmony, balance and health in the individual.

Here it needs to be emphasized that among orthodox Hindus any infringement of these rigid dietary rituals can lead to all kinds of illness – both mental and physical. Although there is little evidence to demonstrate the psycho-physiological efficacy of such practices, by linking ideas of treatment with ideas of illness, they do offer cultural reassurance to family members.

One of the first questions which Indian patients persistently ask of their doctors both in India and in Britain relates to what foods they should eat and what foods they should avoid. The lack of an adequate, psychologically reassuring answer leaves patients with a vague sense of disappointment.

It should be borne in mind that the heating and cooling properties of foods, the relationship of food to the three body humours and their resultant temperaments *(rajas*, *tamas*, and *sattva)*, and the Indian ideal of balance and harmony between the body and the psyche, arise out of the ancient cultural beliefs acquired through Ayurvedic practices. They play an important part in traditional Indian medicine and are significant in many religious rituals.

Among Muslims too, there are definite restrictions and prohibitions related to diet. As is common knowledge in Muslim doctrine, beings are divided into clean and unclean. So is food. There are prohibitions on the eating of pork, the drinking of alcohol and the consumption of a whole series of reptiles and animals. Muslims eat beef, but avoid pork because of a belief in its impurity. Muslims will only eat *halal* meat – that is, meat which has been slaughtered in a particular way. All other meats are considered to be impure (or *haraam*). Devout Muslims are expected to abide by these dietary prohibitions and the problem becomes more acute during the month of Ramadan. It is expected that all Muslims (with exceptions being made for children below the age of 12, the infirm and expectant mothers) to undertake a dawn to dusk fast for the 29 days of Ramadan.

In addition to food, water is also believed to be especially pollution prone. To avoid any form of spiritual contamination, orthodox Hindus always carried with them urns and jugs of water whenever they undertook any long journeys. The practice of carrying water is still prevalent among many sections of Hindu society. My family members, for instance, never undertook a long journey without carrying their own supply of water. Whenever we went on our holidays, which involved a two- or a three-day train journey, my father made sure that we carried several urns and jugs of water with us to see us through the journey. The number of urns and jugs often exceeded all other baggage that we carried with us. On one or two occasions, however, the supply of water that he had brought with him ran out. He forbade us all from drinking water from the restaurant car of the train. At the next station, he arranged for all the jugs and urns to be filled with water from the station water pump. The fact that that water may not have been safe from a hygienic point of view was of little concern to him. What mattered was that the water from the station tap had not been touched by another human hand. Ritual purity took precedence over hygiene.

To remain unaware of the complex dietary practices of Asians, or to ignore them as being trivial, may prevent a therapist from 'picking up' vital cues, or from responding to questions which on the surface might seem innocuous and not worth the bother.

Astrological therapies

Beliefs in astrology and the malevolent (and benevolent) influences of planets on one's life are strongly ingrained in the Indian psyche. It is quite customary to have a child's horoscope cast upon its birth. The heavenly configuration of planets at the moment of birth is seen as a determinant of life chances. A carefully cast horoscope reveals a person's fate which is written on a person's forehead (Fuller 1992). The first step taken by parents, eager to find the 'right' marital match for their children, is to exchange the horoscopes of the couple involved. Were any planetary mismatch in the horoscopes of the couple to be discovered, the parents might decide not to proceed with the betrothal of their respective children. In other words, some of the most enduring and lifelong decisions are taken on the basis of horoscopes.

There is often the fear that misfortunes may occur as a result of the malevolent influence of the planets, particularly Saturn (*shani*).

Shrines containing images of Saturn and other planets are found in all parts of India. On the day when Saturn moves from one house to another, people all over India offer prayers. Some express relief at having survived the last 30 months, and others are fearful and anxious at having to get through the *next* 30 months without calamitous misfortunes (Fuller 1992) Still others may decide to undertake arduous religious ceremonies to reduce the evil influences of the planets.

Such astrological formulations permit explanations and the acceptance of untimely deaths and sudden deaths, including suicides and murder. Pandey *et al.* (1980), in a study of informants of psychiatric patients in India, found that the most commonly stated cause of psychotic disorder and other traumatic experiences was sins and wrong deeds in a previous or present life, and/or the patients' horoscopes. Such findings are not uncommon and have been corroborated by Srinivasa and Trivedi (1982) who, in their study of 266 respondents selected from three villages in south India, attributed, among other factors, 'God's curse', and 'fate' as the most common causes of stress leading to mental disorder.

Yoga therapy

In the last two to three decades ideas concerning yoga have become increasingly popular in western countries. However, the term 'yoga' and what it signifies is not easily understood. In the West, yoga is often seen as a series of physical exercises which involve acquiring certain bodily postures and breath control. It is believed that regular yogic exercises supervised by a trained teacher will lead to a physically (and hopefully mentally) healthy lifestyle.

Although partially correct this is a simplistic view of yoga, and divorces it from its religious, spiritual and karmic roots, including the very complex and poignant theory of detachment – yogic renunciation at a materialistic way of life. The history of yoga is long and ancient. Its origins are associated with Patanjali, the great Sanskrit scholar about whom very little is known (Eliade 1975). According to Patanjali's *Yogasutra*, the main purpose of yoga is to still or silence the mind so that it can reflect accurately and arrive at an understanding of objective reality (Ravindra 1989). The term yoga is related to several others in Indo-European languages, including the English *yoke*, the German *Joch* and the Latin *iujum*, which all have the same meaning (Eliade 1969; Feuerstein 1996). The term yoga itself is derived from the Sanskrit root *yuj*, which when translated into English means to control, to yoke, to unite. Yoga is seen as a discipline of asceticism, renunciation and meditation, which through sustained practice leads to spiritual experience and enlightenment into the nature of existence (Flood 1996). It is a method (or technology) by means of which the mind and senses can be restrained, one's ego controlled and subjugated and transformed into higher states of consciousness, which eventually leads to salvation and the liberation of the individual from the cycle of birth and rebirth. Thus in yogic practice the unsettled and wandering mind can be set into repose by developing the eight aspects of the yogic path: moral restraint (*yama*), breath control (*pranayama*), sense withdrawal (*prayahara*), bodily postures (*asanas*), practice of virtues (*niyama*), concentration (*dharana*), meditation (*dhyana*) and a state of trance (*samadhi*).

Yoga itself has several forms or paths. The most popular form in western countries is the *hatha* yoga, which is occasionally referred to as the path of inner power. The word *hatha* means 'force' and refers to that branch of yoga that is aimed at self-transformation and self-transcendence through exercises, bodily postures, breath control and other forms of physical purification (Feurstein 1996). Because its philosophical and spiritual foundations remain relatively unknown in the West, it is often seen as a form of gymnastic activity which is run alongside other fitness training courses.

In India the followers of yoga often see it as a solution to most if not all their physical and mental problems. In addition to yoga, there is among Indians a greater reliance on indigenous therapeutic treatments for their physical and psychological problems. The World Health Organization (WHO) (1978) points out that there are over 108 colleges of indigenous medicine in India, with over 500,000 practitioners of one of the following indigenous forms of healing: Ayurveds, Unani and yoga. But yoga appears to be the most popular form of treatment used in psychological disorders all over the country. Evidence of the efficacy of yoga therapy is quite convincing (Satyavathi 1988). Encouraged by the results of yoga therapy, Vahia (1982) even suggested that it offers a new conceptual model of health and disease. Although several studies have pointed to the effectiveness of yoga therapy (Neki 1979; Bhole 1981; Dharmakeerti 1982; Nespor 1982) it is not seen as a panacea for all types of disorder.

Religious counselling

Since illness, distress and afflictions are often perceived as visitations from the gods – or God's curse – it is an accepted practice to take the afflicted person to a well-known shrine, temple or Muslim *darga*. In this instance there is a powerful pragmatic mixture of religious beliefs. Hindus frequently visit Muslim *dargas*, and Muslim families may also visit a temple or meet with a well-known guru attributed with divine healing powers. Distress blurs religious divisions. Visits to shrines, temples and mosques may take several forms. The afflicted person 'surrenders' his or her will to the guru by sitting near and 'feasting' his or her eyes on the guru. The *darshan* (blessed vision) of the guru is attributed with immense spiritual and healing powers. In other instances, the guru may encourage the person to recite prayers, meditate, read from the scriptures or to perform religious rites, all of which are believed to have healing properties.

Special emphasis is paid to the intense and symbiotic relationship between the guru and the follower (Sinha and Sinha 1990). The guru-follower therapeutic procedure tends to adopt a directive – even didactic – approach rather than a non-directive one. The guru attempts to guide the afflicted person through all his or her afflictions, offers hope and offers prayer. In return it is beholden upon the follower to abide by all the teachings and prescriptions of the guru. For the therapeutic enterprise to progress smoothly, it is essential for the guru to be perceived as being a person of immense sagacity and wisdom. The guru must have no obvious pecuniary interests in the outcome of the treatment and must also be seen to be living on the 'margins' of society. In other words, the guru, in keeping with Indian cultural traditions, must be seen as being truly and totally detached from material comforts and aspirations.

The guru may also recommend – to those who can afford it – that the afflicted person be taken on a pilgrimage to the holy cities, such as Benaras, Hardwar, Vrindavan and Rishikesh. There they would be expected to perform elaborate religious ceremonies and cleansing rituals, feed hundreds of mendicants and bathe in the river Ganges, which is attributed with divine cleansing powers. At home, the women would be expected to pray, undertake regular fasts, and practice severe austerity to ensure the restoring of the victim's mental and physical health.

Before bringing this chapter to a close let us raise a few concerns, the first of which is 'cultural expertise'. How many western therapists would have the necessary cultural expertise to consider and handle any or most of the above issues were they to be presented to them during the course of therapy? Would it make sense to a therapist trained in the art of one-to-one therapy if the relatives of the client also sat in on the therapy sessions? Would the therapist feel comfortable taking on a directive and didactic role as part of the treatment procedure? Would the therapist relish the idea of being seen as a wise guru? Would the therapist countenance offering advice on the client's diet, religious practices, yogic exercises and a variety of other factors with which they may not be conversant? Would the therapist recommend pilgrimages, visits to temples, the wearing of charms and amulets? Even if the therapist were trained in these indigenous techniques, would they even wish to employ them? No immediate answers come to mind.

Would an Asian therapist fare any better? This question cannot be answered without prior knowledge concerning the cultural expertise of the Asian therapist. Most Asian therapists are trained in the West, and most Asian therapists, it is reasonable to assume, are second- and even third-generation Asians, whose parents and grandparents would have emigrated from the Indian sub-continent, Africa and elsewhere. What are the chances that the Asian therapist would have acquired and imbibed a deep and sophisticated understanding of the complexities of Hindu and Islamic cultures? What are the chances of the therapist even being able to speak the language(s) of Asian clients? Such therapists are trained in western counselling and psychotherapy and follow western theoretical and therapeutic models. The chances of their faring any better than their white colleagues when dealing with Asian clients remains slim.

It is only lately that culture-centred counselling and therapy has become a focus of attention among therapists of all persuasions. In the past, when cross-cultural issues arose, they were often discussed tangentially. In recent years the tenor of the discussions has changed and interrelated issues of political correctness, racism, multiculturalism and the use of indigenous therapies are being vigorously debated and contested.

There are other related issues which are also of concern. One of the central questions to which one would need to find answers is that of validity. When and under what conditions is a given therapy known to work? What are the factors that lead to its success (or failure)? Are Asian clients best 'handled' by Asian therapists? In other words, is there any merit in matching clients with therapists (and vice versa)? Does matching lead to positive outcomes of therapy? Ought matching to become standard practice?

Finally, there is the epistemological problem of commensurability. Is it possible to compare one therapeutic approach with another in terms of a variety of parameters: superiority, efficacy, success rates, duration of treatment, cost etc.? Are such comparative studies possible to undertake? What kind of methodological techniques might one adopt for such research undertakings? Even a cursory consideration of these questions is likely to get us into a state of nervous apprehension.

It is as though Pandora's Box has been prised open and the problem of culture-centred therapy has come out into the open. However, one might recall that the last thing that came tumbling out of Pandora's Box was hope. It is my hope that in the next chapter, after we have examined the major issues related to culture-specific or culture-centred counselling and therapy, we may be able to come up with a few tentative answers.

Chapter 7

A meeting of cultures? 'Matching' clients and therapists

In England there is growing concern among many therapists of different ethnic origins, including white therapists, that ethnicity might be an extremely important factor in intercultural therapy. There is a feeling that clients from a particular cultural group are likely to feel more at ease with a therapist from that same cultural group. In other words, the mutual sharing of a set of common cultural beliefs and values, which may include language, proverbs and metaphors, religious practices, rites and rituals, leisure pursuits and other familial and social patterns of behaviour, may have the desired positive effect on the process and outcome of therapy. This does not imply that clients and therapists who come from different cultural groups will be at a mutual disadvantage. They may be. They may not be. At a common-sense level, the argument related to matching clients with therapists seems understandable, rational and eminently desirable. However, the issue of 'matching', as we shall soon see, is far more complicated than it appears at first sight. The issue raises a variety of political, philosophical, racial, social, linguistic and practical problems which one would need to examine.

Matching involves finding or locating the 'right' counsellor/therapist for a client and the 'right' client for a counsellor/therapist. This is akin to finding the right job for the right person and the right person for the right job. Equally, choosing marital partners in India among Hindus is normally based on a careful matching of horoscopes of the 'boy' and the 'girl'. Horoscopes are exchanged. The Brahmin priest involved in these delicate negotiations for the two families concerned, studies the horoscopes and interprets the influences (benevolent and/or malevolent) of the stars, the moon, the sun and the planets on the future lives of the couple involved, leaving it to the parents to take the final decision. Strange as this might sound to a westerner, one of the most interesting cultural features of such an arrangement is that in many orthodox Hindu families, the prospective bride and bridegroom are seldom allowed to disagree or question the parental decision. It is their *duty* to obey and abide by these decisions. Orthodoxy in many instances leads to ludicrous extremes. In many villages in India, particularly those in some of the states in north India, the parents do not shy away from arranged betrothals of their very young children, in some cases even infants. And barring any unforeseen events or mishaps, the betrothals are binding. The marriages are solemnized when the children reach marriageable age or even earlier, and thus is family honour (*izzat*) preserved.

But whether matching by horoscopes is accurate and/or effective is a contentious issue. Most psychologists, because of their dogmatic belief in the authority of the method of the natural sciences tend to be dismissive of astrological speculations and predictions. However, Feyerabend (1975), the 'anarchic' philosopher of science, is of the opinion that astrological predictions ought not to be dismissed without a proper hearing.

These epistemological issues do not in any way affect the Brahmin priest involved in the comparative study of horoscopes. He remains in an impregnable position regardless of the future outcome of the arranged marriage. If the marriage succeeds within the accepted norms of the social and cultural system, the priest takes the credit for his accurate predictions. If the marriage fails the Brahmin merely attributes other factors (such as an evil eye, a curse, past karma, bewitchment etc.) to that failure.

If the therapy between the ethnically matched client and therapist leads to a successful outcome (although it is extremely difficult to define what a successful outcome is), the therapist can 'keep the credit' (and of course the cash!) for the success because of his or her superior and intimate knowledge and understanding of the client's culture. If, however, the outcome is negative, there are a variety of ways in which the therapist can rationalize the lack of success. The most common one is 'the client was really quite unwilling to confide his or her intimate problems to a person of his or her own cultural background' etc.

Counsellor/client or therapist/client matching

In recent years a lot has been written on the subject of client/therapist counselling; much of it tends to be painfully repetitious. For a comprehensive review the reader is referred to the following sources: Sattler (1977); Jones (1978); Draguns (1981); Atkinson (1983); Helms (1984); Casas (1985); Pederson (1985, 1987); Alladin (1986, 2001); Garfield and Bergin (1986); Roland (1988); Lago and Thompson (1989); Sheikh and Sheikh (1989); Sue and Sue (1990); Ponterotto and Casas (1991); Wade and Bernstein (1991); Kareem (1992); Pederson *et al.* (1996); Triandis (1997); Laungani (1999d); Jewel (2001); Palmer (2001).

Let us first examine the issues of client-counsellor/therapist matching in terms of white counsellors/therapists and non-white clients. Several arguments have been put forward in defence of matching. The first one is concerned with therapist-client relationship.

Uneasy relationship between white therapists and non-white clients

It has been argued that members of ethnic minorities do not have easy access to counselling and/or therapeutic services. This, it is suggested, is due to the unfounded belief among white counsellors and therapists that members of ethnic minorities, particularly those from Asian backgrounds, do not always feel the need to take up the services on offer. It would appear that their close-knit family structures provide them with the required security and comfort. There is also a strong feeling among black and Asian clients that white counsellors often tend to impose their own embedded western values onto their clients.

The members of ethnic minorities look upon these western values as being of little or no relevance to their existential, religious, spiritual, familial and social needs. Some of the more outspoken critics see this form of counselling and psychotherapy as a thinly disguised form of paternalistic imperialism which, among other things, also asserts the moral and racial superiority of western values over other value systems.

Let us consider one more point before we turn to other issues. Most theories of counselling and psychotherapy emphasize the view that counsellors and therapists, in order to help their clients in understanding and dealing with their psychological and existential problems, need to acquire and cultivate those qualities which would facilitate the therapeutic process, namely empathy, trust, suspension of one's personal judgement and neutrality. These considerations form the very substance of counselling theories. Besides, few would dispute that counselling and psychotherapy are noble, honourable, humane and caring professions. People who choose to enter them do so to a large extent out of a desire to help others. To accuse white therapists of adopting dual standards, one for blacks and the other for whites, seems harsh and unfair to say the least. Let us for a moment dismiss the implied racist and imperialist tendencies of white counsellors/therapists as products of a paranoid imagination; let us return to them the integrity and honesty which each professional regardless of his or her skin colour or ethnic origins merits. What then?

Inadequate training courses in cross-cultural understanding

Does the situation get any better? Does counselling/psychotherapy proceed along mutually satisfactory lines? The simple answer given by the critics is no. The problems, as the critics see it, lie firstly in the kind of training given to counsellors/psychotherapists. Their training is almost exclusively eurocentric. All the major theories of counselling are of western origin; they are a product *of* western culture and are located *in* western cultures. Given these conditions, it is hardly surprising that their approach would of necessity be western-oriented – an area of knowledge and expertise in which they feel comfortable and confident.

There is little in the training manuals or on training courses which deals systematically and comprehensively with cross-cultural understanding. As a result white counsellors/therapists occasionally acquire ludicrous, superficial and stereotypic understandings of the lives of people from other cultures. A few years ago I had the sad experience of being asked by a white British therapist if I spoke *Hindu*. I felt so embarrassed by his ignorance that I could not bring myself to correct him – just as he might have been had I asked him if he spoke 'British'. As a result of their inadequate and quite superficial training, many British therapists are unable to crawl into the psyche of their culturally different clients and see the world from their perspective.

Let us assume that a few training courses (such as those run by those organizations which are concerned with cross-cultural and/or trans-cultural counselling and psychotherapy) were to be launched and made available to white counsellors/therapists. The question is this: which cultural group or groups would the white counsellors/therapists be trained to understand, relate to and deal with professionally? One imagines that the types of course on offer would be directly related to the available cultural expertise and experiences of black and/or ethnic minority counsellors. Having said that, one still runs into another problem.

It is not unreasonable to assume that most black and/or ethnic minority therapists wishing to get involved in planning, designing and launching such training courses are more likely, because of their age, to be second- if not third-generation settlers in Britain. As a result they would inevitably have been brought up and educated in Britain and to a large extent would have imbibed and internalized the dominant norms and values of British culture as well as their own indigenous one. Having said that, would they have necessarily acquired a deep and sophisticated understanding of their own cultural background? Their language(s)? Their customs? Would they be able to launch satisfactory courses aimed at educating trainee therapists from different cultural backgrounds? The fact that one is able to trace one's ancestry to another culture and can even speak the language is obviously a desirable asset. But it does not in itself guarantee expertise in one's ancestral culture. Lest this be seen as needless nit-picking let me present the reader with a personal example.

A couple of years ago I was involved in editing a five-volume series entitled *Death and Bereavement Around the World* (Morgan and Laungani 2002) with my friend and co-editor, Professor Jack Morgan. Jack suggested that I should write a long, comprehensive chapter entitled 'Hindu Spirituality in Death and Bereavement' for the first volume. I did not pause to consider what I was letting myself in for, and without batting an eyelid I agreed. My brash confidence grew out of the fact that being a Hindu myself, having been born and raised in a traditional and conservative Hindu family in India, I felt that I had the accoutrements to write an interesting and insightful chapter.

Moreover, right from childhood, I had participated in all the prayers and the religious ceremonies related to birth, marriage and death, both at home and outside. I had performed the daily rites and rituals, imbibed the instructions and the teachings of my teachers, undertaken pilgrimages to the holy cities and shrines, bathed and 'cleansed' myself on the banks of the holy river Ganges, studied Sanskrit at school and then in college, and was familiar with many of the Hindu scriptures. What more did one need?

But when I began to think about the probable contents of the chapter, the number of pages that would need to be written, and the eventual shape and structure it would take, I began to have second thoughts about the project. I realized that I had made the oldest mistake of all. I had assumed that because I was born into a particular religious and cultural background, and because I could read the scriptures, because I could speak a few Indian languages, it was axiomatic that I should have a deep and profound understanding of my own religion and culture. This, I realized, was total nonsense: a merchant seaman may sail round the world a dozen times and know nothing of any significance about the countries and the people visited.

I was appalled by my own ignorance and the thought of abandoning the chapter – 'losing face' seemed a desirable option and I almost succumbed to the temptation. But a few days of reflection convinced me that the actual business of writing the chapter, regardless of the intellectual and emotional costs involved, would be far less painful than loss of face. It was a long, hard and arduous journey, both metaphorically and literally. I had to undertake a trip to India to talk to several scholars and refresh my understanding and interpretation of the scriptures before putting pen to paper. I am still not sure that I have done justice to the chapter.

I do not expect any sympathy from the reader, for it would seem that I brought this problem upon myself. But that is not the point I am trying to make. The point is that no matter how long one may have lived in one's culture, no matter what values one may have imbibed, no matter whether one speaks one language or several, it still does not follow that one thereby becomes an expert in one's culture. 'Expertise' is not conferred. Nor is it acquired as a matter of right or through birth. It is achieved (if, at all) through unrelenting graft and dedication.

This therefore brings us back to the question of the expertise of those black and other ethnic minority counsellors/therapists who plan courses in 'cultural understanding' or 'cultural awareness training' for their white compatriots. One is not disputing their claims to expertise but one would like to know the bases of their claims. I have come to the humble conclusion that experience alone, without genuine scholarship, is a far worse intellectual and moral crime than scholarship without experience.

If the black and the Asian therapists are united in their view that the way forward lies in launching courses in cultural awareness, it is then incumbent upon them to ensure that they operate from the highest scholastic standards. They would need to offer courses which are found to be meaningful, objective, insightful and useful. It is essential that such courses provide the learners with deep and even profound insights (uncontaminated by banal and dangerous stereotypes) into the subtle workings of the culture, perhaps even a glimpse into the psyche of the people of that culture. Watered-down and oversimplified courses, hastily improvised courses, courses peddling inane stereotypes, courses disseminating trivial and banal factual information, courses designed to ensure the tenure of one's job at an institute, or courses used as stepping stones to expand one's 'empire', all these in the long run are likely to run into serious difficulties. Instead of building bridges, they may create chasms.

Assumptions concerning access of ethnic minorities to therapy

There appears to be a widespread belief among several black and other ethnic minority counsellors, psychotherapists and other health professionals that members of ethnic minorities do not have easy access to counselling, therapeutic, health and other social services (Troyna 1981; Skellington and Morris 1992). This, it is argued, is due to the belief among many white counsellors and other health professionals that members of ethnic minorities do not normally feel the need to take up such services. Their close-knit family structures provide them with the required care, security and comfort. Although the pattern of family structures is undergoing a change, it is true that members of ethnic minorities from Asian backgrounds, to a large extent, tend to live in close-knit family structures, but it does not follow that they do not feel the need to take up counselling services. The low take-up rate among this group may in fact be due to different reasons altogether.

It has also been suggested that Asians tend to somatize their psychological and emotional problems, particularly those related to anxiety and depression, and as a result their problems go unnoticed. Recent studies on postnatal depression among Asian women (Sethi

1986; Cox and Holden 1994; Kumar 1994; O'Hara 1994; Laungani 2000a) offer some support of the somatization hypotheses. But the findings from these studies are by no means unequivocal. Consequently, one needs to be cautious in concluding that as a result of somatization the members of Asian communities do not perceive their problems in emotional and psychological terms. As I have stated elsewhere:

> the reason for 'somatising' depression is due largely to the following factors: a) depression as a psychological concept is not easily understood in India; b) psychological disorders of any kind arouse all sorts of fears and negative evaluations; and, c) for a woman, in particular a young wife, who has just given birth to a baby, to present a psychological problem, e.g., postnatal depression, might be construed as bringing disgrace and shame upon the family. To gain the sympathetic attention and concern from her husband and the rest of her husband's family members, it is essential therefore that she 'presents' problems of a somatic kind – problems which the family members understand, are able to identify with, relate to, and are in sympathy with, and consequently, would actively seek medical intervention to such problems.
>
> (Laungani 2000a: 87)

As Johnson and Nadirshaw (2001) point out, to assume somatization is to give rise to stereotypes. Stereotypes are dangerous. If unchecked, they lead to incalculable harm. When they are allowed to gain currency and turn into 'self-evident truths' they deprive members of ethnic minorities from easy access to the counselling and therapeutic services.

Uneasy relations between white clients and non-white therapists

It is not just the 'consumers' of health services who feel they are short-changed. There is among many black counsellors and therapists a growing sense of unease concerning their own dyadic relationships with their white clients. Several black and other ethnic minority counsellors and therapists have expressed serious concern at the nature and pattern of professional relationships which they form (or are unable to form) with their white clients. Many of them have pointed out that in the course of their work with white clients they are occasionally subjected to ridicule. The idea that a black or an Asian counsellor or therapist can even deign to understand the psychological, existential and cultural problems of a white client is seen as being utterly ridiculous. Such racist prejudices, the therapists claim, are communicated to the therapist within the first few sessions, or even earlier. Any progress in therapeutic sessions then becomes a virtual impossibility.

How has such a situation come about? The majority of black therapists strongly believe that racism has been and continues to be an endemic feature of western society (Sattler 1977; Jones 1978; Littlewood and Lipsedge 1982; Atkinson 1983; Ridley 1984; Garfield and Bergin 1986; Pederson 1987, 1988; Lago and Thompson 1989; Sue and Sue 1990; Kareem 1992; Palmer and Laungani 1999; Alladin 2001; Jewel 2001). Racism is slowly and remorselessly beginning to spread its poisonous vapours into the field of counselling and psychotherapy. Whether intentional or unintentional, individual or collective, overt or covert, institutional or personal, religious or secular, racism is an inescapable disease of western society and no counsellor – black or white – can ignore its impact on the process of counselling. To ignore or avoid its malevolent power is to deny its importance. Avoidance is unlikely to guarantee immunity. The question which black counsellors and psychotherapists ask is this: what ought a black (or Asian) therapist to do under such conditions? How should he or she deal with a prejudiced white client? Many therapists have adopted their own strategies to deal with this problem, and these are some of the options that are open to black and Asian therapists:

- *Rejection*: the therapist may refuse to work with white clients.
- *Avoidance*: the therapist for a variety of reasons may deliberately decide to avoid any reference to or any discussion of racial issues and their possible impact on their interpersonal (dyadic) relations in the course of counselling/therapy. The therapist may remain silent and leave it to the client to raise the problem.
- *Confrontation*: right at the outset, the therapist may challenge the (inherent) attitudes of his or her client: 'Let's clear the air before we go any further'.
- *Conscious denial*: in this case, the therapist may adopt what is referred to as a colour blind approach – i.e. that people are people are people, and their skin colour, ethnicity and social

class have very little influence on the course of therapy. Or the therapist may believe that there are no serious racist implications involved in their work. The denial may be deliberate and intentional, or it may be unconscious.

- *Appeasement and conversion of white clients:* some black therapists may attempt to make white clients aware of their racist attitudes and in so doing hope to foster the desired changes in their attitude. The danger in adopting an appeasement approach lies in the possibility of being patronized and subjected to ridicule by white clients.

Uneasy relations between white, black and Asian therapists

There is a strong feeling among many black and Asian therapists that white therapists in general are grossly ignorant of the cultural values and lifestyles of black and ethnic minorities. They are unable to visualize the 'world' of their clients from their clients' perspective. They tend to see their clients' world from their own western perspective. Western values (particularly those related to the ideology of individualism and secularism) imbibed and internalized by white therapists tend to get imposed onto their non-white clients. Western values are seen as being of little or no relevance as far as the existential, religious, spiritual, familial and social needs of non-white clients are concerned. Many outspoken critics see this form of therapy, which Cushman (1990, 1995) refers to as therapy on the 'empty self', as a form of paternalistic imperialism. It tends to create a sense of unease, distress and disappointment among members of ethnic minorities, who see it as an attempt to marginalize and alienate ethnic minorities in Britain.

Although such criticisms 'across the cultural divide' are generally expressed in 'acceptable' academic language, when stripped of their academic niceties they are hurtful and damaging. There are two questions that follow from these assertions. The first is of a philosophical nature: how do these assertions come into being? It is clear that they are based on the subjective (but nonetheless empirical) observations of individual therapists, but do they arise out of any first principles? Are these assertions grounded in a universal theory (e.g. a theory of 'human nature', or a theory of 'motivation', or a theory of 'natural justice', or a universal theory of personality)? Is it in the 'nature' of human beings to display hostility, suspicion and prejudice towards people who are 'different' from them in terms of culture, skin colour, etc.? Does one group see itself as being 'naturally' superior to another group? And would they increasingly display such patterns of behaviour were they not restrained through processes of socialization and by the inhibiting powers of the rule of law? But since not all Asian and black therapists see their white counterparts (and vice versa) in such negative terms, it follows that negative assessments are not grounded in any universal theory, but arise out of the personal experiences of black and Asian therapists in their direct or indirect encounters with white therapists.

And this brings us to our second question, which is concerned with validity: is there any truth in these assertions and accusations? Do white therapists wittingly or unwittingly impose their own values on Asian and black clients? Do white therapists in so doing attempt to assert their own moral and racial superiority?

It is of course possible that subjective assertions or accusations that are based on personal experiences may be true. But subjective knowledge, as is well known, varies from person to person. It may also vary within the same person at different times, thus making it self-contradictory. This is not to deny the importance of subjective assertions, but experiential perceptions are not always a reliable source of objective knowledge. In the final analysis, one is concerned with truth – or objective knowledge, as Popper calls it.

And this is where we run into a serious problem. How does one arrive at objective knowledge? This is one of the most fundamental problems in the philosophy of science. Let us examine it carefully. In this context, it is worth quoting the prophetic lines of the pre-Socratic philosopher Xenophanes (sixth century BC) who said:

> As for certain truth, no man had known it,
> Nor shall he know it, neither of the gods,
> Nor yet of all things of which I speak,
> For even if by chance he were to utter
> The final truth, he would himself not know it:
> For all is but a woven web of guesses.
>
> (Quoted in Magee 1998)

The problem of objective knowledge has perturbed philosophers and scientists for over 2,500 years, and as Popper points out in his book *Conjectures and Refutations* (1963), we have not come any nearer to solving it.

Truth, however 'pure', and however innocent and unprejudiced the mind of the perceiver, is not self-evident, as David Hume claimed over two centuries ago. Truth comes neither through divine revelation nor through authority, tradition or strong belief: 'If the strength of beliefs were a hallmark of knowledge, we should have to rank some tales about demons, angels, devils, and of heaven and hell as knowledge' (Lakatos 1978: 1). Truth cannot be established by fiat. One might, in this connection, recall the doomed attempts by the Stalinist regime to promote the Lysenkian theory of genetics in opposition to Mendelian genetics because the former was in keeping with communist ideology. Incalculable harm was done to Soviet agriculture as a result. Several geneticists of worldwide reputation, including Vavilov, who opposed the spurious theory, were incarcerated and died of severe cold, hunger and malnutrition.

Nor can truth be established by consensus, even though this is a popular and even hallowed theory. In most countries it forms an integral part of the criminal justice system, where a jury of just and rational beings are expected to arrive at a consensus concerning the guilt or innocence of the accused. Yet it is not unknown for the guilty to be found innocent and the innocent guilty.

To return to the point – just because there appears to be a resounding chorus of accusations by black and ethnic minority therapists concerning the implicit (and explicit) racist tendencies of white therapists, this does not mean that such accusations are true. There are some therapists who believe – perhaps rightly so – that the kind of truth one is referring to is virtually impossible to collect with any acceptable degree of objectivity (Sollod 1982). In the final analysis people have to rely on their own subjective and professional experiences.

At a personal level – both as a member of an ethnic minority and as a professional psychologist – I am in great sympathy with these sentiments. I earnestly, whole-heartedly believe that the subjective sentiments expressed by many therapists have more than a hint of truth about them. One has no reason to disbelieve them; they are persons of honour and integrity. And their accusations are based on their own professional experiences. But to accept the validity of their claims at an objective level on the basis of their subjective and experiential sentiments is to engage in what might turn out to be self-deception. This situation has created a personal dilemma for me. Whether I agree or disagree with the critics, I find myself in a 'no win' situation; I'm damned if I do and I'm damned if I don't.

However, let us pursue this argument further. There is no denying that all the major theories of counselling and psychotherapy are founded on certain sets of assumptions, which have a strong eurocentric (or western) bias. What the eurocentric biases and assumptions are have already been discussed in Chapters 3 and 4. Most counsellors and psychotherapists, despite the variations in their individual styles, approaches and emphases, operate from within these major theoretical frameworks.

Socrates pointed out over 2,500 years ago that all human relationships – from the trivial and the transient to the profound and the enduring – have an underlying moral basis. Appealing though this claim is, it is based on a form of rationalist dogmatism because no underlying first principles have been postulated from which the source of such an assertion can be drawn. It was Immanuel Kant who, 2,000 years later, in his brilliant *Critique of Pure Reason*, and *Critique of Practical Reason*, formulated the 'categorical imperative' which posits a rationalist universal moral nature of human relations. Kant argued that one ought to treat each human being as an end in himself or herself and not as a means to an end. These are sound universal moral imperatives. One would therefore need to take it as axiomatic that the dyadic relationship between client and therapist rests on sound universal moral foundations. Reimers and Treacher (1995) point out that counsellors and psychotherapists must accept ethical issues as of primary consideration in therapy. That is indisputable.

However, not all therapists and counsellors live by such axioms. There is substantive evidence to show that many professionals working in the area of counselling and psychotherapy have not always acted in accordance with the highest moral standards. Over the years there have been serious lapses and misdemeanours in the maintenance of high moral (and legal) standards of behaviour (see Holroyd and Brodsky 1977; Bates and Brodsky 1989; Masson 1992; Stean 1993; Jehu 1994a). Be that as it may, it does not seem right to condemn the entire profession on the basis of a few rogue elements. Such harsh, uncompromising judgements besmirch the reputation of the profession and one might therefore wish to err on the side of caution and believe that therapists – white or black – in general adopt the highest possible moral, ethical and 'knowledge-based' standards in the course of their work.

The pros and cons of matching

The idea of matching, as has already been stated, has found favour among several therapists both in the USA and in Britain (Draguns 1981; Alladin 1986, 2001; Garfield and Bergin 1986; Fernando 1988; D'Ardenne and Mahtani 1989; Lago and Thompson 1989; Carter 1995; Moodley and Dhingra 2001). The importance of matching, it is believed, cannot be overstated. To ignore the issue – given its apparent advantages – would be to take a retrograde step. Yet there are other voices of dissent. Some therapists are not entirely convinced about the form, the mechanics and the techniques of matching, nor that matching would be a step in the right direction. The very process of matching, they fear, may lead to consequences other than those intended. Instead of bringing counsellors and therapists of different ethnic and cultural groups together, matching may in fact drive a wedge between them and succeed in alienating them from one another. In the long run the entire exercise may turn out to be counterproductive and even painful both for the counsellors and their clients.

There are a few on the other hand who are opposed to the whole idea of matching, Patterson (1978, 1986) being the most outspoken critic. Patterson argues that counselling and therapy require a set of skills and strategies which, when perfected and used judiciously, humanely and with great sensitivity, can be applied to good effect on clients from different cultural groups. Thus, there might be a need to modify counselling strategies to fit different cultures but not necessarily therapists to 'fit' clients.

Although Patterson does not say so directly it is worth drawing an analogy from Patterson's comments. To rephrase Gertrude Stein's classic rhetoric concerning a rose, one might assert that 'a medical doctor is a medical doctor is a medical doctor'. This would mean that doctors qualified in medicine, regardless of their skin colour, race, ethnicity, gender, age etc. are professionally and legally empowered to attend to a sick person (regardless of the patient's skin colour, race, ethnicity, gender etc.) in a professional capacity. Medicine is thus seen as a knowledge-based and skills-based profession. The personal attributes of the doctors, although important, are not seen as being essential to their being accepted as experts. Nor are such attributes recognized as being crucial to the treatment and recovery of patients. (Whether they ought to be or not is an extremely sensitive and contentious issue, which is beyond the scope of this book.) However, the sheer complexity of diseases has resulted in the creation of specialists whose specialist positions are knowledge-based, not culture based. Such is not the case in counselling and psychotherapy. Here, the psychological, cultural, racial and other attributes of the counsellor, rightly or wrongly, are often assumed to be far more important than their professionally recognized skills and qualifications.

The proponents of matching argue that all the major factors – race, political correctness, gender, age, ethnicity, culture, language and social class – of both counsellor and client enter into the therapeutic equation. Matching would ease and facilitate the process of therapy and enable the client/counsellor/therapist to get off to a good start because of their common cultural, educational, racial and other bonds. Both the client and the counsellor are likely to feel comfortable in such a relationship because of their common cultural, racial, and/or other associations. Matching, it is believed, may also be a way of combating racism.

Let us consider some of the major arguments related to matching.

The 'likes' with 'likes' argument

This proposal carries within it the idea that only 'likes' can understand 'likes', and therefore likes should treat likes. At first sight it seems a good, rational and commendable idea. Let us explore it a bit further. How will such an aim be achieved? What form would the matching process take? How does one define 'like' with 'like' in this context? Would a Gujarati-speaking Ismaili counsellor from Africa be a good culture-match for a Punjabi-speaking Sikh client from Jamaica? Would a Tamil-speaking Hindu from Chennai (Madras) be a good culture match for an Urdu-speaking Muslim from Lucknow? Would a young and highly educated second-generation Punjabi female counsellor be a good match for a first-generation French-speaking, elderly male Hindu client from Mauritius? Would a Bangladeshi housewife from Sylhet feel at ease with a Buddhist Sri Lankan counsellor? Remember neither speaks the other's language. Neither shares the other's food and dietary practices. Neither worships the other's gods. What they share in common is their Indian ancestry. Is that sufficient to merit it being called a reasonable culture match?

The idea that only 'likes' can understand 'likes', and therefore only 'likes' ought to counsel 'likes', when carried to its logical conclusion, would advocate that only men ought to counsel men, women, women, blacks, blacks, whites, whites, gays, gays, lesbians lesbians and so on. Not only would colour differences and gender differences come into play but age, social class and caste differences would also be involved in the mechanics of matching. Pursuing such a line of reasoning in practice would be absurd.

There is another danger to which Alladin (2001) alerts us. He points out that to insist on ethnic matching of client and therapist would be to invite the risk of segregation. In other words, there is a danger of creating counselling or therapeutic 'ghettos'. And, as Kareem (1992) argues, this form of inflexible matching can create its own prisons both for the client and the therapist. Kareem is right in making this point. Were matching to become the preferred norm of therapy, in theory at least it would seal the fate of both white and black counsellors who would then be expected to deal largely with those clients with whom they are suitably matched. From a purely pecuniary point of view, the implementation of such a rigid and inflexible form of matching would make it difficult if not impossible for therapists (and in particular, black therapists) to acquire clients from different cultural, racial and ethnic backgrounds. (Even counsellors and psychotherapists, despite their noble profession, need to earn and eat and live!)

Is there a way out? Given the fact that one can at best only hope for limited and partial matching, one needs to have a clear idea of what is to be matched with what. The major parameters related to matching can hardly be decided on the grounds of intuition, impulse, or one's professional experiences as a therapist, or even on the theory of consensus.

The moral prescription argument

Those in favour of matching are committed to the view that it is beneficial to both the client and the therapist. Whether such a claim is based on carefully gathered empirical evidence, or on a set of a priori propositions, or on the intuitions of therapists is not the point. What emerges from these claims is the theme of moral prescription related to the entire issue of matching. It is not the aim of this chapter to get entangled in complex metaphysical debates concerning the relationship between 'ought' and 'is' and between 'theoretical' (pure) reason and practical reason. At the same time it needs to be said that because such and such ought to be so (because it is a good idea *if it were so*) is not a good enough reason for its implementation. This is because there may a valid and powerful argument for considering exceptions to the moral prescription, as Parekh (2000) has argued with reference to a variety of cross-cultural social issues, including female genital mutilation, and because there is no way of predicting the outcome of the action. In practice it might turn out to be counter-productive. How can one be sure that the advocated moral prescription is indeed the correct one, and that it will lead to its intended consequences? The moral prescriptions underlying matching appear to be based more on a caveat of faith than on sound logic, reason, and empirical evidence. Popper (1963, 1972) points out that human actions may lead to intended consequences, but they may also lead to unintended consequences, which may turn out to be the opposite of what one might have desired or intended.

The relativistic argument

Relativism in this context means that each culture develops its own conceptual system of rules, norms and values to which people subscribe. Therefore, any problems which may arise within that culture (e.g. depression, anxiety) would need to be understood in accordance with the norms and values of that particular culture. An outsider (e.g. a white therapist) unfamiliar with the value systems of that culture would not be able to make sense of the situation and consequently would not know how best to deal with it.

A relativistic formulation would have other advantages too. It would put an end to any form of pejorative (or racist) judgements of other cultures because one would be attempting to understand the client from within the client's cultural system of rules and not from the counsellor's cultural standpoint. Thus, there would be no need to grade or order cultures on a measurable scale of superiority or inferiority, civilized or primitive etc. The adoption of a relativistic approach would also help to dilute, if not dissolve altogether, the oft-voiced accusations of scientific, educational and economic imperialism which have been levelled against western countries by the developing countries.

Although one can see the value of adopting a relativistic position, it does not lend itself to ready acceptance. Relativism as a valid explanatory concept has come to be seriously questioned by, several writers, including Stace (1958), Musgrove (1982), Gellner (1985), Williams (1985), Doyal and Harris (1986) and Bloom (1987). It has also been argued that relativism in recent years has come to acquire a variety of ideological connotations, and is often used as a gag to stifle any acknowledgement of genuine differences in opinions, beliefs, values and behaviours of people. It is, in that sense, potentially dangerous. Its acceptance creates no room for any real understanding of cross-cultural differences in a variety of fields, including counselling. And as Popper (1972, 1988) has pointed out, the *uncritical* acceptance of relativism leads to an epistemological cul-de-sac. Above all, it does not permit one to transcend one's cultural boundaries. One is forever trapped, even imprisoned within the narrowly defined boundaries of one's culture.

An example will help. The idea of female circumcision, or female genital mutilation as it is now referred to, arouses among certain sections of the population in the West perhaps the same degree of repugnance which is reserved for cases of infanticide and the *sati* practice (the burning of widows) in India. Female genital mutilation affects more than 80 million women and girls all over the world. It is practised in West, East and North Eastern parts of Africa, including Nigeria, Sierra Leone, the Ivory Coast and Ghana in North West Africa, in Sudan, Somalia, Mali, Djibouti, Ethiopia, Egypt, Kenya, Uganda and Tanzania. Despite its cultural legitimacy in the countries mentioned above, the practice has come under severe attack by several western countries. With the Prohibition of Female Circumcision Act in 1985, it has been made illegal in Britain. It is illegal too in most, if not all, other western countries. Regardless of how one construes the problem, regardless of which perspective one chooses to defend or attack the practice, the most powerful argument related to its prohibition is a moral one: one must not inflict any needless pain and suffering upon any living being. This is a clear example of a universalistic moral injunction. In questioning and opposing the legitimacy of female circumcision practised in the cultures mentioned above, it questions and challenges the approval of and acceptance of cultural diversity. But here too, as Parekh (2000) points out, exceptions can be found which might make us pause and reconsider the universality of the moral injunction. As Parekh argues, western countries, for a variety of reasons, not the least of which are related to their economic, technological and militaristic might, are in a much stronger position to impose their beliefs, values and practices on the rest of the world than the rest of the world is able to impose any values on them.

If, on the other hand, one adopted an uncritical relativistic position one would have to condone such practices and justify them in terms of ethical relativism. This would distort the entire issue of cultural variations and undermine the richness of cultural diversity. A rigid adherence to a relativistic position cannot be justified on the grounds of political correctness. A position of ethical relativism in the above instance is not only indefensible but naïve and dangerous.

This is not to suggest that relativism does not have an important role to play in counselling and psychotherapy. It does. Nor should the above point be seen as an attempt to defend an inflexible universalistic position. But one needs to be aware that the adoption of an inflexible (culturally or ethically) relativistic position or an inflexible universalistic position can often turn out to be counter-productive.

Conclusion

It is time to take stock. In this chapter we have examined the arguments for and against the problem of matching. Let us summarize the main arguments:

- In theory, matching seems a desirable idea. In practice, it is likely to run into serious problems.
- The call for matching does not arise out of any large-scale empirical findings supporting the need for it.
- Accurate matching on the basis of cultural similarity (or cultural identity) is virtually impossible to achieve.
- Accurate matching cannot be implemented *en masse* because when carried to its logical conclusion it would lead to infinite regress.
- A rigid adherence to a matching philosophy would lead to the espousal of a relativistic stance, which in the long run would lead to the creation of counselling and psychotherapeutic 'ghettos'.
- Although the need for matching is supported by seemingly plausible rational arguments there are equally plausible rational counter-arguments which do not support it.

A dark cloud of depression and pessimism looms over the chapter. It seems that the entire business of matching clients with therapists and therapists with clients is beset with insurmountable obstacles.

The problem of matching extends into a more general one, which is concerned with 'getting on' with peoples of other cultures, with trust, integrity and in peace and harmony. The problem of living in a multicultural society is not an isolated one affecting any one or two individuals. It affects us all.

Chapter 8

Case studies

Introduction

In this chapter we shall be concerned with describing and analysing two case studies. The first concerns a Gujarati family living in London. The study revolves round the theme of cultural and inter-generational conflicts. There are serious conflicts between the family members, and inter-racial conflicts between the members of the family and the indigenous whites. What the nature of the conflicts are and how they are successfully resolved, and what my own role was, shall become clear as we get into the case study.

The second case study is a tragic and heartbreaking account of a sexual assault and the tragic consequences to which it leads. The study extends over several years and moves from one city to another, from one country to another, from one continent to another, ultimately ending where it began. At a personal level, I was involved with this study sporadically for a period extending over 10–12 years. I confess that I have never ceased worrying over this case and am still unable to decide whether I might have handled it differently and helped to avert the tragic consequences. But I shall let readers decide for themselves after they have read it.

Before we get into describing and analysing the two case studies, it would be useful to say a few words about the nature of case studies: their functions, their uses and misuses, and the role they play in explaining subtle and complex feelings, emotions, sentiments, fears, anxieties, hopes and aspirations.

The nature of case studies

The case study is a much-respected qualitative methodological approach favoured by psychologists, sociologists, anthropologists, psychiatrists, medical doctors and other health professionals. In certain instances, a case-study approach is the only viable way of investigating an ongoing phenomenon, such as was done by the famous social psychologist Festinger and his colleagues (Festinger *et al.* 1956) when they set out to investigate the claims made by Marion Keech who prophesized the end of the world to her followers and admirers in Salt Lake City. Such an approach allowed them to test a variety of hypotheses related to their theory of cognitive dissonance.

Strictly speaking, the above study would be referred to as a field study, which may involve examining over time an ongoing situation, event, ceremony or ritual etc. Such a study may involve more than one investigator. However, the lines between field studies and case studies (or case histories) are not always clearly defined (Fisher and Fryberg 1994). Just as the therapist is involved in observing his or her client's behaviours, so too are the investigators in a field study. And just as the therapist is also a participant observer in a therapeutic session, so are the persons involved in field studies, as was the case with Festinger.

Some of the finest case studies – again of an ongoing situation or experience – are the ones recorded by Freud. Many of his case studies (e.g. The Case of Dora, The Case of the Rat Man, The Case of Little Hans) are too well known to merit further discussion. One might also recall the classical psychological case study, *The Three Faces of Eve* (Thigpen and Cleckley 1957), which concerned a woman who during the course of psychotherapy revealed three separate personalities: Eve Black, Eve White and Jane.

One of the interesting features of a case study is that it can be written in a personalized, informal style. This lends greater flexibility to the report, making it more interesting and even stimulating to read. Such ease and flexibility is often quite hard to achieve in formal academic writing. Moreover, a case study allows one to discuss issues, observations and interpretations which are often difficult to discuss in other ways. It enables one to speculate on subtleties, nuances, intuitions and the interplay of the main characters involved directly or indirectly in the case study.

Another advantage of a case study is that the observations and interpretations may lead to serendipitous discoveries, which allow us to deduce a fresh set of hypotheses that can then be subjected to rigorous empirical tests.

However, case studies, by their very nature, do not permit large-scale empirical research in which standardized psychometric instruments are used or experimental manipulations are implemented. They are more concerned with introspective interpretations based on the clinician's experience and expertise, and in general are confined to a sample size of one. However, this need not be seen as a disadvantage.

The merits or otherwise of employing a sample size of one have been extensively discussed and commented upon by several distinguished experimental psychologists, including B.F. Skinner, and therefore need not concern us here. Suffice it to say that Skinner (1953) himself was extremely critical of group experimentation designs, using complex statistical methods. He was personally in favour of single-participant research methods, with their emphasis on repeated measures and replications. For a critical understanding of the issues related to the use of single sample studies, the interested reader is referred to McGuigan (1993).

It has been argued that a case study breaches an important convention. There is a much-respected (even hallowed) tradition within the natural and biological sciences which involves the separation of the experimenter from the objects of his or her study. Such a separation has always been considered to be of paramount importance to any scientific enterprise. Scientists believed, and many still do, that clear separation from the objects of a study enables the scientist to maintain total objectivity. It is therefore incumbent upon scientists to take great care not to allow the phenomena under observation and, in the case of psychology, the people being studied, to influence their observations in any way. The extent to which scientists succeeded in controlling their observations was generally considered as indicative of the level of objectivity of a study. But is that really the case? Do psychologists ever succeed in separating the subject from the object and in so doing maintain complete objectivity in their observations and experimentations? It turns out that the so-called objectivity of observations in an experimental situation is a myth: in 1927, when formulating his principle of indeterminacy in quantum mechanics, Heisenberg discovered that the presence of the scientist along with his or her instruments influences the phenomena under observation, which seriously compromises the notion of total objectivity (see also Kuhn 1962; Scheffler 1969;

Lakatos and Musgrove 1970; Veatch 1972; Feyerabend 1975; Brush 1976; Gillies 1993). Although scientists assert the need for objectivity and prescribe normative standards of research (Popper 1988), the activity of science itself is pursued in a clumsy, subjective and ad hoc manner (Lakatos 1970). Objectivity is best realized in terms of degree, ranging from low to extremely high levels.

Before we turn to the first case study it is important to bear in mind that despite the merits of case studies, they all have one fatal flaw. One cannot 'go beyond' the case study and make any unequivocal general statements. One needs to confine one's interpretations and explanations to that particular case study.

Case study I

This case study concerns a Gujarati family living in London. In order not to cause any embarrassment or distress to the family, the names of the people involved and their place of residence have been changed. None of the people involved in the study is likely to be recognized – not even by their closest relatives. The family are Hindu Gujaratis, belonging to the Vaishya caste (see Chapter 3 for a detailed explanation of the Indian caste system).

The family

It should be emphasized here that whether the family had originated from East Africa, or from South Africa, from India or from Pakistan, from the West Indies or from Mauritius, is irrelevant; most Hindus carry their caste with them almost as openly as most of us carry our skin colour. Although many Hindus lack a comprehensive awareness of their caste and sub-caste, (their *varna* and their *jatis*) their day-to-day behaviours within their own group and with outsiders are often regulated by the rituals and practices demanded by their caste. Caste-related behaviours are part of the socialization process, becoming an integral part of one's psyche through family dynamics. Suffice it to say that any counsellor involved in dealing with a Hindu family would find it exceedingly useful to have an astute, although not necessarily a scholastic, understanding of the caste system and how it works in the day-to-day lives of people. By a similar token, one would expect a counsellor dealing with a Caucasian client to be reasonably conversant with the social class of his or her client, since a variety of attitudes, values and behaviours, not to mention the use of language (in particular, metaphors), tend to be class-related. Such knowledge is essential in helping us to understand complex values and behaviours and the impact which subtle nuances have on the lives of people.

We are concerned with a member of a three-generation, extended family. The father and the mother were first-generation immigrants into Britain. They came during the early 1960s when immigration into Britain posed hardly any problems. On reaching London they settled down in Ealing, where the father, Mr Rashiklal Vanvaria, with the help of a distant cousin, started a small garment business in Greenford. He had no experience of the garment trade, and not surprisingly the business collapsed. On the advice of one of his relatives, he left Ealing and moved with his family to Hackney, where he opened an off-licence. His relatives assured him that Hackney was a multicultural, up-and-coming area and there was ample scope for this type of business. He opened the shop on the ground floor of the house in which they lived. He was a devout and orthodox Hindu, a teetotaller; he had never had a sip of alcohol in his life (other than the occasional medicinal brandy which was forced upon him by his mother in India) and had even forbidden his sons from drinking. It seemed strange and totally out of character, not to say naïve, that he should want to open an off-licence. Given that he had no experience of running this kind of business, or any other kind of business (in India he had worked for most of his life in an insurance company) the off-licence, like the garment business, also collapsed. Unwilling to move yet again, he auctioned all the cases of alcohol and started a small grocer's shop on the ground floor of the house. Much to his amazement, the shop thrived; unbeknown to him, it was the only large shop within a radius of half a square mile in the area.

The Vanvarias have five children: two daughters and three sons. The daughters, both of whom are married, live with their husbands and their in-laws in Ahmedabad in Gujarat, India. Of the three sons, the youngest lives in California with his American wife. (He is, in that sense, out of the picture.) The father and the mother, their two sons and their wives, all live together. The eldest son has no children, but the youngest has two daughters, both of whom go to a local primary school. Thus, the house consists of three generations of the family, all living together.

Mr Vanvaria phoned me and asked if I would be willing to meet with the family and help his younger son to 'sort out his problems'. He had got hold of my name through a complex network of contacts

– the cultural grapevine. It appears that both the elderly parents were extremely worried about their son's 'future' (or rather the lack of it). Since the mother is an invalid – she has arthritis and is unable to walk without pain and discomfort – it was suggested that I should go and visit them at their home in Hackney, which I did.

I felt it was important for me to get a 'feel' for the family and their background, to see them in their own domestic surroundings, interacting with one another, before I took any decisions of a professional nature. My visit would also give all the family members, particularly the father (who I assumed was the head of the family) the opportunity to 'size' me up. In most extended families, the authority of the father to a large extent remains undisputed (Laungani 1997b). I was certain that the decision to have his son counselled by me or by someone else would depend on him and him alone – not on his son.

Even before I went to see them, I guessed that there were at least four points which worked in my favour: I had come highly recommended (by whom, I was never able to find out); I was male; I was not too young; and I was able to understand and speak Hindi, Urdu and Gujarati. It should be mentioned that Indians in general, 'relate' better and have greater confidence in an older male counsellor or therapist than a young, recently trained one, particularly a female. Given the hierarchical nature of Indian society, male elders are placed at the top and are accorded greater deference. Status, position and power are positively correlated with age and gender (Kakar 1981; Roland 1988; Laungani 1999d).

I chose to go just after lunch. It was a time when I was sure I would not be persuaded to join them for lunch or dinner. From my own experience in dealing with Indians, I have found that one is easily enticed into partaking of their hospitality which can often be quite lavish. However, this form of hospitality can often act as a double-edged sword. On the one hand, one is overwhelmed by the selfless and spontaneous generosity of one's host; on the other, one can get entrapped within this hospitality. Having eaten off their dinner plates, it becomes difficult, if not impossible, to deny them any 'favours' which they may then feel emboldened to ask at a later stage. One does not, as the crude but apt Indian saying goes, 'piss in the dinner plates off which one has eaten'. E.M. Forster cautions the reader regarding this significant feature of Indian life in his novel, *A Passage to India*.

Acceptance of hospitality can also bring about a subtle change in the nature of the relationship between guest and host; functional and formal relationships get transformed into friendly and informal ones. Evidence suggests that people from the Indian sub-continent, in general, feel more comfortable and more at ease in informal emotional, hierarchical relationships, than in formal, cognitive, horizontal and/or hierarchical relationships – which act as 'comfort-zones' for most westerners (Weber 1959; Roland 1988). This unique feature of relationships has also been confirmed by many of the GPs, social workers and hospital doctors I have spoken to over the years.

As a therapist or as a counsellor, one needs to exercise discretion in this matter. Sometimes of course it is impossible to avoid accepting hospitality. However, the easiest and the safest way of avoiding the proffered hospitality without causing embarrassment or offence is to state very clearly that one is undertaking a fast. Undertaking fasts both by Hindu (and Muslim) men and women is considered to be an act of immense religious piety (Esposito 1988; Maruta and Chittick 1996; Singh and Nath 1999). This excuse has let me off the hook, so to speak, on many occasions. But whether a Hindu or a Muslim family will 'buy' this form of reasoning from a Caucasian therapist remains an empirical question. Try it.

We sat in a large disorganized living room. Framed pictures of Hindu gods and of Guru Nanak, and of Sai Baba, their family guru, hung on the walls. A corner had been turned into a temple and icons of Krishna, Shiva and other Hindu gods were clearly visible through the glass doors of a cupboard. The father and the mother sat on a sofa, and the two sons spread themselves around the room. The children, at that hour, were at school. I was given no chance to offer my rehearsed excuses related to my religious fasts; no sooner did I enter their house than one of the daughters-in-law, within the twinkling of an eye, produced a tray which contained a variety of vegetarian Gujarati snacks, followed by sweetened *masaala* (spiced) tea. I spent over an hour with the entire family, eating, drinking, chatting, listening and taking stock.

Mr Vanvaria did most of the talking; like most Indians I have known he had the remarkable ability to move from language to language: he would start a sentence in Gujarati, switch into Hindi halfway through and end the sentence in English. All the other members in the family remained silent when he spoke. The mother interjected from time to time, but she was more concerned with describing the nature of her own illness, which had led to her serious incapacity. I had the feeling that she left the discussion of her son's problem (I had yet to learn what it was) to her husband. The two sons remained silent and spoke only when responding to questions put to them either by their father or when I spoke to them directly. Only one of the daughters-in-law was at home; the second one, the eldest son's wife, was at work. I learnt subsequently that she was a biochemist and worked as a research scientist in a hospital.

Mr Vanvaria, from what I could gather, seemed a traditional, orthodox and devout Hindu given to daily recitations of the *Vedas*, prayer, and regular visits to the local temple. He had attempted to inculcate in all his children the merits of Hinduism and Indian culture and was very keen for both his sons to imbibe all the familial, cultural, religious and spiritual norms and values which he believed would enable them to live within the extended family network in peace, harmony and mutual coexistence. This was the only way that they could acquire a secure Indian identity. Having acquired such an identity, they could then learn to integrate into the mainstream of western culture, or distance themselves from it, or even discard it, if they chose. He made it clear that he wasn't against his sons imbibing western values, for that was inevitable. However, there were quite a few western values – the dissolution of the family, being one – which were divisive, pernicious and inimical to leading a life based on Hindu notions of *dharma* and *karma*, which, he believed, had sustained and perpetuated Hindusim for 4,000 years. All values, he asserted, collapse when the family collapses and disintegrates. Their family, by the grace of God, he said was still intact, and all his sons (including his youngest son) were 'good boys'; but of late, one of them appeared to have lost his way. That was precisely how he put it. How and in what way he had lost his way he did not care to elaborate.

Mr Vanvaria did not express himself succinctly; he rambled, he interrupted himself, he repeated himself, he turned to his wife when he was lost for words, but the gist of what he was trying to convey was fairly obvious. He spoke softly, without rancour, without aggression; he seemed sad and disappointed. His son, whose name I learnt later was Mahesh, did not meet his father's eye, nor did he make any attempt to defend himself. He sat in an armchair, staring at the ugly stains on the carpet. It would have been impossible to guess what was going through his mind at that precise moment.

Mr Vanvaria turned to me for help. Looking at me with pleading eyes, he said, 'Help my son. He is a good boy. He needs guidance.'

Before leaving, I arranged for Mahesh to come and see me. I made it clear that I was a stickler for timing; I did not like to be kept waiting, neither did I like appointments being broken, and therefore it was important that he was punctual.

I have now seen Mahesh for ten consecutive weekly sessions, each lasting an hour. Occasionally, a session would 'run over', and I would let it, particularly when I sensed that he was on the verge of revealing something of importance. Western counselling and/or therapeutic sessions normally do not run over; therapists are quite particular about ensuring that they begin and end on time. My own experience would suggest that a western approach of abiding by rigid time schedules may have some disadvantages, such as inhibiting a client, when he or she is about to gather the courage to make important revelations. It should also be pointed out here that there are significant differences in perceived notions of time between eastern and western cultures (see p. 73).

Mahesh's case history

Mahesh is 42 years old. He was 5 when he first came to England with his parents and his older brother, Arvind, who is six years older than him. His youngest brother, Rakesh, and their two sisters were all born in England. While his two brothers went to university and obtained degrees, Mahesh drifted from job to job after leaving school. After a great deal of pressure he agreed to help his father in the running of the grocery shop. His heart was not in it. His work was indifferent and sloppy. He quarrelled with his customers and came and went as he pleased. Much to his father's annoyance, he had started to smoke. But what hurt his father the most was that he had even started to eat meat. As a devout Hindu and a strict vegetarian, he felt humiliated by his son's blatant impiety; it was an act of diabolical defiance. His father, upset at the sight of his son straying away from the path of Hindu *dharma*, pleaded with him cajoled him, bullied him and threatened him. As a last resort, he had even tried shaming his son in the presence of the rest of the members of the family, but that only made matters worse. Shaming is often seen as the most effective weapon of social control in family relationships (Lewis 1971; Roland 1988). Given the interdependence of relationship patterns among Indians, shaming serves as an effective method of socialization of children. However, Mahesh remained unrepentant, refusing to mend his ways.

In despair, Mr Vanvaria consulted with his relatives in England and in India. He even consulted a couple of temple priests in

England in the hope that they would advise him on the best course of action. One of them suggested that he should take his son to India on a pilgrimage, which would change the course of his destiny. Roland (1988: 299) points out that Indians 'are deeply concerned with the unfolding of destiny [they] tend to be constantly on the look-out for signs and predictors, relying a great deal on the magic-cosmic to arrange and manage their practical affairs and relationships – marriage, education, career, children, health, wealth, and power'. The second priest suggested that Mr Vanvaria should get Mahesh married. It should be pointed out that among Indians marriage is often seen as an excellent therapeutic cure for sons with problems. This is because Indian culture itself oscillates between the erotic and the ascetic. At one end of the religious dimension lies sexuality and sensuality, and at the other lies religious renunciation and asceticism (Roland 1988). So the second priest's advice was sound and in keeping with traditional beliefs and customs.

Mr Vanvaria did both. Leaving his shop in the charge of one of his relatives, he and his son went to India, where after spending a month or so visiting the holy cities, they went to Ahmedabad in Gujarat. It did not take long for Mr Vanvaria to find a suitable bride for his son. Horoscopes were matched, dowries were negotiated and the auspicious date of marriage was fixed. In less than three months, Mahesh was married in Ahmedabad. The young bride had to wait for almost a year for all her immigration papers to be sorted out before she could join her husband and his family in England. Three years later they had their first child, and two years after that their second, both daughters. For a few years, Mahesh appeared to 'settle down' and even took greater interest in running the grocery shop; but gradually, he drifted into what his father described as his 'old ways'. Worse was to come. He had even started to drink! Now that Mahesh was a married man, with two young daughters to bring up, his father and his mother were extremely anxious about his future.

His parents tried everything. They even sought the help of their eldest son and his wife; the entire family tried whatever was within their means to help Mahesh to overcome whatever it was that was troubling him. Prayers were offered in temples, religious ceremonies were held, astrologers and palmists were consulted. Nothing worked. Mahesh's condition worsened. He took to staying at home, lying in bed for virtually the whole day. He started to neglect his appearance, didn't shave for days on end, went off his food and whenever anyone questioned or admonished him, he left home and disappeared for the entire day. Where he went no one knew; what he did with himself also remained a mystery. Returning home quite late in the night, he refused offers of food and went straight to bed. His wife too was at her wit's end. She cried, she prayed, she undertook fasts in the hope that her actions of piety would have a beneficial effect on her husband's mental state. It was not just his wife; it was the entire family that was being torn apart by Mahesh's strange behaviour which no one could understand, let alone resolve.

Mahesh's approach to counselling

The above information came to me in dribs and drabs. It was only after the first three or four sessions that I was able to piece it all together. Mahesh seemed tense, nervous and unsure of himself when he arrived for his first session. Although he sat in a comfortable armchair, he kept fidgeting with his body as though trying to find a comfortable position in which to settle. Every other minute or so, he would shift his position, appear to settle down, and a minute later start all over again. He also kept clenching and unclenching his hands; from time to time, he'd remove his handkerchief and wipe his face with it.

'Why are you so nervous?' I asked him, after watching him for several minutes; he wasn't sweating, but wiping his face seemed like a comforting ritualistic gesture.

'I don't know. I'm always like this when I'm nervous.'

I laughed at his unintended witticism. That seemed to break the ice between us. He smiled and seemed to relax a little. I explained to him that there was nothing to feel nervous about: certainly not me. I was there to help him, if I could. But for me to help him he would need to come clean and give me some idea, some indication of what had been troubling him for all these years.

For the first three weeks he addressed me as 'Doctor'. But gradually, he started adding my surname after the title. He never got round to calling me by my first name, which is what many of my western Caucasian clients slip into without any effort. Again, it is worth pointing out that Indians in general tend to establish or try to establish personal, informal relationships, but the hierarchical nature of our professional relationship, compounded by the fact that he was on my 'territory' so to speak, prevented any such attempt on his part. He remained deferential throughout the ten sessions.

By the second or third week he had 'imbued' me with extraordinary powers; he began to see me as his mentor, his guide, his talisman, his guru – he saw me as a person who, by waving a metaphorical magic wand, would solve all his problems. I felt distinctly uncomfortable with such an assessment, but kept my feelings to myself. To have tried to get our relationship going on an even, egalitarian footing, which is what gets established with most Caucasian clients within the first or second week of counselling, would have been impossible because such a step would have gone completely against his entire Hindu upbringing. For such a metamorphosis to occur would have involved a total reappraisal of his beliefs and values and the idiosyncratic norms and rituals that he had imbibed and internalized as a child. I did not know how such a startling metamorphosis could be achieved. Besides, I was not at all certain of its potential value had it been possible. At any rate, to bring about such deep-rooted internal, intrapsychic structural changes in his psyche was far beyond my capabilities; I am not a psychoanalyst, nor have I any desire to become one.

I accepted the fact that I was his mentor, that I had been imbued with extraordinary magic-cosmic powers which could be used to alter his destiny. Thus, to him, I was more than a therapist who was trying to make some sense of his conflicts, confusions and conundrums. I decided to use the unique position in which he had placed me to advantage. Adopting a directive approach instead of the popular non-directive (or person-centred) approach, I started by asking him a series of questions which I had considered during the preceding week. I hoped to learn more about the conflicts and the problems which had upset Mahesh's life. I was aware that if his conflicts were not resolved they would soon have a deleterious impact on his wife, his parents and perhaps even on his brother and *his* wife.

When I first confronted him with direct questions, he seemed intimidated; his replies were vague and insubstantial. Sometimes he fell silent, unwilling to answer any questions. I kept reminding him that I could only help him if he was prepared to help me. Without his help, I was powerless. I could sense that he was seeking irrevocable assurances from me concerning my magic-cosmic powers to help him. Although it was impossible for me to offer him such assurances, I did assure him that I would do my best. That was all I was prepared to promise. Given the unconditional adulation, reverence and respect one receives, one can easily be seduced into believing in one's own feelings of omnipotence and infallibility. Freud in his writings on transference and countertransference commented on this very issue. Putting aside his personal feelings, Freud took great pains to safeguard his own position by training himself to handle the transference and the countertransference situation objectively. He saw it as an unconscious attempt on the part of the 'patient' to identify with the analyst as his or her ego ideal, and in so doing permeate the ego-boundaries which had kept him or her apart from the analyst. In India, such a situation can be observed within the *bhakti*, the devotional movement, where the devotee, through intense emotional involvement, hopes to be merged with the god, goddess or incarnation, 'and in turn through the merger expects the reciprocity of divine bliss' (Roland 1988: 295). We shall not go into the question whether there is any substantive evidence to even justify the notion of transference, let alone the putative effect it has on the therapeutic outcome. Suffice it to say that I had to be careful, even vigilant, in ensuring that my feelings of warmth and empathy for Mahesh did not run away with me because of the magic-cosmic powers he had chosen to imbue me with.

Mahesh's psychological problems

Let me list the major problems which Mahesh mentioned. They are not listed in any order of importance but arranged in chronological order in terms of his life.

- As a child, he had been very unhappy at school. He had been subjected to taunts and abuses, and had been victimized by the white kids. For reasons he could not understand, he was called 'Paki' at school. He had occasionally turned to his elder brother for help, but for reasons he could again not understand, it had never been offered. Mahesh had approached his father, who recommended forbearance, outlining the Gandhian principles of turning the other cheek. He had grown up to hate all the white kids. He hated England, he hated the cold and he hated the way of life he was forced to lead.
- He was envious of his brother who did exceedingly well at school, and later at university. After graduation, his elder brother found an exciting and well-paid job in a large, multi-national organization, thus escaping the drudgery of working in a grocery shop. Mahesh left school without completing his A levels, and joined his father in the grocery business. He hated it.

- Soon, he fell into what he described as 'bad company'. He went out with some black and white kids from the neighbourhood and experimented with sex, cigarettes and alcohol.
- His parents were alarmed at his misdemeanours, which he was unable to conceal from them, but they said nothing to upset him. Being closely attached to his family, he felt ashamed of his actions and also angry with his parents.
- His arranged marriage was not a happy one. He felt angry at having consented to the marriage. He was also angry with his father who he felt had forced him into a marriage which was not of his choice. He was angry too that he felt unable to voice his anger. He felt imprisoned in this situation. It was too late to do anything about it. He had often thought of running away from home, but had neither the courage nor the means. Besides, he was deeply attached to his two daughters and he could not bear the idea of being parted from them.
- The sexual pleasures which to a large extent had sustained his marriage had evaporated soon after the birth of their second child. His wife, he confessed, had lost all interest in sex; she saw herself as a mother whose duty it was to look after her daughters and bring them up with love, care and affection. His wife devoted most of her time to looking after the two girls. She submitted to Mahesh's sexual advances without joy and without reciprocity.
- Mahesh said he felt lonely, isolated and misunderstood. He found it difficult to talk to his father who, although not unwilling to listen to him, was inflexible in his own views concerning right and wrong, truth and untruth, and the manner in which one ought to lead one's life, in accordance with the principles of Hindu *dharma*. His mother on the other hand was totally absorbed in her own illness and took little interest in her son's problems other than to cry whenever they were raised at home. His brother, who was busy with his own family life and work, had little time for him. Mahesh found his brother's judgements of him harsh and unforgiving. Mahesh was in too great an awe of his sister-in-law, who had a Ph.D. in biochemistry and worked in a hospital, to want to confide in her.
- He said he had no friends worth speaking of. His school friends who he used to hang around with had long since disappeared. He had been unable to make any friends after his marriage, and now that he found it difficult to communicate with his

wife he had no one with whom he could talk and unburden his soul.
- At some stage, he said that he had even thought of committing suicide; but luckily, he had never considered it seriously.

My own feeling about his idea of committing suicide was one of doubt. Although I could not discount the possibility completely I felt he was testing the waters, trying to impress me in a perverted, narcissistic way – as though to say, 'You'll be sorry when I'm dead!' But his statement worried me, partly because of what he said and partly because he had chosen to turn me into a paternalistic figure – his father's ego ideal. It was a role which I had no intention of playing.

Therapeutic interventions

I showed Mahesh the shortened version of the above list I had prepared for him and asked him for his comments. 'If I have to help you I need to know two things: one, do you think the list I have made is fair, and that it reflects the problem areas accurately? And two, are there are any important events or facets in your life about which you have told me nothing? I need to know.'

Mahesh sat across the desk, staring into space. He thought long and hard. Without appearing to, I watched him carefully as he frowned to himself. The frown deepened, the vertical furrows on his forehead turned rigid, as though cast in stone. He seemed to be grappling with an overpowering emotion. He took a deep breath, his mouth opened as though he were about to speak; a hissing sound, like steam escaping from a leaking pipe came out of his parted lips, but no words emerged. He fell silent. I waited. Our eyes met. He looked at me imploringly, as though begging me not to ask him to reveal whatever it was that he had on his mind. I smiled at him encouragingly. He started hesitantly, 'My wife Radhika,' he muttered, and then, once again, fell silent.

I waited, not daring to utter a word. I could sense that he was on the verge of taking a crucial decision. The clock on the opposite wall indicated that his session had come to an end. I ignored the clock and waited.

Finally, after what seemed an eternity, it all came tumbling out in a frantic rush. He spoke without stopping, as though a pause would put an end to his confession. His words tumbled out in a higgledy-piggledy fashion and there was no order to what he said. I listened in silence, not daring to interrupt him, lest it break the spell which he appeared to have cast upon himself.

This is the gist of what he confessed.

We already know that he had been very unhappy about his arranged marriage to Radhika. The thought of standing up to his father and refusing to go along with his wishes remained an unvoiced one; he thought about it, brooded over it, but could not bring himself to put his disagreements or defiance into action. He had never questioned his father's judgement in all his life and had grown up to accept his father's wisdom. His father, he believed, was an honourable man, who acted from the highest and purest of motives concerned with ensuring the happiness and prosperity of all his children. At the same time Mahesh was fully aware that his consent to the arranged marriage would have an irrevocable effect upon his future and possibly change the entire course of his life in ways which he could not as yet predict. On the other hand the thought of getting married did not seem unattractive. Having had but a limited number of sporadic and furtive sexual encounters in England, he relished the idea of being able to have sex legitimately, regularly and on demand.

His sexual relations with his wife Radhika were not the voluptuous ecstasies which his fantasies had invented, but he was not unhappy. Although she was not particularly forthcoming, she responded to his overtures with little inhibition and with some degree of passion. What irked him, annoyed him, angered him, and finally broke him, was the fact that on days that were considered to be auspicious and holy she refused to yield to his sexual advances. Her strict Hindu upbringing in these matters could not reconcile the demands of the flesh with those of the spirit. They fought over this continuously. She refused to yield.

The final blow was struck a few years after the birth of their second child. To use a cliché, she 'turned religious'. She spent long hours in prayer and even got her two daughters to participate. Her parents-in-law, noticing the change, were proud of her and looked upon her as a model daughter-in-law, unlike the older daughter-in-law who was busy with her work in the hospital and had little time for such religious practices.

Radhika lost all interest in sex. She yielded to Mahesh's demands but there was no joy, no passion in their lovemaking – just silent submission. She also insisted that all the lights were turned off when they made love. This had never happened before. Her strictures meant that they could never have sex during the day. Mahesh was mystified. He could not get her to talk about the problem. For a while he colluded in the bizarre demands she made, but gradually he began to turn way from her and from all other activities.

'It's not me who is in need of treatment,' he said angrily, his voice overflowing with emotion. 'It's *she* who needs therapy! Not me! Whole day, whole day, she is doing *puja*! If she spent even half the time chasing me, instead of chasing God, I would be the happiest person in the world. But chasing God is like chasing your own shadow. You can never catch it.'

He lost interest in the grocery shop and his enthusiasm for the cinema, for cricket, and all other activities which in the past had given him pleasure. He became morose, stayed up late or slept unusually early, went off his food, neglected his appearance – I have already dealt with all the changes that took place in Mahesh.

As a therapist, what was one expected to do in such a situation? What advice would an astute therapist offer? Which therapeutic model would one use? Which seemed to be the most appropriate? Would the adoption of a particular model achieve some degree of success? How would one define success in Mahesh's case? I spent several days brooding over Mahesh's problems. I knew that when he returned the following week I would need to initiate a form of therapy, which hopefully would deal successfully with his problems. But the more I thought about it, the less clear I became as to what I meant by success. Would it help if Mahesh's wife could be persuaded to attend a few sessions with her husband?

If what Mahesh said about his wife was true – I had no way of corroborating his story – I did initially wonder if it was Radhika and not Mahesh who needed counselling and therapy. However, a moment's reflection convinced me that I was totally wrong. Such an analysis was nothing but an exercise in self-deception. The fact that I had even considered such an idea seemed to me to be morally and professionally suspect. I had taken Radhika's sexual inhibition (if indeed it was inhibition) out of its cultural context and given it a prominence which I am not sure it deserved. It had seemed an easy solution to single out a clearly identifiable specific symptom. This would then have made the 'disorder' seem more manageable and treatable.

The fact that in the last few years Radhika had been totally disinterested in sex (and perhaps was even revolted by it) was hardly reason enough to assume that she had a serious psychological problem and was the cause of Mahesh's conflicts. It is not always recognized that loss of interest in sexual activities among traditional, middle-aged Hindu women is not as uncommon as one might be led to believe. To lay the blame for Mahesh's problems at his wife's door was the easy alternative. I was ashamed of my own naïveté.

Even if there had been some truth in my initial analysis of Radhika, it was unlikely that she would consent to come to one or two sessions with her husband. It should be stressed here that within an orthodox Indian setting, such a scenario is difficult to visualize. Asian women, by and large, find it difficult, if not impossible, to confide in a male therapist. And for them to disclose and discuss problems of a sexual nature with a total stranger, albeit a well-meaning and concerned professional male, would be anathema. The very idea was preposterous! One needs to bear in mind that Radhika is a first-generation Indian; the reader will recall that before coming to England she had lived all her life in India. Her sister-in-law, on the other hand, is a second-generation Indian; she was born and educated in England. Had the need arisen, *she* might have been persuaded to come along to the counselling sessions. But not Radhika.

Her life, from what Mahesh described during the sessions, was tied up with looking after her children, in keeping house, cooking and caring for her aged in-laws. She was deeply religious and even attempted to inculcate all her religious values in her children. If she was disappointed at her husband's inability or unwillingness to take greater responsibility for his life and attempt to make a success of the grocery shop, or set out on his own, she kept her disappointment to herself. A strong belief in the law of karma inures one to the assaults and vicissitudes of life (O'Flaherty 1980; Prasad 1989; Reichenbach 1990; Laungani 1999d; 2000d; 2002c; Sharma 2000).

To put this particular pattern of behaviour within its proper cultural context one needs to understand the manner in which young girls are often socialized in traditional Hindu families. Mythological figures are held up as models, or ego ideals, whose virtues young girls are expected to emulate. The stories of the steadfastness of *Sita* from the epic *Ramayana*; the silent suffering of *Draupadi* from the *Mahabharata*; and the persistence of *Savitri*, who rescued her dead husband from the god of death, thus restoring him to life, are told and retold in Hindu homes. In traditional Indian homes, a woman's identity is almost entirely defined by her relationship to others (Bruner 1959; Lannoy 1975; Kakar 1978; Crossette 1993).

In marital relationships a woman's intimate needs are largely fulfilled through the other women of the family, through their children, through looking after the elders in the family, through prayer and other socially accepted activities. When placed within the context of her orthodox cultural upbringing, Radhika's sexual inhibitions do not seem in anyway neurotic, requiring the professional attention of a therapist.

Five sessions had gone by. I was anxious not to extend the sessions beyond the ten weeks I had stipulated at our first meeting. I also knew that it was not Mahesh but his brother Arvind who was paying for the therapy and I had no wish to put his brother or his father to any needless expense. Mahesh had turned up every week at the appointed hour. It should also be noted that on a couple of occasions he had even phoned me at home to seek my advice on matters which on reflection seemed quite mundane and trivial. But he had seemed so keen on seeking my approval that I had not the heart to take exception at his innocuous familiarity. Roland (1988) in his excellent book *In Search of Self in India and Japan* points to the fascinating differences between his American and his Indian clients. While his American clients, in order not to intrude upon his privacy, seldom phoned him at home, his Indian clients on the other hand seldom hesitated to phone him at home to take his advice and seek his approval on matters unrelated to their psychological problems.

The sixth session was crucial. As usual Mahesh turned up at the appointed hour. With a certain degree of shyness, he placed a box of Indian sweets on my desk and sat down in his usual chair. Before I could even react to his gift, he said that it was Lord Krishna's birthday today, and after his early morning visit to the temple with his wife, he had decided to buy sweets for the family and also for me. Unlike the western custom of opening gifts in the presence of the donor, Indians normally tend to open their gifts in private. I put the box aside and then asked him the usual question of how he had been during the course of the week.

'You know, Doctor, in the last one or two weeks, I am beginning to feel better.'

I wondered if he was merely being polite. I smiled and said, 'I am delighted to hear this. If that is how you feel, perhaps we should consider terminating your therapy. Shall we make this the last meeting?'

Mahesh was horrified.

Obviously there were more sessions to come. I persuaded him to tell me in what ways he thought he was getting better. Presently, he settled down and told me about his improved relations with his wife. He said that basically she was a good woman. Religion to her was like blood, which flowed through her body. She would die without it. His conversations with me had made him realize that beyond any doubt. As for himself, he had never been disinterested in Hindu religion, but he resented having to conform to all the rituals which were expected of him – the silly fasts, the regular feeding of Brahmin priests on festive occasions, the observance of *Shradha* and a hundred and one other routines.

'You remember, you said the only way I could win back my wife was through prayer. Not praying *for* her, mind you, but praying *with* her. I don't pray with her at home. I feel too embarrassed to do that. But we go to the temple together – at least twice a week.'

I asked him if he found prayer comforting.

'It makes my wife very happy,' he answered truthfully. 'It is bringing us closer to each other once again. And that is what I really care about most. I know she really loves me and cares for me. I have even started reading the *Gita*. Even our two daughters are much happier now when they see us together. One of them, Doctor, the youngest one – her name is Chetna – used to wet her bed at least once or twice a week. For the last two to three weeks, nothing! I think this is a good sign. What do you think, Doctor?'

Over the next three sessions, Mahesh and I discussed the 'problems' which he had been unable to resolve. New problems had also arisen in his life. Both he and his parents were saddened by the fact that his older brother Arvind and his wife were buying a house of their own. Their extended family, which had survived for over 40 years, would soon be breaking up. But luckily, they were planning to move to Stoke Newington, which was not far from where they lived, and they would be able to see one another regularly. Mahesh was not certain that Arvind would continue to contribute towards the running of the house. At first, Mahesh had resented his brother's decision, finding it cruel and selfish, but after talking to me, he had come to accept the wisdom of it. His brother, he said, had every right to lead his own life in his own way.

'You are right. You can hardly expect your brother to be your keeper all your life.'

Mahesh's resentment, luckily, was short-lived. It was just the 'shot in the arm' that he needed. He said that he had begun to take a greater interest in running the grocery shop. His father was getting old and was unable to devote enough time and energy to run the shop single-handed. His father and he, between them, had arrived at a workable arrangement. Since Mahesh had never been an early riser, his father agreed to open the shop in the mornings. Mahesh would take over the running of the shop from midday onwards, his father joining him once again at closing time. The father and son decided that unlike many other Indians who kept their shops open seven days a week, their shop would remain closed on Sundays. Sundays could then be devoted to joint family activities. He had even phoned his younger brother Amit, in San Diego, inviting him and his wife to come and spend some time with them in London. Amit was delighted to hear from him and said they would try and come in October, during the Diwali festival.

It would be untrue to say that life with Mahesh was one long, rosy dream, but all in all, many of the ill-fitting pieces in his life were beginning to fall into place, and he was beginning to get a grip on some of his problems. On the sexual side, his wife was still reticent to have the lights on when they made love, but he had persuaded her to have the bedside lamp on, which could be turned off without any interruption.

Finally, our agreed ten therapeutic sessions came to an end. Mahesh was reluctant, even stubbornly unwilling to cease therapy. For the last ten weeks, I had been his lifeline or rather he had seen me as his lifeline, and suddenly it was being taken away from him. Not surprisingly, he was frightened. This was by no means unusual; many therapists and counsellors often encounter this situation in the course of their work. Despite my attempts to keep my 'distance' from him and prevent him from forming 'emotional relatedness' with me, I had not succeeded completely. He was saddened and even hurt at the prospect of not being able to see me every week. Nonetheless, he did manage to squeeze one concession out of me. I promised to visit him and his family members during the Diwali festival, which was three months away. That visit, I thought, would bring the entire counselling encounter to an end. It had started with my visiting them, and there it would end.

Discussion

The case described above is in some senses atypical. It involves not just one person but others in Mahesh's life. Although they did not make a direct appearance, their involvement was not inconsiderable, and their impact on Mahesh's life not insubstantial. The first point which emerges from this is that I was dealing not just with one client, but with all his family members. In that sense, therefore, it was not a typical one-to-one therapeutic situation, but a family therapy situation.

To have ignored the strong but faceless 'presence' of all the family members and focused exclusively on Mahesh's problems would, to my mind, have created further problems for Mahesh. To have done so would have meant taking Mahesh's problems out of their cultural context. Such an approach might be of relevance when dealing with Caucasian clients who have imbibed and internalized all the dominant western values related to individualism, cognitivism, freewill, determinism etc. but as far as Mahesh was concerned, he was, as was evident from my discussions with him, firmly rooted in his own Indian, Hindu culture. Suffice it to say for the moment that to take an individual out of his or her cultural context and examine his or her problems from another cultural context would be like measuring your body temperature with a barometer! It is not often realized nor is it always fully appreciated how firmly we are all rooted in our cultures.

Mahesh's case (luckily for me) did not contain ingredients of high drama. Mahesh's moods did not swing from one extreme to the other, there were no sudden, unpredictable outbursts, no accusations, no wild threats against the world at large or against any of his family members. For most of the time, he exercised reasonable control over his emotions, although from time to time he bemoaned his fate, beat his forehead and cried. Mahesh also made it clear that he was not on any medication; he had refused to go and see his GP, arguing that there was nothing wrong with him physically that required any medical attention. He was so completely absorbed in his own problems that he showed hardly any curiosity concerning the social, political and racial problems in Britain. When questioned on these issues, he explained that each country produced its own unique problems, and who was to say that the problems of racism in Britain were more serious than the problems of untouchability in India? He wasn't by any means defending racism or untouchability; he was merely 'accepting' the universality of human cruelty. 'It's the same, everywhere, wherever you go, Doctor.'

His attitude was one of non-involvement. He had not come to England to fight battles against racism; there were far greater battles he could fight in India if he wanted to. He had come not by his own choice, but by his father's choice. England had been and would remain his home.

The point that emerges from this is that it would have been pointless to discuss with Mahesh anything related to racial, social and political injustices. He just wasn't interested. Racism appeared not to have made the slightest impact upon his psyche. Thus, there seemed to be no merit in pursuing this line of enquiry.

But among several western counsellors and therapists there is a strongly held belief that the problems of identity are inextricably linked with the problems of racism in western society. Therefore it becomes necessary to explore this area with a client to determine the extent and the manner in which it affects the growth and development of one's identity. Clearly, there is a great deal of truth in this proposition, and western therapists are right to pursue this line of enquiry, but it does not follow that this area is worth exploring in all cases.

What the reader has sampled is a form of culture-centred counselling. Let us list the strategies that were used, comparing them with western forms of counselling and therapy.

- Prior to accepting the client, I agreed to meet with the entire family. The need to meet with the family was seen as being important both from the family's point of view and also from my own. I needed to know about all the people involved, their interrelations and the level of influence which they wielded over Mahesh. Asian cultures tend to be family-oriented and emotionally and functionally interdependent. An individual ego is often submerged into the collective ego of the family. Western societies tend not to operate on a familial and communal network, which emphasizes emotional, material and functional interdependency.
- Asian societies tend to function on a hierarchical model, where power and status tend to reside in the male elders of the family. They are deferred to, and their authority, to a large extent, remains unquestioned. This knowledge affected my own strategy. It would have been difficult, if not impossible, to operate on a non-hierarchical western model of equality. Mahesh would have found it impossible to cope with such a situation.
- Within the first week of counselling, it became clear that a non-directive model (or a person-centred) model was inappropriate.

A person-centred model assumes, among other things, that most individuals are capable of realizing their own potentialities; the role played by the counsellor or the therapist is that of a facilitator not a guide in the literal sense of the word. Mahesh had already chosen to see me as his mentor, his guru; having gilded me with magic-cosmic powers, he expected me to guide him, direct him and lead him from 'darkness' into 'light'. Again, this involved a change in strategy: I used my position as his 'mentor' to ask direct questions. Although I offered no direct help, the questions I asked evoked answers which helped me to clarify some of the issues which were of concern to him.

- Since the religious beliefs and behaviours of the entire family played a major role in their individual and joint lives, it seemed more than appropriate to bring religion into the therapeutic process. This contrasts sharply with counselling and psychotherapeutic practices in western countries which tend to be scrupulously secular in their orientations. Religious beliefs and religious practices of both the therapist and the counsellor are seen as being private and personal and have no role to play in the therapeutic process. But as Tanaka-Matsumi *et al.* (2001) have pointed out, there is a close relationship between basic cultural concepts and specific forms of intervention, and therefore it was perfectly legitimate that I should take religious beliefs and practices into the therapeutic framework.
- The therapeutic process was greatly assisted by the fact that both Mahesh and I shared a common worldview and common sets of beliefs concerning the nature of his problem and the manner in which it might be handled. Sharing a common worldview is considered to be a universal feature of effective therapy in its cultural forms (Frank and Frank 1991).
- Tanaka-Matsumi *et al.* (2001) tend to see the goal of therapy as a form of 'social restoration'. I prefer the phrase 'maintenance of familial and communal closeness and harmony'. My aim was to bring about closeness within the family and restore family harmony.

My reasons for offering such a detailed exposition and analysis of this case study is to bring home two general points which are relevant to our discussion:

- It has been shown that behaviours considered aberrant and therefore undesirable in one culture may seem perfectly reasonable and desirable in other cultures. For instance, promoting family harmony and thereby assuring mutual interdependence seemed a perfectly reasonable goal to achieve within the context of Indian culture. In an individualistic culture, such as America, Britain and other western European countries, the accepted philosophy of individualism would militate against the creation of societies based on emotional and functional interdependence.
- It is clear that the western theoretical models of counselling and psychotherapy are themselves culture-bound or 'culturally encapsulated' (Wrenn 1985). Wrenn explains cultural encapsulation in the following manner: reality is defined by one set of cultural assumptions, which are then assumed to be the correct ones, regardless of observed cultural variation. Counsellors ignore or become insensitive to cultural variation and believe their view is the only right one. Solutions are sought in technique-oriented strategies, or in the form of quick and simple recipes. Pederson (1997) goes a step or two further and argues that the entire profession of counselling is far more encapsulated now than it was in 1985, when Wrenn published his original article.

Counsellors in western societies must alert themselves to the fact that while individualism may be the ruling philosophy of people in the West it is of hardly any relevance to people from non-western cultures, where the 'cultural cookie' crumbles in different ways. In their continued obstinacy in preserving and promoting their culturally encapsulated counselling and other psychotherapeutic intervention strategies, they expose themselves to attacks of bigotry, paternalism and racism (Pederson 1988; Sue and Sue 1990; Ponterotto and Casas 1991; Ridley 1995; Ponterotto 1998). Western counsellors must learn that western notions of reality constitute but one form of reality. There are several others. To ignore or dismiss other cultural realities as products of undisciplined or under-developed minds is hardly likely to endear counsellors to people of non-western cultures. It hardly needs reiterating that such condescending attitudes are inimical to the promotion of genuine cross-cultural counselling and therapy.

Case study 2

Let me start with a question, which at first sounds rather cryptic. When is a case study *not* a case study? For a case study to be legitimately called a case study, does it need to fulfil a set of clearly defined criteria? If so, what are the criteria, which when combined in certain ways, allow us to refer to a particular study as a genuine case study? How have such sets of criteria been formulated, and by whom, and why have they come to be accepted? Are there certain rules and guidelines which need to be followed scrupulously? For instance, is it an essential criterion that a case study is written in the third person singular, as no doubt many are? Some of the world's greatest case studies (e.g. those written by Freud) were written in the first person singular. Does a case study have to be brief, succinct and written without the use of any 'frills' which may have no direct bearing on the study? These are extremely important questions which deserve serious consideration. I have left this discussion to the last and final chapter.

For the moment, let us content ourselves by referring to what you are about to read – a case study. The study (the word 'tragedy' would seem a more befitting term) by all accounts has all the ingredients of high drama. It deals with a series of very sad, depressing, violent and heartbreaking problems which befell the parties involved, a wife and husband; problems which they were unable to resolve satisfactorily by themselves. In desperation the husband turned to me for help, which looking back on it I agreed to offer with far more haste and foolhardiness than caution and sagacity.

I have brooded over this problem for several years, and although I made copious notes as and when I was 'involved' in it, I have not had the courage to write it as a 'proper' case study until now. My diffidence was due to the fact that first of all I was uncertain about the manner in which this particular study needed to be written and secondly whether I would have the skill and the ability to do justice to the study which ran over several years. Finally, the main reason for my inertia was the fact that the parties involved were my very, very dear friends. This of course made it even more difficult for me to sit down and put pen to paper. The fear of betrayal never stopped haunting me; it brought to my mind the remarkable statement which E. M. Forster was reputed to have made when he said that if he had to choose between betraying his country and his friend, he hoped that God would give him the courage and the strength to betray his country.

Why then, have I changed my mind? Why have I decided to bring this case study to your attention? Two reasons can be offered: one, it is an extremely unique study, complex and convoluted and offers fascinating insights into the fragility of human relationships, their 'making' and 'breaking', the important role that 'chance' often plays in our lives and the inability of many persons to prevent themselves from roasting their hands in the fire, knowing that fire burns. Second, one of the two people around whom the study revolves is now dead. He died very suddenly under extremely tragic circumstances and I shall discuss that event at the appropriate point. His wife now lives in India. You shall meet her too, by and by. But before I introduce you to these two wonderful people, let me assure you that it has taken me far longer to devise subterfuges and stratagems to conceal their real identity than it has taken me to write the study itself. I have ensured that in life and in death they shall remain not unsung, not unpraised, but certainly unrecognized.

Introduction

This case study revolves around two people: Hardeep Gupta and his wife Reena. Hardeep is a Punjabi; his family are from Delhi, where he was born. But for a variety of reasons his father, a construction engineer, sensing opportunities of large-scale commercial development, migrated to Bombay, which is where Hardeep grew up.

Over the years, Hardeep's name underwent a change. At first it was shortened to Hari, and subsequently another r was added to the first r, and the letter i was dropped in favour of a y; he became known as Harry ever afterwards. His 'mates' (in the naval sense of the word), most of whom were English, found it easier and comforting to call him Harry. Hari too, felt comfortable at being called Harry, largely because he could not bear his name Hardeep being mispronounced by his English and other European friends and workmates. To his intense exasperation, he knew that the English were either unwilling or unable to roll their 'rs', nor could they pronounce 'deep' as 'thee' followed by a p – 'theep', which is what the correct pronounciation of his name would have entailed.

A thumbnail sketch of Harry and Reena

Harry, as you have no doubt guessed, is a 'shipping person'. Soon after leaving school he trained as a marine engineer and joined the

Merchant Navy. As a strong, healthy, good-looking bachelor, with voracious and wide-ranging appetites and desires, he thrived on the unsettled life which he was obliged to lead in the course of his work. He went round the world several times, did his job conscientiously, and within a few years became first officer with a medium-sized Indo-Australian shipping company, which had its head office in Sydney. He preferred working on cargo ships. He found it difficult to work on passenger liners because he couldn't stand rich, demanding and overbearing passengers. More to the point, cargo ships often dropped anchor at a variety of exotic ports in the Pacific Ocean. Nothing gave him greater pleasure and joy than when their ship dropped anchor and he was able to spend a few idyllic days on any one of the many islands in the South Pacific – particularly Pago Pago – until all the cargo was loaded and they were ready to weigh anchor and set sail to Sydney or Tokyo.

Although he was reasonably happy with the type of life he lived, his parents were keen for him to get married; he was their only child and heir. Much to their astonishment he agreed. He married Reena, a Punjabi girl whom he met via an 'arranged' meeting organized through his father's network of close relations. To the unsuspecting it might have seemed a fortuitous coincidence that both Reena and Harry came from the same caste and virtually the same professional and educational background. But all these factors had been carefully orchestrated, prior to the exchange of horoscopes and the subtle discussion of dowries – which Reena's father, who owned a medium-sized factory in Faridabad near Delhi, agreed to without a murmur. However, at Reena's father's insistence, they married in Delhi, but soon moved to Bombay, where through his father's business contacts in the construction business, Harry acquired a small but smart flat by the sea. Coming as she did from Delhi, Reena was fascinated by Bombay and enchanted by the sea. It was not long before she managed to find her way into a circle of friends of her own kind. While her husband was away at sea, she spent a considerable amount of her time with her new friends, all of whom shared interests which, given their affluence, were not too difficult to pursue.

Having acquired a degree in the social sciences from Jawaharlal Nehru University, Reena had initially contemplated doing a masters degree, but her marriage to Harry had put paid to her academic ambitions. With time on her hands, she even considered the idea once again, but somehow it didn't seem such a priority. She wanted Harry to settle down in Bombay and not go wandering off to distant lands for months on end. She tried to persuade him to give up his sailor's life and settle down on terra firma in Bombay. Besides, she wanted to have children, and understandably she had not the slightest intention of bringing them up on her own. But Harry had no plans to settle down in Bombay while he was still hopelessly, madly in love with the South Pacific Islands. He could not bear the anguish of not being able to swim off any one of the many coral islands, or to lie on the shore and see the waters set ablaze by the crimson sun dipping into the distance.

Reena nagged him constantly, but without success and they reached an impasse. At some point he tried explaining to her that he was unfit for work of any kind other than that of a marine engineer. That was what he was qualified to do and if he were to give up his job, how were they going to survive? Moreover, he loved his work and was good at it. Eventually they arrived at a compromise. He said the best he could do would be to apply for a temporary or permanent transfer to Australia. Most of the ships of the company he worked for sailed from Australia to New Zealand and further east to Samoa, and sometimes even as far as Japan before returning to Sydney. Some ships, on the other hand, sailed westward from Australia to Papua New Guinea, thence to South-East Asia and back. Australia seemed the best place to be: whichever direction he sailed in, he'd be back home in less than a month. He applied for a transfer and much to his amazement was offered a three-year (renewable) contract based in Sydney.

Reena was disappointed at having to leave Bombay; she loved her style of life, her friends and acquaintances, not to mention the retinue of servants who made her day-to-day life more than comfortable. She had serious reservations about moving to Sydney, but she'd rather her husband stayed with her on a more permanent basis and with some trepidation she consented to the move.

The Australian experience

For the first two or three years, Reena was charmed by Australia and fell in love with Sydney. The shipping company had done them proud. They had arranged for them a fairly large and spacious flat to move into which overlooked the harbour and the opera house. It did not take them long to make friends; they entertained and were entertained by all: Australians, Greeks, Chinese and Indians. Harry earned enough for them to be able to lead a fairly comfortable and affluent life, to which of course Reena had always been accustomed.

But as the months and years went by, Reena began to question her life in Australia. For a start she missed her parents; she also missed the retinue of servants, which one took for granted in India; and finally she found the Australians she came into contact with, mainly Harry's naval friends, coarse and uncouth. All they could think and talk about was sex, beer and sport. She was also extremely disturbed by their blatant prejudices against all minority groups, which included the Aborigines, the Chinese, the Malaysians, the Greeks and even a few Indians.

On a more personal and worrying note was the fact that during their three years of stay she had had two miscarriages. Reena, needless to say, was extremely distressed and her health suffered. She wanted to return to India to be among her own people, particularly her mother, whom she missed dearly. She would have loved her mother to come and stay with her for a few months, but since she suffered from asthma and high blood pressure she was unwilling to risk taking the long flight from Delhi to Sydney.

Reena, however, had been to Delhi twice, staying for three months on each visit. On returning to Sydney, she felt even more unsettled and pined for the simple pleasures of Delhi: the *dabba* (roadside) restaurants, the musty bookstalls in Connaught Circus, the early morning walks along the River Jamuna, the Indian cinemas, the sweet shops around Chandini Chowk, even the noise, the dirt, the pollution, the traffic and the crowds, which she had left behind.

At this point, the reader might wonder how I became privy to this personal and relatively, intimate information. Here, I need to take a slight detour to explain to the reader that despite Harry's moving to Australia, it made no difference to maintaining contact with each other. Prior to their moving to Australia, we met a few times in London, whenever his ship brought him into Southampton or Tilbury. On a couple of occasions, we even met halfway round the world, in India, which was (and in my case, still is) our ancestral home. Harry and I kept in touch with one another: birthday greetings, Diwali greetings, invitations to weddings, Christmas cards, pretty picture-postcards from the exotic ports at which Harry's ship loaded and/or unloaded cargo. Harry was by no means an intrepid correspondent; he hated writing letters, but enjoyed sending postcards – and he loved the telephone. Regardless of the cost involved, he phoned me at regular intervals from Sydney, or India, or Pago

Pago or Tahiti, or Tokyo, or wherever his ship docked. I had got used to his phoning me at odd hours of the day and night – he was either careless of time differences between countries, or indifferent – to bring me up to date with all that was happening in their lives in Sydney. Thus, our contact never withered. Although we didn't get to meet for several years at a time, time always stood still when we did meet.

One such phone call disturbed me intensely. Without so much as a preamble, Harry said that Reena had been taken into hospital.

'What! Where are you phoning from?'

'Where do you think, you fool!'

He seemed very agitated. I remained silent and waited for him to continue. Harry did not sound very coherent. He kept interrupting himself, he went backwards and forwards, he did not even make it clear whether he was speaking from Sydney or India, or from the high seas.

'She's had her third miscarriage. But this one is very serious. There has been a lot of bleeding. She had to be taken into hospital.'

'Were you there when it happened?'

'That's just the point. It wouldn't have happened if I had been at home.'

'What do you mean?'

'I was in Japan when I received the phone call from the hospital.' He was given compassionate leave and took the first available flight to Sydney. 'If only I'd been there . . . I would have prevented it.'

'Prevented what?'

'Never mind.'

Was it just his agitation or was there something of significance that he wasn't telling me? Reena had already had two miscarriages and this third, from Harry's passionate but incoherent account, seemed very serious. I wondered if it had put an end to any hope of her being able to have children.

'She's very distressed. She keeps crying all the time. She's also very weak.'

I did not know what to say.

'The police have been very helpful.'

I was nonplussed.'What have the police got to do with this?'

'Our flat was burgled that night!'

So *that* was what he meant when he said that he could have prevented it.

'That's probably what brought about the haemorrhaging.'

My heart went out to Harry and Reena. I wished there was something I could do for them. We spoke for a few more minutes, during which he said that he should have paid heed to Reena's advice to give up his job; he was sure if he had tried hard enough, he could have found a 'land' job in his area of expertise. He might have even found a job in a hydraulic company, where his expertise as a marine engineer would have come in handy. One could see he was berating himself as though to reduce the self-blame and guilt that he felt over what had happened.

A few days later he phoned again. He said he had decided to resign from his job. He had no idea what he wanted to do with his life, but for the moment he was more concerned about Reena's health and recovery than anything else. Nothing else mattered. As soon as she was better, they would take a long vacation to India, where she could stay in Delhi with her parents if she wished, or in Bombay, either at their flat or with his parents.

Four years later

I heard from Harry a few more times, and then suddenly, for no reason at all, I lost contact with him for almost four years. I had tried phoning him in Bombay and then in Delhi, but to no avail. I left messages, which he did not return. I even tried phoning them in Sydney, but I learnt that the flat was occupied by someone else – no doubt a new first officer. I even wrote to Harry; but my letters remained unanswered.

I could not stop wondering why Harry had so suddenly and abruptly dropped out of my life. We had always been good friends; not what one would call soulmates, but certainly good friends.

I was full of feelings of guilt. I often wondered if there was something, some little thing that I might not have done for him, which may have eased the pain of their suffering. That she was totally traumatized was evident from the way he had described her condition. And then, one day, out the blue, Harry phoned. He said he was in London; he and Reena had arrived a few days ago. They had come to attend the wedding of one of her cousins and had rented an apartment. They were planning to stay in London for about six months, if not longer.

I must confess I did not take kindly to his phone call. I was peeved that he hadn't phoned me during the last four years, causing me not inconsiderable anxiety. And now he had suddenly dropped back into my life, without as much as an apology or a word of explanation. I was brusque and even quite short with him. He sensed my injured pride and apologized profusely.

'But before you judge me harshly, my friend, there are things I need to tell you – in the strictest of confidence. Wait till you have heard me through.'

I enquired after Reena.

He seemed non-committal. He said he wanted to come and see me on his own. 'Then, if you are a good boy, I shall introduce you to my wife.'

The meeting in London

I was shocked by Harry's appearance. He had changed dramatically, and without sounding unkind, for the worse. Gone were his handsome youthful looks, his lean cheeks, his rugged, chiselled face, his sleek black hair, his narrow waist and broad shoulders; he looked like a huge shapeless sack, which one might have expected Santa Claus to heave over his shoulders. He had not just put on weight: weight, as though by some mysterious volition, had grown upon him! His hair, with streaks of grey in it, had thinned and there were visible bald patches on his crown. His breathing had become shallow and rapid, as one might notice in a patient suffering from asthma. I had always known him to be a meticulous and even fastidious dresser; now he seemed old, haggard and unkempt. Even his shoes were scuffed.

'How's Reena?' I enquired.

'Not too bad, under the circumstances.'

'What do you mean?' I found it difficult to comprehend that even after four years she had been unable to overcome the trauma of the burglary. But then, never having met Reena, one could not tell the impact which the event had had on her. 'Is she still bothered by the burglary?'

Harry said nothing. He looked at me for a long time; there was a frown on his face, as though he was trying to make up his mind. A strange look came over him – it might have been anger, desolation, sadness; I could not tell.

'You don't know half the story, do you?'

I waited.

'It wasn't just a burglary!'

'Oh, God!'

'Yes.'

Neither of us could bring ourselves to utter the vile word.

He awoke as though from a dream. In a voice heavy with emotion, he said that that was what he had come to discuss with me, and also to seek my help.

It took me a series of long, painful and arduous hours of reflection, checking and cross-checking the snippets of information that Harry volunteered over several meetings we had at home, before I began to make some sense of each piece of the jigsaw puzzle, and bit by bit, transform it into a coherent pattern.

It would serve little purpose to try and reproduce the detailed conversations and discussions I had with Harry – I couldn't, even if I tried. The reader needs to bear in mind that Harry was also my friend and there were lots of things that we spoke about – people we knew in our past, our old friends, the 'good times' we had had as young kids. They have no bearing whatever on the traumatic experiences he and Reena had suffered. What follows is an abbreviated summary of the 'missing' four years.

The missing four years

Reena, it appeared, had tried to conceal from Harry the savage violation which had been perpetrated on her, but since the police were already involved, not to mention the doctors looking after her in the hospital, it was impossible for Harry to remain in the dark for more than a couple of days.

True to his word, he resigned from his job with the shipping company, who were very sympathetic to say the least. They allowed him the use of the flat for another six months, which would give him the time and the space in which to make whatever arrangements he felt were necessary. They also agreed to bear all the expenses of Reena's treatment. Although he had not the slightest notion of what he wanted to do with his life and how he was going to earn a living, Harry's main concern was to ensure the recovery of his wife. He promised himself that he would do everything within his power to hasten her recovery. She had been devastated by the experience, and it was clear that it would take a long time before she recovered and put the horrendous experience behind her – if at all.

Harry was plagued by conflicting and contradictory emotions: rage, bitterness and a sense of injustice. He was wrestling with guilt, sorrow and depression. If only he had listened to Reena and had found a land job, this wouldn't have happened. What a fool he had been to disregard her sound advice! They would have lived in India among their own people. Why, oh why had he been mad enough to come to Australia?

In the months that followed, Harry's guilt and self-flagellation gradually gave way to a form of protective defence. Without being fully aware of it himself, he was angry with himself because something in him – some deep-rooted primeval prejudice – prevented him from seeing the trauma from *Reena's* point of view. He saw it as an assault on himself, on his manliness, on his own image of himself. He was not crass enough to blame her for the assault, but one got the feeling that he did occasionally wonder if she could not have defended herself more vigorously than she claimed she did, and in that sense she had 'failed' him. Thus, he did not feel entirely responsible for the tragedy that had disrupted their lives. He also believed that he had chosen to come to Australia only because of Reena, only because she couldn't reconcile herself to staying in Bombay on her own during his long voyages. If only they had continued to live in Bombay! But these were futile and painful speculations.

Gradually, Reena began to take a renewed but altered interest in life once again. They were back at the flat, but she could not bear to be on her own. She was unwilling to go back to India, which surprised Harry. He could not understand why, as such a move would have offered her the refuge she so sorely needed. It took him a long time to work out why.

'Why doesn't she want to go to India?' I asked, half guessing the answer.

'I have thought about it a great deal. I think she was – and still is – frightened of disclosure.'

Although the chances of discovery seemed quite remote, Harry explained, one could never be certain. An indiscreet word by the people who knew, the doctors and the nurses at the hospital, the ambulance men, the neighbour in their block of flats who had summoned the police on hearing her screams – any one of them could have let the secret out, and the poisonous air of gossip, travelling faster than the speed of light, would have choked and suffocated her even before their arrival in India.

Having dealt with a case which was in some ways similar to Reena's I could understand what Harry was trying to convey. An assault of this nature has long-lasting repercussions. It can take years for the public stigma and the private scars on one's psyche to heal. But with genuine help, care and tenderness, the cruelties can be laid to rest, if not exorcized for good.

However, in India, the stigma of such an event is seldom or never laid to rest as it might be in most western countries. The woman concerned is seldom seen as the victim, deserving of care, concern and sympathy. Instead, she is often seen as being the 'temptress', the *apsara* (siren) of the Vedic period who, through her wily, sexual charms, arouses lust even in men who are considered to be holy, noble and totally free from all earthly and carnal desires. Hindu religious texts are replete with examples of how an *apsara* (Meneka being a prime example) was sent down by a demi-god to disrupt the attempted transcendental meditations of a great guru by exploiting her wily sexual charms.

This tendency to blame the woman is also enshrined in the great Indian epic, *The Ramayana*. Sita, Lord Rama's wife, is abducted by Ravana, the demon king and brought to his kingdom in Sri Lanka. Rama, with the help of Hanuman and his army of monkeys, wages war against Ravana, rescues his wife and returns with her to his kingdom in Ayodhya. On his return he begins to doubt her innocence and questions her virtue and fidelity. To test her innocence, Sita is then subjected to a 'fire' test, the results of which shall determine her innocence and virtue. Sita's situation, as one can see, was similar to those women in Europe during the Dark and Middle Ages who were pronounced witches and could only establish their innocence by similar 'no win' tests: they were innocent if they drowned and guilty if they didn't.

It needs to be stressed that all over India, right from ancient times to the present day, Sita is held up as the epitome of modesty, virtue and truthfulness and is seen as the role model for every young female child to learn from and emulate. Parents in bringing up their daughters lay particular emphasis on the virtues of Sita, and expect their children to acquire her noble qualities.

Harry was not unaware of the consequences of disclosure: it would carry a lifelong stigma, a shame which Reena could no more disentangle herself from than from her shadow. The shame, he knew, would also fall upon the rest of the members of his and her family, including himself, making it difficult for the elders to find suitable 'matrimonial matches' for their children and grandchildren.

Harry was at his wit's end. In order for Reena not to be alone and frightened, he used whatever influence he had on his 'contacts' in high places, and managed to import a maid from India, who agreed to come and work for them in Sydney. Reena left the cooking and the day-to-day running of the flat to the maid, but she did all the washing and cleaning.

But Sydney had soured on her. She hated going out. At her behest they declined invitations from friends and did not invite any of them home. She stayed at home for most of the day, doing next to nothing. She bathed and washed herself several times during the day, and spent the rest of her time reading from Hindu religious texts, sleeping and looking out from their balcony, which overlooked the opera house. Harry, now that he was out of work, went out for several hours in the morning, roaming from bar to bar, befriending lost souls, until it was time to stagger home for lunch. During lunch, when the mood got to him, which of course was quite often, he managed to down another bottle of wine, and slept off its effects in a blind stupor, until it was time to start a fresh round of drinks.

Their six-month stay at the flat was coming to an end, and decisions had to be taken. Harry had made token attempts to find a land job, but his heart was not in it, for he was certain that Reena had no desire to live in Sydney any more, after their term of six months expired.

'What did you do?' I asked.

'We went to Tahiti.'

He must have noticed the stupefied look on my face. He smiled for the first time.'I knew you wouldn't believe me.'

I waited for an explanation.

India, he said was out of the question because Reena was firmly set against it. So was Sydney. They could not move to London because it was too far away (from where, he did not explain) and given his present altered circumstances it was too expensive for them to maintain the kind of lifestyle to which they were both accustomed.

'Why Tahiti?'

'You know my love for the islands in the South Pacific.'

'Is that a good enough reason?'

'Find me a better one! I think it is a mistake to always expect rational reasons for all one's actions. We just went. Can't you accept that?'

'What about Reena?'

'She didn't care so long as we left Australia. Secretly, I think she was quite pleased at the idea. So we went, and stayed there for a year or so. But Papeete, which is where we lived, is tourist-infested and over-commercialized – thanks to Marlon Brando's generosity when they were filming *Mutiny on the Bounty*. And we both had difficulty with French and the local languages. We also missed Indian food. Not a single Indian restaurant for 2,000 miles! From the Windward Islands, we even moved to the Leeward Islands and for a while lived in Bora Bora. They are all, as you know, part of The Society Islands in French Polynesia. Bora Bora, I'm not joking, is the most beautiful coral island one can ever set one's eyes upon. But one can't eat beauty! So later on, we moved to Samoa – on the American side, to Pago Pago – and that is where we have been staying for the last three years.'

Living there, he explained, was cheaper than living in The Society Islands and far more comfortable. The people were warm and friendly. Not so much the Americans, but the locals were terrific. Local culture and family arrangements were not dissimilar to their own. Harry had opened a garage where they repaired cars, specializing in the repair of American cars and jeeps. As a qualified marine engineer, repairing motor vehicles was dead easy to learn. Life in Pago Pago was easy, relaxed and comfortable; he loved the climate, which of course included the beaches, the sea and all the fish one could catch. Financially too, they were doing pretty well.

'What about Reena? How has she taken it?'

'Doesn't say much. Keeps to herself most of the time.'

It appeared that her routine remained unchanged. They had employed a few maids, which freed her from the day-to-day cooking, cleaning and the running of their house. She spent most of her free time reading from Hindu scriptures, and about three evenings a week their chauffeur drove her to a Hindu temple, which was not really a temple, but a shrine which had been set up in the home of an Indian family that had been living there since the 'dawn of civilization'.

'Is she happy?'

'That's what I have come to see you about. She needs help. Some kind of therapy.'

I didn't see that as a problem. 'I could certainly recommend one or two people I know and respect, who, I am sure, would be quite willing to help.'

'Therapists are one a penny. I could find them anywhere – even in Pago Pago. I want *you* to help her.'

'But Harry, you're a friend. You can't . . .' I objected.

'All the more reason. A friend in need . . .'

His request came out of the blue. I should have anticipated it, but I didn't because I had chosen to see him as a friend and not as a client in need of therapy. It put me in a quandary. What was I to do? A moment's reflection ought to have convinced me that I had more reasonable and viable alternatives at my command, the most sensible of which would have been to recommend a therapist or two who lived in London. Yet I prevaricated. Harry was nothing if not persuasive.

It seemed churlish, even unkind and, dare I say, immoral to refuse the help asked of me. A little voice of caution, which whispered to me, went unheeded. How could one stand by and watch the sufferings of one's friends? Would he not have not done the same for me had I been in his place, I kept asking myself, running through infantile hypothetical arguments. I must confess that I partly 'blamed' (if that is an appropriate word to use) Immanuel Kant for having inculcated in me an attitude which I can only describe as 'moral priggishness' (Bertrand Russell was probably right in suggesting – with tongue in cheek – that the acceptance of Kant's categorical imperative often turns people into crashing bores). And it was over twenty years ago that I was first seduced by the writings of Kant. What a bore!

Eventually, I plunged into their problems headlong. Was it vanity, or an inner moral stricture to which I was responding – or perhaps a bit of both? It was like diving from a precipice into the swirling waters of a raging torrent a million miles below! I was plagued by doubt and wondered if I had the required skills, the calm, and the experience to deal with this unique and complex situation. There was also the fear of overstraining our friendship because of what might come tumbling out when the lid of Pandora's Box was prised open!

I laid down one or two conditions. First, I asked Harry to try, in so far as it was possible, to maintain a client-therapist relationship during the sessions. It was imperative that both Reena and he, regardless of the types of interpretation and analyses which emerged during the sessions, understood them within that formal framework, independent of our long-standing friendship. Our friendship was sacrosanct and would remain inviolate. Second, for a few sessions,

I wanted to see the two of them together; then I wanted to see each of them individually. Finally, to 'round off' the sessions, I wanted to see the two together again. Harry raised the question of fees; I stifled the discussion by saying that he was my friend and there was nothing more to be said. To bring home the point, I said, 'Had you been a brain surgeon, and I needed a tumour removed, would you not have performed the operation free?'

Harry laughed. 'Don't flatter yourself. I'd be hard-put to find *any* grey matter inside your thick skull.'

The relaxed conviviality gave me my first opportunity to ask the question which had been bothering me for quite some time.

'Harry, I'd like to ask you a few questions.'

'Shoot.'

'Since the tragic event, have you continued to lead a normal sexual life with your wife?'

His long silence gave me the answer.

'For a year or so, she could not even bear being touched.'

'Not even a comfort touch?'

'We slept in separate beds. Still do.'

'What about now?'

'Occasionally.'

I waited for him to volunteer further information, but none was forthcoming: I was left to my own guesses. The fires had long since burned out; they merely stoked cold ashes.

I changed tack. 'How long do you think you will continue to live in Samoa?'

'I don't know. Until she's ready to return to India, I guess.'

'But doesn't everyone wonder why you're both living there?'

'With us Indians, as you well know, out of sight is out of mind.'

I decided not to pursue this line of thinking. I left it to later. (The reader is referred to Chapter 3 for a detailed discussion on the Indian approach to time, friendship and hospitality.)

'Tell me something. Did the police ever find out who the culprit was?'

He shook his head. 'I don't think they tried hard enough. Why would the Australian police wish to worry about the fate of an Indian woman?' His voice was devoid of anger but filled with bitterness. 'I am sure they have better things to do with their time. Why should they care? In any case, what purpose would it have served? Some smart-arsed lawyer would probably have got him off free.'

As he spoke, it became clear to me that it was not only his wife but also Harry who needed counselling and therapy.

The therapy sessions

They came, as arranged, on a Friday evening. Harry brought me a gigantic bottle of cognac, enough to disintegrate a million superegos!

Reena, who I had never met before, surpassed my wildest imagination. She had the kind of beauty of which dreams are made and poems written. Nothing was out of place. Her pale blue sari matched her turquoise-necklace and bracelets, and her turquoise-coloured handbag. Perfect, oval-shaped eyes, dark eyelashes, arched-eyebrows, a dimpled face, dark, shoulder-length, silky hair – a face that would have easily launched a thousand ships! Yet there was a graveyard-like sadness about her, which reminded me of the cold, dark catacombs I had seen in Rome.

Neither of them seemed relaxed or happy, not even when they chanced to look at each other. Silence, like a heavy, faded curtain obliterating any sunshine hung over the room. Conversation did not flow, but sputtered, hissed and stopped; and after several moments of agonized silence, started again, creating a feeling of utter gloom.

Although I wanted to, I refrained from asking any questions, lest I asked the wrong question at the wrong time. I waited. In the meantime, Harry took off his blazer, loosened his tie, kicked off his shoes, ran his hand through his soggy hair, wiped the sweat pouring off his puffed face and filled his glass almost to the brim. After he'd had a long and deep drink, he seemed more relaxed, as though he were ready to 'open up'.

But it was not Harry who made the first move.

'I *hate* Australia! Oh God, I loathe the Australians! God, how I hate them – the smug, stupid, mean little bastards!' In her rage, Reena almost threw her wine glass away.

Like the proverbial criminal returning to the scene of the crime, she too was returning to the scene of the crime – although in her case, she was the victim and not the perpetrator. I was stunned by her violence. After her sudden outburst she withdrew into herself and refused to meet my eye. I looked at each of them, from one to the other: Harry sat with his glass of wine in his hand, staring into space.

A long time went by. And then, the dam burst. It all came gushing forth. They both spoke at once, each interrupting the other, each picking up when the other paused for breath, each repeating what the other had just said. It took me a long time and several meetings with each of them individually and then jointly to put all the bits and pieces of their lives in Samoa together.

Once again, I shall content myself with summarizing the main problems. Let us start with Harry.

Harry

From the several sessions I had with him (he kept his word and came punctually at the arranged times) I had the feeling that there were several unresolved problems in Harry's mind, which I have listed below.

- Harry, in the four to five years that had gone by, had never once asked his wife for any details of what actually transpired on that fateful night. He could not bring himself to find out because he too felt violated and abused by the tragic event and wanted to put it out of his mind.
- To have asked for and been given all the details of Reena's violation would have meant an explicit acknowledgement that some other person, a stranger, had laid hands on her body, and in so doing had appropriated the exclusive 'right' which he as her husband had over her. Although he could not bring himself to utter the word, in his heart he felt that she had been soiled by the violation.
- He harboured an unvoiced grudge against Reena, which grew out of proportion because of her unwillingness (or inability?) to lead a normal conjugal life with him once again.
- He 'played the field' and made no attempt to conceal this from Reena. Whether this was revenge or indifference one could not tell. They appeared to lead fairly independent lives, making sure that neither got in the way of the other.
- He seemed resigned to live out the rest of his life in Samoa and although he missed India and what it might have offered him were they to return, he accepted their new life.
- He had taken to drink, had put on an incredible amount of weight, and was not far from becoming an alcoholic. But he didn't seem to care. Nor did he seem to worry too much about his high blood pressure and the occasional 'arrhythmic twinges' in his heart, which momentarily unsettled his equanimity.

- His business thrived. His easy, carefree charm combined with his generosity endeared him to his workmen and also to his customers. But underneath the carefully cultivated façade and bonhomie one had the feeling that he was very unhappy.
- Harry persuaded Reena to take holidays with him to other islands in the South Pacific, and from time to time they sailed to Fiji, to the Solomon Islands, Hawaii and other smaller islands.
- Although he and Reena retained lukewarm contact with their family members in India, they neither invited them over, nor took a trip there.

What was one to do, I wondered? How was one to deal with this problem?

Reena

For understandable reasons, Reena was far more difficult to deal with than Harry. I had never met Reena before; she obviously knew of me and had heard of me, but our meetings were hardly what one would have described as social and friendly. The agenda had changed. Talking to me would have also meant a revelation of her innermost traumas, which she had in all probability kept locked in the innermost recesses of her heart. I felt it was difficult for her to take kindly towards me. Besides, I was unsure whether she had agreed voluntarily to these sessions or had been railroaded into them by Harry. It took several sessions of just sitting with her, just sitting and doing nothing, saying nothing, before I could get her to volunteer any information.

Much to my surprise, she liked living in Samoa. Unlike Harry's, her own interests did not include the sun, the sand and the sea, nor the fish; she preferred to sit under the shade of a beach umbrella, and while Harry swam she spent her time reading and staring vacantly at the changing moods and colours of the horizon in the distance.

She had no desire whatsoever to return to India. On that she was adamant. She did not wish to bring shame upon her family and upon her in-laws. It was her fate to have 'earned' this permanent scar. It had happened. It was her karma. There was nothing she could do about it. She could, however, prevent others from being affected by it. Samoa offered her the very haven that she craved. In a sense, Samoa was akin to the earth that had opened for Sita into which she had been swallowed when accused of infidelity by her husband Rama. Identification with the 'fate' of the Indian goddess made her own life in Samoa more bearable, and allowed her to 'take on' Sita's divine attributes.

I noticed too that she was unwilling to forgive her husband for even daring to cast aspersions on her character. She was intensely disappointed that he had never 'come clean' with his unvoiced suspicions, nor had he ever asked to be forgiven for doubting her in the first instance. Nonetheless, she continued to live with him and would continue to do so; she was after all an Indian wife and it was her duty, her *dharma*, to share her life with her husband. Happiness did not enter into this equation. Duty took precedence.

In any case, she said that she had very little choice in the matter. What other alternatives did she have? She could not return to India for fear of disclosure; she could not leave her husband; she could not live on her own in those godforsaken Samoan islands, beautiful though they were. Her life had come to a premature end after the tragic event. She felt like a zombie. Reading from the ancient Hindu scriptures brought her a sense of relief and restored some meaning into her life, and she had decided to spend most of her time and energies on devotion and prayer.

But in a symbiotic way, both Reena and Harry were inseparably joined. They were both utterly, desperately lonely and they were both unable to, or refused to, countenance this sad fact from their own individual perspectives. Neither of them had decided to bury the past and lay it to rest. Like Banquo's ghost, it kept raising its bloody head again and again and would not go away.

I thought a great deal about what had transpired during the three to four months that I had continued seeing them, at least two or three times a week. I came to the conclusion that their 'problem' was both a serious psychological one and a 'moral' one. I was by no means undervaluing the trauma that Reena had gone through; it was unimaginable, the pain and the suffering that she had endured. I decided to pursue the 'moral' line of therapy at our final joint meetings and then work my way into the psychological issues which continued to torment them and virtually tear them apart. I felt that over the years they had each become entrenched in their own position of moral righteousness. Reena of course had greater cause to feel aggrieved and it was impossible not to be concerned and sympathetic to the stance she had chosen (consciously or unconsciously) to adopt. I felt that a clear understanding of some of the moral issues involved in the trauma, and in their subsequent relationship, might allow them to see their tragedy from a different perspective, the acceptance of which might restore their mutual trust in one another once again.

Final joint meetings

So we settled down to our final sessions. I explained to them that we had been meeting regularly for the last three or four months, during which I had learnt a lot from them. I had come to realize that a large number of emotional problems which people experience, when analysed carefully and accurately, stem from an insufficient or inadequate understanding of their own moral position on those issues. People, I explained, seldom consider the issues of right and wrong, good and bad, evil and virtue, even happiness and sorrow, from a set of general moral principles which prevail in their respective cultures. This is due partly to the fact that many people lack an awareness of the values underlying the moral principles, nor do they have a conscious understanding of the origins of the values which guide their private and social behaviours. Values are often the result of past religious, political and philosophical legacies; they are 'passed on' to us over the centuries, and although their origins are often shrouded in mystery, they nonetheless become an integral part of our psychological and existential being.

An ignorance of the overarching moral principles which guide our daily behaviours often leads to a pragmatic short-sightedness. People often tend to visualize their problems from their own immediate, subjective and pragmatic perspective, where right and wrong, guilt and blame, forgiving and forgiveness, often become labels which are attached to those who they feel have wronged them. They may also turn into slurs and accusations which are hurled at the wrongdoers. Even self-recrimination, under certain circumstances, is easily transformed into recriminations of the other. So strong and powerful is the human need to justify one's actions that it seldom occurs to people in such situations to hold back and reappraise their own beliefs and values before passing judgement. Under such circumstances, one is anything but self-critical.

At this point, Reena began to cry. Harry cleared his throat, pulled out a handkerchief and passed it to her in silence.

'Do you, think,' he asked, 'that is what we have both been doing?'

'I think it is for you both to ask this question of yourselves. Not of me. My own opinion is neither here nor there.'

'What do you think we should do?'

'That again is for the two of you to decide, individually and jointly. But at a general level, I strongly believe that a large number of emotional and psychological problems have in them several unresolved and inadequately understood moral considerations. One needs to have the intellectual ability and the honesty and integrity to appraise and reappraise those problems unflinchingly, without hasty judgement. I am not saying that one should not judge; one cannot help but judge. All I am prepared to say is this – although it sounds pious, a little self-criticism never goes amiss, and perhaps, a little forgiveness too.'

'This sounds like the cliché of the year,' mocked Harry.

'Perhaps the cliché of the century,' I retorted gently. 'But I am prepared to stand by it and allow my own life to be guided by it.'

I added that a detached, dispassionate, objective and critical attitude towards one's life and its vicissitudes was the ultimate path to knowledge and wisdom and also the most desirable way of relating to oneself and to the rest of the world.

Conclusion

I cannot to this very day (it is several years since I met Harry and Reena in London) tell truthfully whether my meetings with them served any useful purpose. All I can say is that it was a great strain on my own psychological resources, and there were times when I almost gave up on them; but to have given up on them would have meant giving up on myself.

With renewed promises to keep in touch and their invitations to me to visit them in Samoa, we parted – as ever on the best of terms.

Four months later Harry died of a sudden heart attack in his garage in Pago Pago, where he was busy fixing the air-conditioning on a jeep that had come in for repairs. Reena stayed on in Pago Pago for another six months, settled her affairs and returned to India.

A few months after Harry's death, Reena wrote to me from Pago Pago, explaining why she had decided to return to India. Luckily, she had been well provided for; they still had their flat in Bombay, and the proceeds from the disposal of the garage and their flat in Pago Pago ensured her financial independence. She would never be a burden on either her in-laws or her own parents. She was aware too that her return to India would probably unleash a new set of accusations: the premature death of her husband would be partly attributed to her misdoings.

The remainder of her life had been 'decided' by her newly acquired inferior status – that of a widow. And now that she was a widow, it did not matter to her if her trauma was discovered or not. Nothing mattered any more.

Chapter 9

The summing up

To write a book on a controversial subject is often fraught with serious dangers. One can never be sure that the issues and the arguments which one has marshalled and presented are sound, logical, rational and valid. But to write a book on a controversial subject in a manner which to say the least is controversial, is to compound the dangers. It is like committing hara-kiri in public – as the Japanese poet Mishima Yukio did in 1970. I have exposed myself to both dangers: writing on a controversial subject and writing the book in a controversial manner. But since I have no desire to emulate Mishima Yukio, and nor do I relish the idea of being pilloried, I really should have played 'safe' and written a relatively 'mild', unchallenging and non-controversial book, as some of them are. No truth is worth a stake.

My main concern has been to articulate the major issues related to counselling and psychotherapy within a western and cross-cultural (Asian) framework. In so doing I have found it impossible not to raise many of the issues which are controversial, to say the least.

The fear of stepping 'over the line', of being construed as a racist, of not being seen as politically correct, of offending the sensibilities of the ethnic minorities, of not being taken for a 'liberal' etc., etc. have often forced many a writer to adopt a rather sanitized, non-controversial approach in their writings on this subject. But privately, I daresay very few therapists would deny the controversial nature of counselling and psychotherapy in western society in general and in cross-cultural settings in particular.

In the first chapter, the reader may recall that we concentrated on arriving at a clear understanding of the term 'culture'. What was clear is that the term culture is not very clear. Imagine the difficulty which such ambiguity forces one into! Trying to understand culture is like trying to capture a pattern or an image through a kaleidoscope; a slight tilt of the hand, and the pattern changes. Add a word here, subtract a term there, and you find that the meaning of the term culture also changes. There were at least five major shifts in our kaleidoscopic formulations: the subjective, the anthropological, the sociological, the psychological and the postmodernistic, each beset with its own problems, its own ambiguities. Which of the approaches seems the most meaningful from a therapeutic perspective? This question is not easy to answer. Is the choice of a particular approach to be dictated by one's training as a therapist, one's theoretical orientations or by one's personal preferences based on one's past experiences? Or, like the eclectic, does one pinch a bit from here and a bit from there, and make up one's own definition? But which bit and how much does one pinch from here and which bit from there? The answer, as one can see, continues to remain undecided. Such a situation does not inspire confidence in the professional work of therapists, nor does it offer a great deal of help to a trainee counsellor or therapist. But the advantage of being placed in an ambiguous situation is that it prevents a therapist from an early 'closure'. In a sense, it compels the therapist to tolerate and come to terms with the ambiguities, uncertainties and contradictions which form an integral part of one's understanding of culture. A therapist would need to be extremely cautious before attributing certain 'atypical', unexplained behaviours in his or her client to their cultural upbringing or cultural influences. This would be akin to using the term culture as a wastebasket into which one discards the behaviours, beliefs and values of the client which defy rational explanation. Adopting such an approach is a short cut to perdition!

Let us now formulate our first rule:

Rule 1: do not use the term culture as a wastebasket to discard anomalies and unexplained behaviours.

In the second chapter we learnt of Indian independence and the break up of India into two separate countries: Pakistan and India, with West Pakistan at one flank. We outlined a brief history of the migratory patterns of Asians living in Britain. This allowed us to look at their lifestyle and the intergenerational differences in their attitudes, values, behaviours and occupations. The last 60 years have witnessed startling changes in the occupations, attitudes to work, material prosperity and lifestyles of the second- and third-generation

Asians living in Britain. Although the Asian community as a whole is united by a set of core values, including strong religious beliefs, living together in extended family networks, even pooling their resources, they are also divided by sharp differences in their approach to education, leisure pursuits, marriage etc. These differences are noticeable particularly at an intergenerational level. But in addition to the obvious differences there are others that are quite subtle and may pass unnoticed by many a therapist. It is important for a therapist to acquire a close understanding of the changes and the variations that have taken place.

To bring out the differences between western and eastern cultures, the chapter paid significant attention to the theme of family life in the eastern and western context, and in so doing considered the issues related to the socialization of children, gender differences and the development of identity. The chapter ended with a vignette of an English family living in India and the serious difficulties the children experienced in coming to terms with a culture which to them seemed alien, despite being born and socialized in it.

Rule 2: even within a single culture, people may be divided more by their differences than united by their similarities.

The third chapter plays a very important role in the book. It presents a conceptual model which highlights the major differences and similarities in beliefs, attitudes and values between eastern and western cultures. Although the book focuses on India and England, the conceptual model can be extended to other countries including Pakistan, Bangladesh, Malaysia and Sri Lanka in eastern cultures, and America, Canada and Australia in western cultures. The chapter demonstrates that our behaviours – from the mundane to the complex, from the religious to the secular – are not random acquisitions within a social setting – they are guided by our past social and cultural histories. This suggests that a mature understanding of behaviours would necessitate our taking into serious consideration the impact of our past legacies on our present behaviours. Behaviours would therefore need to be perceived and interpreted within their appropriate social and historical context. Otherwise one exposes oneself to the danger of misinterpreting behaviours by taking them out of their cultural context.

However, it is fair to warn the therapist that, despite careful considerations, even an experienced practitioner can err in his or her assessments and interpretations of a client's feelings, emotions and values. The client might behave in a manner that is totally unexpected.

Rule 3: always expect the unexpected and prepare to be taken by surprise.

The fourth chapter traced a brief history of counselling and psychotherapy in western society, travelling through Roman times to the present. It also had a critical look at the chequered development of counselling and psychotherapy, and the major theoretical and applied models of psychotherapy that have been developed, some of which have been discarded, altered, changed or resuscitated. Each model has its protagonists and its antagonists. The models have proliferated over the last 50 years, making the problems of validating them even harder than it was five decades ago. We found that the given conceptual frameworks of certain therapeutic models (e.g. the Freudian, the transactional, the transcendental, the person-centred and their variants) are not easily amenable to rigorous empirical scrutiny. Thus the choice of a particular model used by a therapist is not necessarily related to the model's rigour, but to what the therapist has been trained in and what the therapist feels 'comfortable' with. The therapist should not rule out the possibility that regardless of the popularity of a given model (e.g. the person-centred approach or the cognitive behavioural approach) it may be of little use in many cross-cultural settings.

Rule 4: the universal popularity of a theoretical model neither guarantees its usefulness nor its validity. The two are independent.

How clients get to meet their therapists formed the basis of Chapter 5. In the West, we observed that there are recognized avenues by which clients get to meet a therapist: through referral by one's GP, through one's friends, through direct contact, through the internet and so on. We also noticed that barring family therapists, the meeting between a client and a therapist tends to operate on a one-to-one basis. In India and other eastern countries the situation tends to be quite different. Since religion plays an extremely important part in daily life, a 'therapist' may be a guru, a saint, a *swami*, a preacher, an *imam* and so on. Such religious people may often be accorded greater respect and reverence than a qualified western therapist. The relationship between the therapist and the client rests on a hierarchical structure and the therapist's position is recognized as being superior to the client's. Often a therapist is imbued with magico-spiritual powers of healing. The meetings between the therapist and the client do not always operate on a one-to-one basis and the client's entire family may be involved. There is also an expectation that the therapist will be didactic; the therapist leads and the client follows, akin to a guru-student relationship.

Rule 5: there are no standardized norms for dealing with clients from different cultures. What may be relevant in the West may have little or no meaning in the East and vice versa.

Given the strong belief in religion and its power over a human being, illness, pain, distress and sorrow are often attributed to supernatural causes in the East. The cultural norms in such societies permit the acceptance of sorcery, spells, bewitchment, curses and other such evils. Each of these afflictions may require different sets of skills from the healer. Chapter 6 outlined the different models of therapy in eastern cultures, which included within their therapeutic framework a variety of religious and quasi-religious approaches, such as pilgrimages to holy places, visits to gurus, respite in *ashrams*, prayers, yogic exercises, reliance on astrologers and palmists and so on. Thus the term 'therapy' has greater flexibility. It is not confined to a formalized meeting between the client and the therapist but is variable. One's 'illness', distress, anxiety or whatever the client finds stressful may be due to supernatural causes. Since one can never be certain what is going to work, when, how, and under what circumstances, it would seem wise to hedge one's bets and try whatever is available in the hope of a cure. This appears to be the guiding philosophy in several eastern cultures.

Rule 6: wisdom lies in recognizing and accepting the culturally relevant beliefs and practices of one's clients.

Chapter 7 examined the major arguments related to the problem of matching clients with therapists. We found that in many cases the need for matching was quite justified, but its implementation is likely to create a variety of problems. In the long run, even genuine and sincere attempts at matching may, for a variety of reasons, turn out to be counterproductive. Why should this be the case?

My own view is that the entire business of matching is best seen as a symptom, an outer layer of a deep-rooted problem: multiculturalism. The question is this: does one attempt to promote a genuine multicultural society in which people of different cultures, speaking different languages, worshipping different gods, eating different foods, construing their own worlds in diverse ways, join hands and live and work together in peace, love and harmony? Does the creation of such a society fall within the bounds of possibility? Or is it a romantic utopian dream seen through rose-coloured lenses? How do such dreams compete against the present drive by western nations toward economic globalization and homogenization?

So long as stereotypes and prejudices, mistrust and ill feelings continue to 'poison' the cultural atmosphere, multiculturalism will remain a dream. And so long as the boots of economic globalization continue to march to the drums of progress, multiculturalism will remain a dream. If, however, therapists of different theoretical persuasions and from different ethnic and cultural backgrounds were to join hands and work together, it is possible that what seems a dream may one day become a reality.

Rule 7: ask not what you can teach other therapists. Ask instead what you might *learn from* other therapists.

The case studies in Chapter 8 were carefully selected. Both dealt with cross-cultural issues. The main object was to demonstrate that it is possible for therapists, regardless of their ethnic background, their colour, their gender, their age, to deal successfully with the problems presented by their clients from different cultural backgrounds. Space did not permit the inclusion of more case studies. Many of them not included in the book have since been published, and are being published elsewhere (see Laungani, 2003b). Case studies, by their very nature, do not necessarily subscribe to the formalized requirements of academic articles and papers, which demand a specific style of presentation, comprehensive referencing, verification of statements etc. Case studies are more flexible. The introduction of dialogue and reported speech allows the reader to visualize the situation being described and 'come close' to and even empathize with the people whose dilemmas and problems are being analysed.

Rule 8: a case study is like a picture. It reveals more than a carefully written report.

Conclusion

Let me end this chapter, and with it the book, by writing what might perhaps sound like a sermon, though a sermon it is not meant to be.

No one is likely to disagree with the sentiment that counsellors and psychotherapists in their own unique and specialized way are concerned with the promotion of human welfare. Their concern by its very nature does not encompass the whole of humanity, certainly not in the sense in which one might expect preachers, gurus and even poets to operate. Their concern is individualized. It is with their day-to-day encounters with their clients, who come seeking help, guidance and comfort. It follows that the more enlightened, the more humane, a therapist is the better she or he might be able to understand the psyche of the client and offer the required help.

The completion of training, the passing of a course, obtaining a certificate or diploma, a postgraduate qualification and even a doctorate, is merely the first step in the process of development and eventual enlightenment. It is only then that a sensitive therapist becomes aware of the huge uphill task that faces him or her. If we assume that a large number of problems which our clients bring to us are problems that for want of a better phrase are fundamental human problems, we need to develop an antenna which would sensitize us to those problems. The onus is upon therapists to find ways to crawl into the skin (psyche) of their clients and see the world from their perspective, without imposing their own rigid categories of explanations, which may or may not turn out to be relevant.

Thus, whether the client is black, brown, pink, grey or white, male or female, old or young, rich or poor, educated or uneducated, gay or straight, the problem which each of them brings to the therapist is concerned, in the final analysis, with making sense of one's life and living in a productive and meaningful way, which is in keeping with their rational appraisal of their potential strengths and weaknesses. What constitutes a 'meaningful life' might of course be worded and described differently, but in essence it is concerned with the sentiment expressed by Socrates in the fourth century BC, when he posed the question: 'How shall we lead our lives?' This question is as relevant today as it was then. The question posed by Socrates carries within it a moral injunction. For when Socrates spoke of 'the good life' he was in fact proposing a fundamental moral basis for one's relations with oneself and with the outside world. Thus, ethics and morality, in Socratic terms, are seen as the mainspring of all human actions. It is imperative therefore that during the course of therapy, moral issues are brought out into the open and given an airing. The skill of the therapist lies in engendering in the client a need to understand and examine the moral issues underlying his or her problems.

But the picture painted by reality is often in stark contrast to what might seem desirable. Moral problems, if and when they arise, tend often to be underplayed or ignored. Therapists tend in general to focus on the emotional, relational, social and economic problems of their clients. Can anything be done to salvage the situation? I do not know.

But being an incorrigible optimist, I shall continue to live in hope.

References

Alladin, W. J. (1986) Ethnic minorities and clinical psychology: an inside view, *Clinical Psychology Forum*, 5: 28–32.

Alladin, W. J. (2001) Ethnic matching in counselling, in P. Milner and S. Palmer (eds) *Counselling: The BACP Counselling Reader*, vol. 2. London: Sage.

Allport, G. W. (1954) *The Nature of Prejudice*. New York: Doubleday.

Aronson, E. (1992) *The Social Animal*, 6th edn. New York: W. H. Freeman & Co.

Asch, S. (1946) Forming impressions of personality, *Journal of Abnormal and Social Psychology*, 41: 258–90.

Asch, S. (1952) *Social Psychology*. New York: Prentice-Hall.

Asch, S. (1955) Opinions and social pressure, *Scientific American*, 193(5).

Atkinson D. R. (1983) Ethnic similarity in counselling: a review of the research, *The Counselling Psychologist*, 11: 79–92.

Barnlund, D. C. and Araki, S. (1985) Intercultural encounters: the management of compliments by Japanese and Americans, *Journal of Cross-Cultural Psychology*, 16: 9–26.

Bartlett, F. C. (1923) *Psychology and Primitive Culture*. Cambridge: Cambridge University Press.

Bartlett, F. C. (1937) Psychological methods and anthropological problems, *Africa*, 10: 410–19.

Basham, A. L. (1966) *The Wonder That Was India*. Bombay: Rupa & Co.

Bates, C. M. and Brodsky, A. M. (1989) *Sex in the Therapy Hour: A Case of Professional Incest*. London: Guildford Press.

Bauman, Z. (1992) *Intimations of Postmodernity*. London: Routledge.

Bellah, R. N. (1985) *Habits of the Heart: Individuation and Commitment in American* Life. Berkeley, CA: University of California Press.

Bem, D. (1972) Self perception theory, in L. Berkowitz (ed.) *Advances in Experimental Social Psychology*, vol. 6. New York: Academic Press.

Berry, J. W., Poortinga, Y. H., Segall, M. H. and Dasen, P. R. (1992) *Cross-cultural Psychology: Research and Applications*. New York: Cambridge University Press.
Bhandari, A. K. and Parathi, A. (2000) Empathy and its development, in J. Mohan (ed.) *Personality Across Cultures: Recent Developments and Debates*, pp. 265–83. New Delhi: Oxford University Press.
Bhavasar, S. N. and Kiem, G. (1989) Spirituality and health (*Ayurveda*), in K. Sivaraman (ed.) *Hindu Spirituality: Vedas through Vedanta*, pp. 338–57. London: SCM Press Limited.
Bhole, M. V. (1981) Concept of relaxation in shavasana, *Yoga Mimamsa*, 20: 50–6.
Bisbing, S., Jorgenson, L. and Sutherland, P. (1996) *Sexual Abuse by Professionals: A Legal Guide*. Charlottesville, Virginia: Michie & Co.
Bloom, A. (1987) *The Closing of the American Mind*. London: Penguin.
Boaz, F. (1911) *The Mind of Primitive Man*. New York: Macmillan.
Bochner, S. (ed.) (1982) *Cultures in Contact: Studies in Cross-Cultural Interaction*. Oxford: Pergamon.
Bock, P. K. (1980) *Continuities in Psychological Anthropology: A Historical Introduction*. San Francisco: W. H. Freeman.
Boring, E. (1950) *A history of Experimental Psychology*, 2nd edn. New York: Appleton Century Crofts.
Bougle, C. (1992) The essence and reality of the caste system, in D. Gupta (ed.) *Social Stratification*. Delhi: Oxford University Press.
Boyne, R. and Rattansi, A. (eds) (1990) *Postmodernism and Society*. New York: St. Martin's Press.
Brinton, C. (1962) *The Anatomy of Revolution*. New York: Prentice-Hall.
Brislin, R. (1983) Cross-cultural research in psychology, *Annual Review of Psychology*, 34: 363–400.
Brislin, R. (ed.) (1990) *Applied Cross-cultural Psychology*. Newbury Park, CA: Sage.
Brown, R. (1965) *Social Psychology*. London: Collier Macmillan.
Brown, R. (1987) *Social Psychology*, 2nd edn. London: Collier Macmillan.
Bruner, J. S. (1959) Myths and identity, *Daedalus*, Spring.
Brush, S. G. (1976) Fact and fantasy in the history of science, in M.H. Marx and F.E. Goodson (eds) *Theories in Contemporary Psychology*, pp. 66–86. New York: Macmillan.
Burks, H. M. and Stefflre, B. (1979) *Theories of Counselling*, 3rd edn. New York: McGraw-Hill.
Camilleri, C. (1989) La communication dans la perspective interculturelle, in C. Camilleri and M. Cohen-Emerique (eds) *Chocs de Cultures: Concepts et Enjeux Pratiques de L'interculturel*. Paris: L'Harmattan.
Camilleri, C. *et al.* (1990) *Stratégies Identitaires*. Paris: PUF.
Camus, A. (1955) *The Myth of Sisyphus*. London: Hamish Hamilton.

Carrithers, M. (1992) *Why Humans Have Cultures: Explaining Anthropology and Social Diversity*. Oxford: Oxford University Press.

Carter, R. T. (1995) *The Influence of RACE and Racial Identity in Psychotherapy*. New York: Wiley.

Casas, J. M. (1985) The status of racial and ethnic counselling: a training perspective, in P. Pederson (ed) *Handbook of Cross-cultural Therapy*. Westport, CT: Greenwood Press.

Chandrashekar, C. R. (1989) Possession syndrome in India, in C. A. Ward (ed.) *Altered States of Consciousness and Mental Health: A Cross-Cultural Perspective*, pp. 79–95. Newbury Park, CA: Sage.

Channabasavanna, S. M. and Bhatti, R. S. (1982) A study on interactional patterns of family typologies in families of mental patients, in A. Kiev and V. Rao (eds) *Readings in Transcultural Psychiatry*, pp. 149–61. Madras: Higginsbothams.

Cheng, C. H. K. (1996) Towards a culturally relevant model of self-concept for the Hong Kong Chinese, in J. Pandey, D. Sinha and D. P. S. Bhawuk (eds) *Asian Contributions to Cross-cultural Psychology*. New Delhi: Sage.

Cohen, D. (1979) *J. B. Watson: The Founder of Behaviourism. A Biography*. London: Routledge & Kegan Paul.

Cooper, D. E. (1996) *World Philosophies. An Historical Introduction*. Oxford: Blackwell.

Cox J. and Holden, J. (eds) (1994) *Perinatal Psychiatry: Use and Misuse of the Edinburgh Postnatal Depression Scale*. London: Gaskell.

Crossete, B. (1993) *India: Facing the Twenty-first Century*. Bloomington, IN: Indiana University Press.

Crutchfield, R. (1954) A new technique for measuring individual differences in conformity to group judgement, cited in R. Gross (1996) *Psychology: The Science of Mind and Behaviour*, 3rd edn, p. 479. London: Hodder & Stoughton.

Crutchfield, R. (1955) Conformity and character, *American Psychologist*, 10: 191–8.

Crutchfield, R. (1962) *Individual in Society*. New York: McGraw-Hill.

Cushman, P. (1990) Why the self is empty: toward a historically situated psychology, *American Psychologist*, 45: 599–611.

Cushman, P. (1995) *Constructing the Self, Constructing America: A Cultural History of Psychotherapy*. Washington, DC: American Psychological Association.

D'Ardenne, P. and Mahtani, A. (1989) *Transcultural Counselling in Action*. London: Sage.

Das, C. (2000) *India Unbound*. New Delhi: Penguin.

Davies, P. (1990) *God and the New Physics*. London: Penguin.

Davis, H. and Fallowfield, L. (1991) *Counselling and Communication in Health Care*. Chichester: Wiley.

de Riencourt, A. (1980a) *Sex and Power in History*. New York: Dell Publishing.

de Riencourt, A. (1980b) *The Eye of Shiva: Eastern Mysticism and Science*. London: Souvenir Press.

Deutsch, M. and Gerrard, H. B. (1955) A study of normative and informational social influences upon individual judgement, *Journal of Abnormal and Social Psychology*, 51: 629–36.

Dharmakeerti, U. S. (1982) Review of 'Yoga and cardiovascular management'. *Yoga*, 20(6): 15–16.

Dilman, I. (1999) *Free Will: A Historical and Philosophical Introduction*. London: Routledge.

Doyal, L. and Harris, R. (1986) *Empiricism, Explanation and Rationality: An Introduction to the Philosophy of the Social Sciences*. London: Routledge.

Draguns, J. G. (1981) Psychological disorders of clinical severity, in H. C. Triandis and R. W. Brislin (eds) *Handbook of Cross-Cultural Psychology*, vol. 5. Boston, MA: Allyn & Bacon.

Dryden, W., Charles-Edwards, D. and Woolfe, R. (1996) *Handbook of Counselling in Britain*. London: Routledge.

Dumon, W. (ed.) (1992) *National Family Policies in EC-Countries in 1991*. Luxembourg: Commission of European Countries.

Eliade, M. (1969) *Yoga: Immortality and Freedom*. Princeton, NJ: Princeton University Press.

Eliade, M. (1975) *Patanjali and Yoga*. New York: Schocken Books.

Eliot, T. S. (1969) *The Complete Poems and Plays of T. S. Eliot*. London: Faber & Faber.

Elizur, A. (1985) An integrated development model of empathy, *Israel Journal of Psychiatry and Related Sciences*, 22(1&2): 29–39.

Ellison, R. (1965) *The Invisible Man*. London: Penguin.

Embree, A. T. (1988) *The Encyclopedia of Asian History: Sources of Indian Tradition*. New Delhi: Penguin.

Erikson, E. (1963) *Childhood and Society*. London: Penguin.

Esposito, J. L. (1988) *Islam: The Straight Path*, 3rd edn. Oxford: Oxford University Press.

Eysenck, H. J. (1953) *Uses and Abuses of Psychology*. London: Penguin.

Eysenck, H. J. (1998) *Dimensions of Personality*. New Brunswick, NJ: Transaction Publishers.

Featherstone, M. (1988) In pursuit of the postmodern: an introduction, in M. Featherstone *et al.* (eds) *Postmodernism*, pp. 195–215. London:Sage.

Fernando, S. (1988) *Race and Culture in Psychiatry*. London: Croom Helm.

Festinger, L., Reicken, H. W. and Schachter, S. (1956) *When Prophesy Fails*. Minneopolis, MN: University of Minnesota Press.

Feuerstein, G. (1996) *Yoga: An Essential Introduction to the Principles and Practice of an Ancient Tradition*. Boston, MA: Shambhala.

Feyerabend, P. (1975) *Against Method. Outline of an Anarchic Theory of Knowledge*. London: NLB.

Filippi, G. G. (1996) *Mrtyu: Concept of Death in Indian Traditions*. New Delhi: D.K.

Fisher, C. B. and Fryberg, D. (1994) Participant partners, *American Psychologist*, 49(5): 417–27.

Flood, G. (1996) *An Introduction to Hinduism*. Cambridge: Cambridge University Press.

Frank, J. D. and Frank, J. B. (1991) *Persuasion and Healing*. Baltimore, MD: Johns Hopkins University Press.

Freud, S. ([1953]1976) *The Psychopathology of Everyday Life*, in J. Strachey (ed) *The Standard Edition of the Complete Psychological Works of Sigmund Freud*, vol. 6. London: Hogarth.

Fuller, C. J. (1992) *The Camphor Flame: Popular Hinduism and Society in India*. Princeton, NJ: Princeton University Press.

Garfield, S. L. and Bergin, A. E. (eds) (1986) *Handbook of Psychotherapy and Behaviour Change*, 3rd ed. New York: Wiley.

Geertz, C. (1973) *The interpretation of Culture*. New York: Basic Books.

Gellner, E. (1985) *Relativism and the Social Sciences*. Cambridge: Cambridge Universty Press.

Gellner, E. (1992) *Reason and Culture*. Oxford: Blackwell.

Giddens, A. (1991) *Modernity and Self-Identity: Self and Society in the Late Modern Age*. Cambridge: Polity Press.

Gillies, D. (1993) *Philosophy of Science in the Twentieth Century: Four Central Themes*. Oxford: Blackwell.

Gold, A. R., Christie, R. and Friedman, L. C. (1976) *Fists and Flowers: A Social Psychological Interpretation of Social Dissent*. New York: Academic Press.

Gonsiorek, J. C. (1995) *The Breach of Trust*. Thousand Oaks, CA: Sage.

Gorer, G. (1965) *Death, Grief and Mourning in Contemporary Britain*. London: Cresset Press.

Greenberg, C. I. and Firestone, J. J. (1977) Compensatory response to crowding: effects of personal space and privacy reduction, *Journal of Personality and Social Psychology*, 35: 637–44.

Greenberg, C. I. *et al.* (1994) *Facilitating Emotional Change*. New York: Guilford.

Gulerce, A. (1996) A family structure assessment device for Turkey, in J. Pandey, D. Sinha and D. P. S. Bhawuk (eds) *Asian Contributions to Cross-cultural Psychology*. New Delhi: Sage.

Gupta, D. (1992) Continuous hierarchies and discrete castes, in: D. Gupta (ed.) *Social Stratification*. Delhi: Oxford University Press.

Gupta, D. (2000) *Interrogating Caste: Understanding Hierarchy and Difference in Indian Society*. New Delhi: Penguin.

Habermas, J. (1981) *The Theory of Communicative Action*. London: Beacon Press.

Harris, M. (1968) *The Rise of Anthropological Theory: A History of Theories of Culture*. London: Routledge & Kegan Paul.

Heider, F. (1946) Social perception and phenomenal causality, *Psychological Review*, 51: 358–74.

Heisenberg, W. (1930) *The Physical Principles of the Quantum Theory*. Berkeley, CA: University of California Press.

Helms, J. E. (1984) Considering some methodological issues in racial identity counseling research, *The Counseling Psychologist*, 17(1): 227–52.

Herink, R. (ed.) (1980) *The Psychotherapy Handbook*. New York: Meridian.

Higgins, E. T., Rholes, W. S. and Jones, C. R. (1976) Category accessibility and impression formation, *Journal of Experimental Social Psychology*, 13: 141–54.

Hiriyanna, M. (1949) *The Essentials of Indian Philosophy*. London: Allen & Unwin.

Hockey, J. (1993) The acceptable face of human grieving? The clergy's role in managing emotional expression during funerals, in D. Clark (ed) *The Sociology of Death*, pp. 129–48. Oxford: Blackwell.

Hoffman, M. L. (1976) Empathy, role-taking, guilt, and development of altruistic motives, in T. Lickona (ed.) *Moral Development and Behaviour: Theory, Research and Social Issues*. New York: Holt, Rinehart & Winston.

Hoffman, M. L. (1982) Development of prosocial motivation: empathy and guilt, in N. Eiservberg (ed.) *Development of Prosocial Behaviour*, pp. 281–313. New York: Academic Press.

Hofstede, G. H. (1980) *Cultures' Consequences: International Differences in Work-related Values*. Beverly Hills, CA: Sage.

Hofstede, G. H. (1991) *Cultures and Organizations: Software of the Mind*. New York: McGraw-Hill.

Holroyd J. C. and Brodsky, A. (1977) Psychologists' attitudes and practices regarding erotic and nonerotic physical contact with patients, *American Psychologist*, 32: 843–9.

Honderich, T. (1999) *The Philosophers: Introducing Great Western Thinkers*. London: University College.

Howard, A. (1996) *Challenges to Counselling and Psychotherapy*. Basingstoke: Macmillan.

Hui, C. H. and Triandis, H. C. (1986) Individualism-collectivism: a study of cross-cultural researchers, *Journal of Cross-Cultural Psychology*, 17: 222–48.

Huyssen, A. (1984) Mapping the postmodern, *New German Critique*, 33(Fall): 5–52.

Jahoda, G. and Krewer, B. (1997) History of cross-cultural psychology and

cultural psychology, in J. W. Berry, Y. H. Poortinga and J. Pandey (eds) *Handbook of Cross-Cultural Psychology*, vol. 1, *Theory and Method*, pp. 1–42. Boston, MA: Allyn & Bacon.
James, W. (1918) *Principles of Psychology I*. New York: Dover Publications.
Jehu, D. (1994a) (ed.) *Sexual Abuse in Psychotherapy and Counselling*. Chichester: Wiley.
Jehu, D. (1994b) *Patients as Victims: Sexual Abuse in Psychotherapy and Counseling*. New York: Wiley.
Jewel, P. (2001) Multicultural counselling research: an evaluation with proposals for future research, in S. Palmer (ed.) *Multicultural Counselling*, pp. 238–65. London: Sage.
Jing, Q. and Wan, C. (1997) Socialization of Chinese children, in H. S. R. Kao and D. Sinha (eds) *Asian Perspectives on Psychology*. New Delhi: Sage.
Johnson, A. W. and Nadirshaw, Z. (2001) Working with issues of race in counselling, in P. Milner and S. Palmer (eds) *Counselling: The BACP Counselling Reader*, vol. 2. London: Sage.
Jones, E. E. (1978) Effects of race on psychotherapy process and outcome: an exploratory investigation, *Psychotherapy: Theory, Research and Practice*, 15: 226–36.
Kagitcibasi, C. (1997) Individualism and collectivism, in J. W. Berry, M. H. Segall and C. Kagitcibasi (eds) *Handbook of Cross-cultural Psychology: Social Behavior and Applications*, pp. 1–49. Boston, MA: Allyn & Bacon.
Kakar, S. ([1979]1992) *Identity and Adulthood*. Delhi: Oxford India Paperbacks.
Kakar, S. (1981) *The Inner World: A Psychoanalytic Study of Children and Society in India*. Delhi: Oxford University Press.
Kakar, S. (1982) *Shamans, mystics and doctors*. London: Mandala Books.
Kakar, S. and Chowdhry, K. (1970) *Conflict and Choice: Indian Youth in a Changing Society*. Bombay: Somaiya Publications.
Karasu, T. B. (1986) The psychotherapies: benefits and limitations, *American Journal of Psychotherapy*, 40: 324–42.
Kareem, J. (1992) The Nafsiyat Intercultural Therapy Centre, in J. Kareem and R. Littlewood (eds) *Intercultural Therapy Themes: Interpretations and Practice*. London: Blackwell Scientific Publications.
Kim, U. (1997) Asian collectivism: an indigenous perspective, in H. S. R. Kao and D. Sinha (eds) *Asian Perspectives on Psychology*. New Delhi: Sage.
Kim, U., Triandis, H. C. and Yoon, G. (eds) (1992) *Individualism and Collectivism: Theoretical and Methodological Issues*. Newbury Park, CA: Sage.
Kim, U., Triandis, H. C., Kagitcibasi, C., Choi, S-C. and Yoon, G. (1994) *Individualism and Collectivism: Theory, Method, and Applications*. Thousand Oaks, CA: Sage.
Klineberg, O. (1980) Historical perspectives: cross-cultural psychology

before 1960, in H. C. Triandis and W. W. Lambert (eds) *Handbook of Cross-cultural Psychology*, vol. 1, pp. 31–67. Boston, MA: Allyn & Bacon.

Klostermaier, K. K. (1998) *A Short Introduction to Hinduism*. Oxford: One World.

Koller, J. M. (1982) *The Indian Way: Perspectives*. London: Collier Macmillan.

Kozeki, B, and Berghammer, R. (1992) The role of empathy in the motivational structure of school children, *Personality & Individual Difference*, 13(2): 191–203.

Krishnamurthy, K., Venugopal, D. and Alimchandani, A. K. (2000) Mental hospitals in India, *Indian Journal of Psychiatry*, April, 2.

Kroeber, A. L. and Kluckhohn, C. (1952) *Culture: A Critical Review of Concepts and Definitions*. Cambridge, MA: Peabody Museum.

Kuhn, T. (1967) *The Structure of Scientific Revolutions*. Chicago: University of Chicago Press.

Kumar, R. (1994) Postnatal mental illness: a transcultural perspective, *Social Psychiatry & Psychiatric Epidemiology*, 29: 250–64.

Lago, C. and Thompson, J. (1989) Counselling and race, in W. Dryden, D. Charles-Edwards and R. Wolfe (eds) *Handbook of Counselling in Britain*. London: Routledge.

Lakatos, I. (1970) Falsification and the methodology of scientific research programmes, in I. Lakatos and A. Musgrove (eds) *Criticism and the Growth of Knowledge*, pp. 91–196. London: Cambridge University Press.

Lakatos, I. (1978) Science and pseudoscience, in J. Worrall and G. Currie (eds) *Imre Lakatos: The Methodology of Scientific Research Programmes: Philosophical Papers*, vol. 1, pp. 1–7. Cambridge: Cambridge University Press.

Lakatos, I. and Musgrove, A. (eds) *Criticism and the Growth of Knowledge*. London: Cambridge University Press.

Lannoy, R. (1975) *The Speaking Tree. A Study of Indian Culture and Society*. Oxford: Oxford University Press.

Larson, G. (1987) Ayurveda and the Hindu philosophical systems, *Journal of Philosophy: East and West*, 37(July): 245–59.

Laungani, P. (1988) Accidents in children: an Asian perspective, *Public Health*, 10: 171–176.

Laungani, P. (1990) Turning eastward: an Asian view on child abuse, *Health & Hygiene*, 11(1): 26–9.

Laungani, P. (1992a) Assessing child abuse through interviews of children and parents of children at risk, *Children and Society*, 6(1): 3–11.

Laungani, P. (1992b) Cultural variations in the understanding and treatment of mental disorders: India and England, *Counselling Psychology Quarterly*, 5(3): 131–44.

Laungani, P. (1993) Cultural differences in stress and its management, *Stress Medicine*, 9(1): 37–43.

Laungani, P. (1994) Cultural differences in stress: India and England, *Counselling Psychology Review*, 9(4): 25–37.
Laungani, P. (1995) Stress in eastern and western cultures, in J. Brebner, E. Greenglass, P. Laungani and A. O'Roark (eds) *Stress and Emotion*, vol. 15, pp. 265–80. Washington, DC: Taylor & Francis.
Laungani, P. (1996) Research in cross-cultural settings: ethical considerations, in E. S. C. Miao (ed.) *Cross-cultural encounters: Proceedings of the 53rd Annual Convention of International Council of Psychologists*. Taipei, Taiwan: General Innovation Services.
Laungani, P. (1997a) Replacing client-centred counselling with culture-centred counselling, *Counselling Psychology Quarterly*, 10(4): 343–51.
Laungani, P. (1997b) Mental illness in India and Britain: theory and practice, *Medicine and Law*, 16: 509–40.
Laungani, P. (1997c) Death in a Hindu Family, in C. M. Parkes, P. Laungani, and W. Young (eds) *Death and Bereavement Across Cultures*. London: Routledge.
Laungani, P. (1998) The changing patterns of Hindu funerals in Britain, *Pharos International*, 64(4): 4–10.
Laungani, P. (1999a) Client centred or culture centred counselling? in S. Palmer and P. Laungani (eds) *Counselling in a Multicultural Society*. London: Sage.
Laungani, P. (1999b) Culture and identity: implications for counselling, in S. Palmer and P. Laungani, (eds) *Counselling in a Multicultural Society*, pp. 35–70. London: Sage.
Laungani, P. (1999c) Death among Hindus in India and England, *International Journal of Group Tensions*, 28(1–2): 85–114.
Laungani, P. (1999d) Cultural influences on identity and behaviour: India and Britain, in Y. T. Lee, C. R. McCauley, & J. G. Draguns (eds) *Through the Looking Glass: Personality in Culture*. Mahwah, NJ: Lawrence Erlbaum Associates.
Laungani, P. (2000a) Postnatal depression across cultures: conceptual and methodological considerations, *International Journal of Health Promotion and Education*, 38(3): 86–94.
Laungani, P. (2000b) The changing patterns of Hindu funerals in Britain: cultural and psychological implications, *Asian Journal of Psychology and Education*, 33(1–2): 2–14.
Laungani, P. (2000c) Cultural influences on the development of identity: India and England, in J. Mohan (ed.) *Personality Across Cultures: Recent Developments and Debates*, pp. 284–312. New Delhi: Oxford University Press.
Laungani, P. (2000d) Death: the final end or a new beginning? Cross-cultural evaluations, in A. L. Comunian and U. Gielen (eds) *International Perspectives on Human Development*, pp. 637–62. Zagreb: Pabst Science Publishers.

Laungani, P. (2001a) Culture, cognition, and trauma: cross-cultural evaluations, in J. F. Schumaker and T. Ward (eds) *Cultural Cognition and Psychopathology*, pp. 119–44. Westport, CT: Praeger.

Laungani, P. (2001b) Hindu deaths in India – I, *International Journal of Health Promotion and Education*, 39(4): 114–20.

Laungani, P. (2001c) The influence of culture on stress: India and England, in L. L. Adler and U. P. Gielen (eds) *Cross-cultural Topics in Psychology*, 2nd edn, pp. 149–70. Westport, CT: Praeger.

Laungani, P. (2001d) Hindu deaths in England – II, *International Journal of Health Promotion and Education*, 39(4): 114–20.

Laungani, P. (2002a) Cross-cultural psychology: a handmaiden to mainstream western psychology, *Counselling Psychology Quarterly*, 15(4): 385–97.

Laungani, P. (2002b) The Hindu caste system, in G. Howarth and O. Leaman (eds) *The Encyclopedia of Death and Dying*. London: Routledge.

Laungani, P. (2002c) Hindu spirituality in life, death and bereavements, in J. Morgan and P. Laungani (eds) *Death and Bereavement Around the World*, vol. 1, *Major Religious Traditions*, pp. 9–38. Amityville, NY: Baywood Publishing Company, Inc.

Laungani, P. (2003a) Familial stress and obsessive compulsive disorder, *International Journal of Health Promotion and Education*, 39(4).

Laungani, P. (2003b) Sexual abuse in an Asian family, *Counselling Psychology Quarterly*, 16(4).

Laungani, P. (2004). Some unresolved issues in philosophy and psychology: implications for therapeutic counselling. *Counselling Psychology Quarterly*, 17(1): 109–25.

Laungani, P. and Sookhoo, D. (1995) Myocardial infarction in British white and Asian adults: their health beliefs and health practices. Paper presented at the 4th European Congress of Psychology, Athens, Greece.

Lavine, T. Z. (1984) *From Socrates to Sartre: The Philosophic Quest*. New York Bantam.

Leach, E. (1964) Comment on Naroll's 'On ethnic unit classification', *Current Anthropology*, 5(4): 299.

Leslie, C. (1976) *Asian Medicinal Systems: A Comparative Study*. Berkeley, CA: University of California Press.

Levin, J. (1990) How to define family, *Family Reports*, 1(17): 7–18.

Levine, R. A. (1973) *Culture, Behaviour and Personality*. Chicago: Aldine.

Lewis, H. B. (1971) *Shame and Guilt*. New York: International Universities Press.

Lipner, J. (1994) *Hindus: Their Religious Beliefs and Practices*. London: Routledge.

Littlewood, R. and Lipsedge, M. (1982) *Aliens and Alienists: Ethnic Minorities and Psychiatry*, 3rd edn. London: Routledge.

Luhrmann, T. M. (1996) *The Good Parsi: The Fate of a Colonial Elite in a Postcolonial Society*. Cambridge, MA: Harvard University Press.
Lukes, S. (1973) *Individualism*. Oxford: Blackwell.
Madan, T. N. (1987) *Non-Renunciation: Themes and Interpretations of Hindu Culture*. Delhi: Oxford University Press.
Magee, B. (1998) *The Story of Philosophy*. London: Dorling Kindersley.
Malinowski, B. (1927) *Sex and Repression in Savage Society*. London, Routledge.
Mandelbaum, D. G. (1972) *Society in India*, vol. 2. Berkeley, CA: University of California Press.
Manorama (2002) *Manorama Year Book*. Kottayam, India: Malayala Manorama Co. Ltd.
Markowitz, P. F. (1987) A synthesis of self psychology and ego developmental perspectives: toward a model of empathy, *Psychological Development*, 48(8): 2477.
Maruta, S. and Chittick, C. C. (1996) *The Vision of Islam*. London: I.B. Taurus.
Maslow, A. (1970) Motivation and Personality, 2nd edn. New York: Harper & Row.
Maslow, A. (1971) *The Farther Reaches of Human Nature*. New York: McGraw-Hill.
Masson, J. (1992) The tyranny of psychotherapy, in W. Dryden and C. Feltham (eds) *Psychotherapy and its Discontents*. Buckingham: Open University Press.
Matsumoto, D. (1996) *Unmasking Japan: Myths and Realities about the Emotions of the Japanese*. Stanford, CA: Stanford University Press.
McClelland, D. C. (1961) *The Achieving Society*. Princeton, NJ: Van Nostrand.
McGuigan, F. J. (1993) *Experimental Psychology: Methods of Research*, 6th edn. Englewood Cliffs, NJ: Prentice-Hall.
McLeod, J. (1998) *An Introduction to Counselling*. Buckingham: Open University Press.
Milgram, S. (1974) *Obedience to Authority: An Experimental View*. London: Tavistock.
Miller, G. A. (1969) Psychology as a means of promoting human welfare, *American Psychologist*, 24: 1063–75.
Moodley, R. and Dhingra, S. (2001) Cross-cultural/racial matching in counselling and therapy: white clients and black counsellors, in P. Milner and S. Palmer (eds) *Counselling: The BACP Counselling Reader*, vol. 2. London: Sage.
Morgan, J. D. and Laungani, P. (eds) (2002) *Death and Bereavement Around the World*, vol. 1: *Major Religious Traditions*. Amityville, NY: Baywood Publishing Company, Inc.
Munroe, R. L. and Munroe, R. H. (1980) Perspectives suggested by

anthropological data, in *Handbook of Cross-cultural psychology*, vol. 1, pp. 253–317. Boston, MA: Allyn & Bacon.

Murdock, G. P. (1964) Comment on Naroll's 'On ethnic unit classification', *Current Anthropology*, 5(4): 301–2.

Murdock, G. P. and Provost, C. (1973) Measurement of cultural complexity, *Ethnology*, 12: 379–92.

Murthy, S. P. *et al.* (1992) *Evaluation: Work book on Community-Based Rehabilitation Service*. Adugodi, Bangalore: National Printing Press.

Musgrove, F. (1982) *Education and Anthropology: Other Cultures and the Teacher*. Chichester: Wiley.

Neki, J. S. (1979) Psychotherapy in India: traditions and trends, in M. Kapur, V. N. Murthy, K. Satyavathi and R. L. Kapur (eds) *Psychotharapeutic Processes*. Bangalore: Institute of Mental Health.

Nespor, K. (1982) Yogic practices in world medical literature, *Yoga*, 20: 29–35.

O'Flaherty, W. D. (1976) *The Origins of Evil in Hindu Mythology*. Berkeley, CA: University of California Press.

O'Flaherty, W. D. (1980) *Karma and Rebirth in Classical Indian Traditions*. Berkeley, CA: University of California Press.

O'Hara, M. W. (1994) Postpartum depression: identification and measurement in a cross-cultural context, in J. Cox and J. Holden (eds) *Perinatal Psychiatry: Use and Misuse of the Edinburgh Postnatal Depression Scale*, pp. 145–68. London: Gaskell.

Palmer, S. (ed.) (2001) *Multicultural Counselling*. London: Sage.

Palmer, S. and Laungani, P. (eds) (1999) *Counselling in a Multicultural Society*. London: Sage.

Pande, S. (1968) The mystique of 'western' psychotherapy: an eastern interpretation, *The Journal of Nervous and Mental Disease*, 146 (June): 425–32.

Pandey, R. (1969) *Hindu Samskaras: Socio-Religious Study of the Hindu Sacraments*. Delhi: Motilal Banarasidass Publishers.

Pandey, R. S., Srinivas, K. N. and Muralidhar, D. (1980) Socio-cultural beliefs and treatment acceptance, *Indian Journal of Psychiatry*, 22: 161–6.

Paranjpe, A. C., Ho, D. Y. F. and Reiber, R. W. (eds) (1988) *Asian Contributions to Psychology*. New York: Praeger.

Parekh, B. (2000) *Rethinking Multiculturalism: Cultural Diversity and Political Theory*. Basingstoke: Macmillan/Palgrave.

Patterson, C. H. (1978) Cross-cultural or intercultural psychotherapy, *Hacettepe University Bulletin of Social Sciences*, 1: 119–34.

Patterson, C. H. (1986) Culture and Counselling in Hong Kong, *Chinese University Education Journal*, 14(2): 77–81.

Pederson, P. (ed.) (1985) *Handbook of Cross-cultural Therapy*. Westport, CT: Greenwood Press.

Pederson, P. (1987) Ten frequent assumptions of cultural bias in counseling, *Journal of Multicultural Counseling and Development*, 15: 16–24.
Pederson, P. (1988) *A Handbook for Developing Multicultural Awareness*. Alexandria, VA: American Association for Counseling and Development.
Pederson, P. (1997) *Culture-centred Counselling Interventions: Striving for Accuracy*. London: Sage.
Pederson, P. B., Draguns, J. G., Lonner, W. J. and Trimble, J. J. (eds) (1996) *Counselling Across Cultures*. London: Sage.
Piaget, J. (1970) *Genetic Epistemology*. New York: Norton.
Ponterotto, J. G. (1988) Racial/ethnic minority research: a content analysis and methodological critique, *Journal of Counselling Psychology*, 3: 410–18.
Ponterotto, J. G. and Casas, J. M. (eds) (1991) *Handbook of Racial/Ethnic Minority Counselling Research*. Springfield, IL: Charles C. Thomas.
Popper, K. (1963) *Conjectures and Refutations*. London: Routledge.
Popper, K. (1972) *Objective Knowledge: An Evolutionary Approach*. Oxford: Clarendon Press.
Popper, K. (1988) *The Open Universe: An Argument for Indeterminism*. London: Hutchinson.
Prasad, R. (1989) *Karma Causation and Retributive Morality: Conceptual Essays in Ethics and Metaethics*. New Delhi: Indian Council of Philosophical Research/Munshiram Manoharlal Publishers Pvt. Ltd.
Radhakrishnan, S. ([1929]1989) *Indian Philosophy*, vol. 2 (centenary edition). Delhi: Oxford University Press.
Ravindra, R. (1989) Yoga: the royal path to freedom, in K. Sivaraman (ed.) *Hindu Spirituality: Vedas Through Vedanta*, pp. 177–91. London: SCM Press Ltd.
Reichenbach, B. R. (1990) *The Law of Karma: A Philosophical Study*. Honolulu, HI: University of Hawaii Press.
Reimers, S. and Treacher, A. (1995) *Introducing User-friendly Family Therapy*. London: Routledge.
Ridley, C. (1984) Clinical treatment for the non-disclosing black client, *American Psychologist*, 39: 1234–44.
Ridley, C. (1995) *Overcoming Unintentional Racism in Counselling and Therapy*. Thousand Oaks, CA: Sage.
Riesman, D. (1950) *The Lonely Crowd*. New Haven, CT: Yale University Press.
Riesman, D. (1954) *Individualism Reconsidered*. New York: Doubleday.
Rivers, W. H. R. (1901) Introduction and vision, part 1, in A. C. Haddon (ed.) *Reports of the Cambridge Anthropological Expedition to Torres Straits*, vol. 2. Cambridge: Cambridge University Press.
Rogers, C. (1961) *On Becoming a Person*. Boston, MA: Houghton Mifflin.
Rogers, C. (1980) *A Way of Being*. Boston, MA: Houghton Mifflin.

Rogers, C. R. and Dymond, R. F. (eds) (1954) *Psychotherapy and Personality Change*. Chicago: University of Chicago Press.

Rohner, R. P. (1974) Proxemics and stress: an empirical study of the relationship between space and roommate turnover, *Human Relations*, 27: 697–702.

Roland, A. (1988) *In Search of Self in India and Japan*. Princeton, NJ: Princeton University Press.

Rosenhan, D. (1973) On being sane in insane places, *Science*, 179: 250–8.

Roy, A. (2001) *The Algebra of Infinite Justice*. New Delhi: Penguin Books.

Russell, B. (1961) *Religion and Science*. Oxford: Oxford University Press.

Rutherford, R. B. (1990) Introduction and notes in *The Meditations of Marcus Aurelius Antonius*, trans A.S.L. Faraquharson. Oxford: Oxford University Press.

Rychlak, J. F. (1973) *Introduction to Personality and Psychotherapy: A Theory-Construction Approach*. Boston, MA: Houghton Mifflin.

Sachdev, D. (1992) Effects of psychocultural factors on the socialisation of British born Indian children and indigenous British children living in England. Unpublished doctoral dissertation, South Bank University, London.

Sampson, E. E. (1977) Psychology and the American ideal, *Journal of Personality and Social Psychology*, 15: 189–94.

Sattler, J. M. (1977) The effects of therapist-client similarity, in A. S. Gurman and A. M. Razin (eds) *Effective Psychotherapy: A Handbook of Research*. New York: Pergamon.

Satyavathi, K. (1988) Mental health, in J. Pamdey (ed.) *Psychology in India: The State of The Art*, vol. 3. New Delhi: Sage.

Scheffler, I. (1969) *Science and Subjectivity*. Indianapolis, IN: Bobbs-Merrill.

Schwartz, S. H. (1990) Individualism-collectivism: critique and proposed refinements, *Journal of Cross-cultural Psychology*, 21(2): 139–57.

Segall, M. H., Dasen, P. R., Berry, J. W. and Poortinga, Y. H. (1999) *Human Behaviour in Global Perspective: An Introduction to Cross-cultural Psychology*, 2nd edn. Boston MA: Allyn & Bacon.

Sethi, B. B. (1986) Epidemiology of depression in India, *Psychopathology*, 19 (suppl.2): 26–36.

Sethi, B. B. and Manchanda, R. (1978) Family structure and psychiatric disorders, *Indian Journal of Psychiatry*, 20: 283–8.

Sharma, A. (2000) *Classical Hindu Thought: An Introduction*. New Delhi: Oxford University Press.

Sheikh, A. and Sheikh, K. S. (1989) *Eastern and Western Approaches to Healing: Ancient Wisdom and Modern Knowledge*. New York: Wiley.

Shweder, R. A. and Sullivan, M. A. (1993) Cultural psychology: who needs it? *Annual Review of Psychology*, 44: 497–527.

Sinari, R. A. (1984) *The Structure of Indian Thought*. Delhi: Oxford University Press.

Singh, C. and Nath, P. (1999) *Hindu Festivals, Fairs and Fasts*. New Delhi: Crest.

Sinha, J. B. P. and Sinha, D. (1990) Role of social values in Indian organization, *Journal of Transpersonal Psychology*, 12(2): 127–42.

Sivaraman, K. (ed.) (1989) *Hindu Spirituality: Vedas Through Vedanta*. London: SCM Press Ltd.

Skellington, R. and Morris, P. (1992) *Race in Britain Today*. London: Sage.

Skinner, B. F. (1953) *Science and Human Behaviour*. New York: Macmillan.

Smart, N. (1996) *Dimensions of the Sacred: An Anatomy of the World's Beliefs*. London: Fontana.

Smith, P. B. and Bond, M. H. (1993) *Social Psychology Across Cultures: Analysis and Perspectives*. Hemel Hempstead: Harvester Wheatsheaf.

Sollod, R. N. (1982) Non-scientific sources of psychotherapeutic approaches, in P. W. Sharkey (ed.) *Philosophy, Religion, and Psychotherapy: Essays in the Philosophical Foundations of Psychotherapy*. Washington, DC.: University Press of America.

Sookhoo, D. (1995) A comparative study of the health beliefs and health practices of British whites and Asian adults with and without mycardial infarction. Paper presented at the 53rd Annual Convention of the International Council of Psychologists, Taipei, Taiwan.

Spence, J. T. (1985) Achievement American style: the rewards and costs of individualism, *American Psychologist*, 40: 1285–95.

Srinivasa, D. K. and Trivedi, S. (1982) Knowledge and attitude of mental diseases in a rural community of South India, *Social Science Medicine*, 16: 1635–9.

Stace, W. T. (1958) Ethical relativity, in M. K. Munitz (ed.) *A Modern Introduction to Ethics*. Glencoe, IL: Free Press.

Stean, H. S. (1993) *Therapists Who Have Sex With Their Patients: Treatment and Recovery*. New York: Brunner Mazel.

Stevens, S. S. (1951) Mathematics, measurement and psychophysics, in S. S. Stevens (ed.) *Handbook of Experimental Psychology*, pp. 1–49. New York: Wiley.

Stiglitz, J. (2002) *Globalization and its Discontents*. London: Allen Lane.

Sue, D. W. and Sue, D. (1990) *Counseling the Culturally Different*, 2nd edn. New York, Wiley.

Summers, M. (1994) *The History of Witchcraft*. London: Studio Editions.

Szymanska, K. and Palmer, S. (1997) Counsellor-client exploitation, in S. Palmer and McMahon, G. (eds) *Handbook of Counselling*. London: Routledge.

Tanaka-Matsumi, J., Seiden, D. Y. and Lam, K. N. (2001) Translating cultural observations into psychotherapy: a functional approach, in J. F. Schumaker and T. Ward (eds) *Cultural Cognition and Psychopathology*, pp. 193–212. Westport, CT: Praeger.

Taylor, S. E. (1989) *Positive Illusions: Creative Self-deception and the Healthy Mind*. New York: Basic Books.

Thigpen, C. H. and Cleckley, H. M. (1957) *The Three Faces of Eve*. New York: McGraw-Hill.

Trefil, J. (1980) *From Atoms to Quarks: An Introduction to the Strange World of Particle Physics*. London: Althone.

Triandis, H. C. (1972) *The Analysis of Subjective Culture*. New York: Wiley.

Triandis, H. (1980) Introduction, in H. C. Triandis and J. W. Berry (eds) *Handbook of Cross-cultural Psychology*, vol. 2, Boston, MA: Allyn & Bacon.

Triandis, H. C. (1994) *Culture and Social Behavior*. New York: McGraw-Hill.

Triandis, H. C. (1997) Theoretical framework for the evaluation of cross-cultural training effectiveness, *International Journal for Intercultural Relations*, 1: 19–45.

Trost, J. (1990) Do we mean the same by the concept of family? *Communication Research*, 17(4): 431–43.

Troyna, B. (1981) *Public Awareness and the Media*. London: Commission for Racial Equality.

Tyler, S. A. (1960) *Cognitive Anthropology*. New York: Holt, Rinehart & Winston.

Tyler, S. A. (ed.) (1969) Cognitive Anthropology, 2nd edn. New York: Holt, Rinehart & Winston.

United Nations (1996) *Family: Challenges for the Future*. New York: United Nations Publications.

Vahia, N. S. (1982) Yoga in psychiatry, in A. Kiev and A. V. Rao (eds) *Readings in Transcultural Psychiatry*, pp. 11–19. Madras: Higginbothams.

Valsiner, J. (1989). *Human Development and Culture*. Toronto: Lexington Books.

Veatch, H. B. (1972) Science and humanism, in M. H. Marx and F. E. Goodson (eds) *Theories in Contemporary Psychology*, 2nd edn, pp. 61–5. New York: Macmillan.

Vine, I. (1982) Crowding and stress: a personal space approach, *Psychological Review*, 2(1): 1–18.

von Furer-Haimendorf, C. (1974) The sense of sin in cross-cultural perspective. *Man*, 9: 539–56.

Wade, P. and Bernstein, B. L. (1991) Culture sensitivity training and counsellor race: effects on black female clients' perceptions and attribution, *Journal of Counselling Psychology*, 38(1): 19–45.

Ward, C. and Kennedy, A. (1996) Psychological and socio-cultural adjustment during cross-cultural transitions: a comparison of secondary students overseas and at home, *International Journal of Psychology*, 28: 129–147.

Waterman, A. A. (1981) Individualism and interdependence, *American Psychologist*, 36: 762–73.
Webb, S. D. (1978) Privacy and psychosomatic stress: an empirical analysis, *Social Behaviour and Personality*, 6: 227–34.
Weber, M. (1959) *The Sociology of Religion*, 4th edn. London: Allen & Unwin.
White, L. A. (1947) Cultural versus psychological interpretations of human behaviour, *American Sociological Review*, 12: 686–9.
Whiting, J. W. M. (1964) Comments on Naroll's 'On ethnic unit classification', *Current Anthropology*, 5(4): 305–6.
Williams, B. (1985) *Ethics and the Limits of Philosophy*. London: Fontana.
Woodworth, R. S. (1910) Racial differences in mental traits, *Science*, 31.
Woolfe, R. and Dryden, W. (1996) *Handbook of Counselling Psychology*. London: Sage.
World Health Organization (WHO) (1973) *Report of the International Pilot Study of Schizophrenia*. Geneva: WHO.
World Health Organization (WHO) (1978) *The Promotion and Development of Traditional Medicine*. WHO Technical Report Series No. 622. Geneva: WHO.
World Health Organization (WHO) (1979) *Schizophrenia: An International Follow-up Study*. Geneva: WHO.
Wrenn, G. (1985) Afterword: the culturally encapsulated counsellor revisited, in P. Pederson (ed.) *Handbook of Cross-cultural Counselling and Therapy*, pp. 323–9. Westport, CT: Greenwood.
Yang, K. S. (1997) Theories and research in Chinese personality: an indigenous approach, in H. S. R. Kao and D. Sinha (eds) *Asian Perspectives on Psychology*. New Delhi: Sage.
Zaehner, R. C. (1966a) *Hinduism*. New York: Oxford University Press.
Ziman, (1978) *Reliable Knowledge: An Exploration of the Grounds for Belief in Science*. Cambridge: Cambridge University Press.
Zimmer, H. ([1951] 1989) *Philosophies of India* (Bollingen Series XXVI). Princeton, NJ: Princeton University Press.

Author index

Subject index